Social Work Practice in Africa

Indigenous and Innovative Approaches

Edited by

Janestic Mwende Twikirize

Helmut Spitzer

WITH FUNDING FROM

AUSTRIAN
DEVELOPMENT
COOPERATION

CRISOWO
EAST AFRICA
CENTRE FOR RESEARCH AND
INNOVATION IN SOCIAL WORK

appear

Austrian Partnership Programme
in Higher Education and Research
for Development

FOUNTAIN PUBLISHERS
www.fountainpublishers.co.ug

Fountain Publishers
P.O. Box 488
Kampala
E-mail: sales@fountainpublishers.co.ug
         publishing@fountainpublishers.co.ug
Website: www.fountainpublishers.co.ug

Distributed in Europe and Commonwealth countries outside Africa by:
African Books Collective Ltd,
P.O. Box 721,
Oxford OX1 9EN, UK.
Tel/Fax: +44(0) 1869 349110
E-mail: orders@africanbookscollective.com
Website: www.africanbookscollective.com

This publication was funded by APPEAR, the Austrian Partnership Programme in Higher Education and Research for Development. APPEAR is a programme of the Austrian Development Cooperation.

ISBN: 978-9970-617-92-0

Contents

About the Editors

Janestic Mwende TWIKIRIZE, PhD, is a Senior Lecturer in the Department of Social Work and Social Administration, Makerere University, Uganda. She holds a PhD in Social Work and Social Development. Dr Twikirize served as the Vice President of the Association of Schools of Social Work in Africa (ASSWA) and as a board member of the International Association of Schools of Social Work (IASSW) from 2012 to 2018. She is a member of the editorial board of the journal *International Social Work*. She is the East Africa Regional Coordinator of PROSOWO, a six-member institutional academic partnership project to professionalise social work in East Africa. She has served as a Visiting Lecturer at Gothenburg University, Sweden, and University of Stavanger, Norway. Her research areas and published works focus on social work in Africa, indigenisation of social work, gender and child rights.

Contact: janestic@gmail.com

Helmut SPITZER, PhD, is a Professor of Social Work at Carinthia University of Applied Sciences, Austria. He served as Overall Coordinator of the projects PROSOWO I (2011-2014) and PROSOWO II (2016-2018) on the promotion of professional social work in East Africa. His teaching, research and publications (in German and English) focus on international social work, social work methods, gerontological social work, children in especially difficult circumstances, cross-cultural research, and social work in East Africa. The book *Professional Social Work in East Africa: Towards Social Development, Poverty Reduction and Gender Equality* (2014), which he published together with Janestic M. Twikirize and Gidraph G. Wairire, has become a major reference on social work in the East African region.

Contact: h.spitzer@cuas.at

About the Contributors

Théogène BANGWANUBUSA, PhD, is a Lecturer at the University of Rwanda (UR). He holds a Baccalaureat and Licence in Social Sciences (National University of Rwanda), an MA in Sociology (Stellenbosch University, South Africa), and a PhD in Peace and Development Research (Göteborg University, Sweden). He is Associate Researcher at the Centre for Conflict Management (UR). Among others, he is the author of *Exercice à la Maturation Sociale au Rwanda: Analyse d'un Contexte Post Conflit* (2012); *Conceptualisation des Systèmes de Sécurité Sociale: Un Regard sur l'Expérience Rwandaise* (2011); *The South African Experience of Rural Development: What Is the Relevance for Rwanda?* (2011); *Leadership and Genocidal Violence in Rwanda: Towards a Post-Conflit Era* (2011); and *Understanding the Polarization of Responses to Genocidal Violence in Rwanda* (2009).

Contact: batheogene@yahoo.fr

Alexandre HAKIZAMUNGU holds a master's degree in Social Work and Human Rights. He is currently an Assistant Lecturer and Head of Department of Social Sciences at the University of Rwanda. He is a licensed social work specialist and President of the Rwanda National Organisation of Social Workers.

Contact: alexahakiza@yahoo.fr

Stanley KITIMBO holds a Bachelor of Social Work and Social Administration degree and is currently enrolled in an MA programme (Social Sector Planning and Management) at Makerere University, Uganda. He served as a Project Assistant for the PROSOWO project in Uganda. His evolving research interests and areas include social work with vulnerable children and families, indigenous social work models, and HIV/AIDS among young people.

Contact: kitimbo.stanley@gmail.com

Abigail KIWELU is an Assistant Lecturer in the Department of Social Work, Institute of Social Work, Tanzania. She served as a Project Assistant for PROSOWO II in Tanzania.

Contact: kiweluabigail@yahoo.com

Linda KREITZER, PhD, practised social work in the U.S. and the UK from 1976 to 1994. From 1994 to1996, she taught social work at the University of Ghana,

Legon. She finished her master's in Social Work at the University of Calgary, completing her social work practicum and thesis data collection at Buduburam refugee camp, Ghana. From 1999 to 2000, she worked for the American Red Cross in Armenia. In 2004, she finished her PhD programme at the University of Calgary looking at social work curriculum in Africa. She continues to be involved in African social work issues. Currently, she teaches at the University of Calgary, Faculty of Social Work, Central and Northern Region, and her teaching interests include international indigenous issues, community practice, professional use of self, international social work, and immigrants and refugees. Her book, *Social Work in Africa: Exploring Culturally Relevant Social Work Education and Practice in Ghana*, was published in 2012. Other books include *Lying Down in the Ever-falling Snow: Canadian Health Care Professionals' Experiences of Compassion Fatigue* and *Sherpa in My Backpack: A Guide to International Social Work Practicum Exchanges and Study Abroad Programs*. She currently sits on the Board of Directors for the International Association of Schools of Social Work.

Contact: lmkreitz@ucalgary.ca

Ronald LUWANGULA, PhD, is a Lecturer in the Department of Social Work and Social Administration, Makerere University. He is a social worker specialising in children's rights. He is a child protection scholar, researcher, trainer and consultant. In the field of action research, he tailors his engagement with communities towards identifying locally relevant solutions to contextual social development challenges.

Contact: r.luwangula@gmail.com

Zena Mnasi MABEYO, PhD, is a Senior Lecturer in social work and the Acting Rector of the Institute of Social Work in Dar es Salaam, Tanzania. She has been the Chairperson of the Tanzania Association of Social Workers since 2012 and a Country Coordinator of the project entitled *Promotion of Professional Social Work in East Africa* (PROSOWO), which has contributed immensely to professionalising social work and increasing the visibility of African social work both locally and globally. She is also a member of the Executive Committee of the Association of Schools of Social Work in Tanzania (ASWORT) – a newly formed body for standardising and promoting social work education. She is the East African Representative of the Association of Schools of Social Work in Africa (ASSWA). She has lead research and contributed to publications in the field of social work in her country, particularly in the areas of social protection for older people, the role of social work in poverty reduction, and indigenous and innovative models of social work practice.

Contact: zlyuwo@yahoo.com

William MANYAMA is an Assistant Lecturer in the Department of Social Work at the Institute of Social Work in Tanzania. He is currently pursuing PhD studies in the Department of Sociology, University of Dar es Salaam. His areas of research include parenting, indigenous knowledge systems, reproductive health and developmental social work. He has published several articles in these areas.

Contact: williammanyama@yahoo.com

Susan Wanjiku MUCHIRI is a Lecturer at Hope Africa University, Burundi, where she serves as the Head of Department of Social Work and Community Development. She holds a bachelor's degree in Social Work and a master's degree in Counselling Psychology. She served as Project Co-coordinator of the project PROSOWO II in Burundi.

Contact: muchiriwanjee13@gmail.com

Rodreck MUPEDZISWA, PhD, is a Professor of Social Work (and former Head), Department of Social Work, University of Botswana. He previously taught at University of Witwatersrand in Johannesburg and at the School of Social Work, University of Zimbabwe. His research interests focus essentially on the theme of social development issues.

Contact: mupedziswa@mopipi.ub.bw

Jacqueline MUREKASENGE is a PhD candidate in Development Studies at the University of Vienna, Austria. Before starting her PhD studies, she was a Lecturer and Head of Department of Social Work at Hope Africa University, Burundi. Murekasenge holds a master's degree in educational leadership and a bachelor's degree in Social Work.

Contact: jmurekasenge@yahoo.com

Abu K. MVUNGI, PhD, is a Senior Lecturer in the Department of Social Work at the Institute of Social Work, Dar es Salaam, Tanzania. He has wide experience in teaching sociology, anthropology, and social policy, as well as in research and consultancy. He holds a PhD in Sociology. His areas of interest are governance and leadership, social welfare enhancement and empowerment, economic and environmental issues, child rights, and gender inclusiveness. He has published a number of journal articles in both local and international journals and is involved in several research projects on socio-developmental issues. He was also involved in various consultancy projects funded by the United Republic of Tanzania and development partners.

Contact: kambagha1955@gmail.com

Lengwe-Katembula J. MWANSA, PhD, is a Professor of Social Work, University of Botswana. Previous portfolios include the headship of the Department of Social Work, Universities of Zambia and Botswana; the Presidency of the Southern African Social Sciences Conference and ASSWA, and the Vice-Presidency of IASSW. Areas of interest include social policy, youth, social work education in Africa, and NGOs.

Contact: mwansalk@mopipi.ub.bw

Elijah Macharia NDUNG'U, PhD, is a Lecturer at St. Paul's University, Nairobi in the Faculty of Social Sciences. He has actively been involved in the projects PROSOWO I and PROSOWO II on the promotion of professional social work in East Africa. His areas of interest are in social development, counselling psychology, and social research.

Contact: elijah.macharia@outlook.com

Serges Claver NZISABIRA served as Assistant Project Coordinator for Burundi in PROSOWO II, a project for promoting social work in East Africa. He holds a bachelor's degree in Social Work and Community Development from Hope Africa University, Burundi. He is a member of the National Association of Social Workers, Burundi.

Contact: nzisabirasergeclaver@gmail.com

Morena RANKOPO, PhD, is a Senior Lecturer and Coordinator of Graduate Social Work programmes at the University of Botswana. He is actively involved in research on the themes of community development, indigenous social work education and practice, HIV and AIDS, disaster risk reduction and management, and gender and development.

Contact: Rankopom@mopipi.ub.bw

Charles RUTIKANGA is a Lecturer at the University of Rwanda in the Department of Social Sciences. Currently he is pursuing his PhD studies in the Department of Development Studies at the University of Vienna on an APPEAR scholarship which is linked to the PROSOWO II project. His areas of research include child protection and social development.

Correspondence: crutikanga@ur.ac.rw

Sharlotte TUSASIIRWE is an Assistant Lecturer in the Department of Social Work and Social Administration at Makerere University, Uganda. She is currently pursuing her PhD at Western Sydney University, Australia. Her research interests include older people's vulnerability and resilience, particularly of rural older women, social work with older people, gender-based violence, and community development from below.

Contact: t_sharlotte@yahoo.com

Justus TWESIGYE is a Lecturer and Coordinator of Fieldwork in the Department of Social Work and Social Administration at Makerere University, Uganda. He is also a member of the Board of Directors of Concern for the Girl Child, a child-focused NGO that operates in Kampala city, Luwero and Nakaseke Districts. He has previously served as Senior Psychiatric Social Worker in the Ugandan Ministry of Health.

Contact: justustwesigye@yahoo.com

Consolee UWIHANGANA is an Assistant Lecturer in the Department of Social Sciences, University of Rwanda. She holds a Master of Science (MSc) in Social Work and Human Rights, a Master of Arts (MA) in Development Studies, and a bachelor's degree in Social Work. She has also received training in Psycho-social Support of People Living with HIV/AIDS. Before joining the University of Rwanda, she worked as a trainer for an international NGO, Women for Women International, Rwanda Chapter, and has delivered different trainings and seminars related to social work. She is part of different research teams in social work. She served as the Rwandan Country Coordinator of PROSOWO II, a project on the promotion of professional social work in East Africa.

Contact: uwihanganaconsolee@gmail.com

Abbreviations and Acronyms

ADP	Area Development Programme
AIDS	Acquired immunodeficiency syndrome
APPEAR	Austrian Partnership Programme in Higher Education and Research for Development
ASASWEI	Association of South African Social Work Education Institutions
ASSWA	Association of Schools of Social Work in Africa
ASWEA	Association for Social Work Education in Africa
ASWORT	Association of Schools of Social Work in Tanzania
CFPU	Child and Family Protection Unit (Uganda)
CRISOWO	(East Africa) Centre for Research and Innovation in Social Work
EAC	East African Community
EACs	East African Countries
FGDs	Focus group discussions
FGM	Female genital mutilation
GSM	Global System for Mobile Communications
HAI	HelpAge International
HDI	Human Development Index
HIV	Human immunodeficiency virus
IASSW	International Association of Schools of Social Work
IFSW	International Federation of Social Workers
IMF	International Monetary Fund
LAPEWA	Laroo-Pece Women's Association (Uganda)
LEKIDEA	Legho Kilua Development Association (Tanzania)
LGBTQ	Lesbian, gay, bisexual, transgender, queer
LODA	Local Administrative Entities Development Agency (Rwanda)
MGLSD	Ministry of Gender, Labour and Social Development (Uganda)
NGO	Non-government organisation
NUSAF	Northern Uganda Social Action Fund
PLHA	People living with HIV and AIDS

PPA	Participatory poverty assessment
PROSOWO	Promotion of Professional Social Work (in East Africa)
PRSP	Poverty Reduction Strategy Paper
RACA	Rakai Councillors' Association (Uganda)
RGB	Rwanda Governance Board
RWF	Rwandan francs
SACCO	Savings and Credit Cooperative Society (Rwanda)
SAGE	Social Assistance Grant for Empowerment (Uganda)
SMS	Short message services
ToTs	Trainers of trainers
UBOS	Uganda Bureau of Statistics
UGX	Uganda shilling
UN	United Nations
UNCRC	United Nations Convention on the Rights of the Child
UNDP	United Nations Development Programme
UNESCO	United Nations Educational, Scientific and Cultural Organisation
UNICEF	United Nations International Children's Emergency Fund
UNPD	United Nations Population Division
UPE	Universal primary education
USAID	United States Agency for International Development
US$	United States dollar
UWEP	Uganda Women Entrepreneurship Programme
VICOBA	Village and community banking (Tanzania)
VSLAs	Village savings and loans associations (Uganda)
WSU	Western Sydney University
YLP	Youth Livelihood Programme (Uganda)

Preface

Social Work Practice in Africa. Indigenous and Innovative Approaches is based on the notion that social work can only be meaningful and effective if it provides context-specific and tangible responses to the given social problems in African countries. These responses must be related to the socio-cultural realities in Africa. Owing to the over-dependence of social work education and practice on Western models in many African countries, there is a dire need for research on what we call indigenous and innovative practice models. Empirically based evidence of such models is the key for the profession to be capable of meeting the challenges of contemporary, ever-changing societies on the African continent.

In 2011, a consortium of higher education institutions in East Africa, together with an Austrian partner, linked up in a joint project to promote professional social work to more effectively contribute towards social development and poverty reduction in countries of the East African Community (EAC). The interconnected components of the project, *Professional Social Work in East Africa* (PROSOWO), which ran from 2011 to 2014, included research, capacity-building, dissemination, publications, networking, and policy advocacy. A major milestone of that collaboration was the execution of an extensive empirical study on the status of social work and its contribution to the overall social development of EAC countries. The study generated significant findings and made critical recommendations for social work education, research, policy, and practice. One of the recurrent themes from the research undertaking was the unacceptably high levels of influence of and reliance on theories, models, case studies, and knowledge systems based on Western norms, culture, and epistemology.

From Basic Research to Practice Research

Whilst social work education and formal practice have been in existence in most countries in Africa for over 50 years, and notwithstanding the clarion call for indigenisation, it was unequivocally reiterated from our study that little had been done in Africa and East Africa in particular to lay a strong foundation and establish mechanisms to support the process of indigenisation. A critical argument was that the education and training of social workers continue to heavily rely on Western literature owing to the paucity of documented theories, practice models, and case studies from the region. Filling this gap calls for research that supports theory and model-building from the bottom up and, along with this, to enable an adequate supply of scientific publications from within Africa that support the integration of local thinking and practices into mainstream social work knowledge.

It was in response to this identifiable gap that the PROSOWO project, in its second phase (2016-2018), embarked on an empirical study to collect, analyse, and publish indigenous and innovative models of social work (or problem solving) in East Africa. This book is a product of this effort. The book presents a critical analysis of a selection of indigenous and innovative models of problem solving from Burundi, Kenya, Tanzania, Rwanda, and Uganda to bring to the fore culturally relevant knowledge and practices from the grassroots that could be informative and potentially integrated into social work curricula as well as in policy and practice. All these models and practices are – in one way or the other – underlined by the African philosophical ideal of *ubuntu,* an indigenous African concept of humanness, which refers to the interdependence of human beings.

Acknowledgements

The project, *Professional Social Work in East Africa,* was funded by Austrian Development Cooperation under the Austrian Partnership Programme in Higher Education and Research for Development (APPEAR). We wish to thank the entire APPEAR team for their supportive role throughout the project span. Our appreciation also goes to the authorities of the participating partner institutions of the PROSOWO project, namely Makerere University (Uganda), University of Nairobi (Kenya), University of Rwanda, Institute of Social Work (Tanzania), Hope Africa University (Burundi), and Carinthia University of Applied Sciences (Austria). We also thank Mark Schreiber (Austria) for his good job in proofreading the manuscript of this book.

It is our hope that social work educators, students, practitioners, and policy makers will find this book both informative and instructive in promoting the rich indigenous and innovative practices and knowledge systems in Africa. Whilst it is impossible to document all relevant practices and models in one volume, we do believe that this publication will inspire and stir up more indigenisation-focused research from a social work and social development perspective. Detailed accounts of more country-specific models are provided in the forthcoming research reports and publications.

Janestic M. Twikirize and Helmut Spitzer
Editors

Indigenous and Innovative Social Work Practice: Evidence from East Africa

Janestic M. Twikirize and Helmut Spitzer

Introduction

For five decades now, there have been sustained calls and efforts to rid social work education and practice of its largely Western orientation in order to make it more relevant to African contexts. The move has been informed by the realisation that what is conceived and conceptualised for particular contexts in the Western world may not necessarily produce similar effects in other settings. This is due to differences in cultural orientations, different development stages that imply different sets and magnitudes of social problems, as well as differing social, economic, political, and spiritual realities. All these demand locally relevant knowledge, theoretical bases, models, and approaches. These are best developed from the bottom up. The United Nations Declaration on the Rights of Indigenous Peoples (United Nations, 2007) unequivocally recognises that respect for indigenous knowledge, cultures and traditional practices contributes to sustainable and equitable development and proper management of the environment. Spitzer and Twikirize (2014) similarly assert that locally relevant cultural practices, indigenous knowledge systems, and African ethical concepts are very important elements for the success of any social work intervention on the African continent.

Many authors have sustained the discourse of indigenisation and kept it on the agenda for social work and social development in Africa (e.g. Walton and Abo El Nasr, 1988; Osei-Hwedie, 1993; Mupedziswa, 2001; Gray and Coates, 2008; Gray, Coates and Yellow Bird, 2008; Gray and Coates, 2010; Rankopo and Osei-Hwedie, 2011; Kreitzer, 2012; Twikirize, 2014; Spitzer, Twikirize and Wairire, 2014; Spitzer, 2017). The findings of a major empirical study on social work in East Africa, conducted in Kenya, Uganda, Tanzania, and Rwanda (Spitzer, Twikirize and Wairire, 2014), had revealed gaps in terms of social workers' abilities to deliver culturally appropriate practices. Such gaps emanated from a type of social work education that paid little attention to local knowledge systems and indigenous approaches to problem solving.

The quest for indigenisation has also become evident in two recent social work conferences on the African continent. In a major conference in Rwanda, organised under the auspices of the PROSOWO project[1], the theme of indigenisation and locally relevant social work education and practice permeated the discussions. The theme of this conference was *Professional Social Work and Sustainable Development in Africa.* It was clear that social work cannot effectively contribute towards sustainable social development in Africa, when it is still struggling to find its own domesticated identity. Another conference held in South Africa in 2017 had been exclusively devoted to the theme *Rethinking Social Work in Africa: Decoloniality and Indigenous Knowledge in Education and Practice.*[2] This theme was formulated towards 'the need to construct a social work profession that is embedded in post-colonial and indigenous contexts, that speaks to the unique and local nature of these contexts, in critical dialogue with the historically dominant voices in the discipline from the Global North' (ASASWEI, 2017, 4). The need for more research, theory building and case studies from within – and from the bottom up – has been consistently reiterated in these major events.

Generally, the process of developing indigenous knowledge and cultural competence cannot just start with practice but rather with research and education that aim to integrate these knowledges and practices into the mainstream, teach them in the classroom, and competently apply them in practice.

The research referred to in this volume as well as the publication itself is an attempt to move towards closing some of these gaps. This chapter provides a general discussion on indigenisation and the importance of researching, analysing, documenting, and mainstreaming indigenous and innovative approaches of helping, healing, and problem solving, thus referring to some empirical evidence of a study conducted in the East African countries of Burundi, Kenya, Rwanda, Tanzania, and Uganda. A brief discussion on practice research as a critical element in indigenisation is provided and the specific methodologies and approaches used in the study upon which most of the chapters of this book are based are laid out. The chapter ends with a mapping of what the reader should expect in the subsequent chapters.

---

[1]   The acronym PROSOWO that is mentioned throughout this book stands for 'Professional Social Work in East Africa' and refers to a major project at the core of which is the professionalisation of social work in countries of the East African Community (see also in the Foreword). The said conference took place from 19 to 22 March 2018 in Kigali.

[2]   This conference took place from 8 to 11 October 2017 in Boksburg, South Africa.

The Enduring Case for Indigenisation of Social Work in Africa

The concepts of as well as the debates on indigenisation of social work are not new by any means. As far back as the 1970s, educators in Africa recognised the need to make social work more responsive to the contexts and specific needs of communities, groups, individuals, and development agendas in Africa. The Association for Social Work Education in Africa (ASWEA), which was formed in 1971, spearheaded the move towards making social work more relevant to African contexts. Gray, Kreitzer and Mupedziswa (2014, 101) note that ASWEA was

> guided by a decolonising agenda, as social work education sought alternatives to dominant Western approaches to service delivery and social work training. It set the stage for social work educators to consider local and regional issues and make the profession relevant to African settings.

The authors argue that besides the bid to rid social work of its Eurocentric values and cultural norms, the broader post-colonial political Africanisation movement called for the construction of scholarly knowledge based on African cultures and values in post-independence Africa. In fact, such indigenous knowledge – which should be seen as a rather dynamic, and not a static set of ideas, beliefs, and practices – abounds (Mawere, 2015; Mawere and Awuah-Nyamekye, 2015), despite oppression, hegemony and arrogance on the part of the former colonial powers, contemporary Eurocentric scholars, and some African elites.

The late Kenyan Nobel Laureate Wangari Maathai contended that, as much as foreign heritages might be wonderful and enriching to human experiences, they remain other people's experiences and heritages. And yet, through their strong power of suggestion, these heritages and cultures may reinforce a sense of inadequacy and nurture an inferiority complex in those constantly exposed to them and urged to perceive them as 'better' (Maathai, 2009, 172). In the perspective of social work, the move towards indigenisation and the adoption of culturally appropriate models and knowledge has had to grapple with such challenges. In the context of an education largely informed by the colonial heritage and still attached to the trappings of Western development aid as well as the forces of modernisation and globalisation, there are predominant voices across different population groups in Africa, including the elite, that conspicuously consider Western culture, knowledge and ways of knowing as superior, and, hence, promote these at the expense of their own cultural heritage.

Conversely, some authors (cf. Twikirize, 2014) have questioned whether some aspects of social work practice, particularly in East Africa, have been consciously or sub-consciously indigenised or contextualised to suit local realities. Twikirize (2014) raises the issue of the extent to which seemingly localised or indigenised models of practice fairly adopted by grassroots community development organisations have found their way into social work curricula.

A good example can be traced from Rwanda. The Rwanda government that took over after the 1994 genocide embarked on a development agenda built on the philosophy and practice of 'home-grown solutions' (see Ndahiro, Rwagatare and Nkusi, 2015). The key argument was that what is relevant to the people of Rwanda was the only means and way of developing Rwanda rather than adopting external models, theories, and practices (Kalinganire and Rutikanga, 2015). In this regard, a number of traditional and innovative models of social development were adopted and mainstreamed into national development plans, poverty reduction papers, and other critical social policies, such as those that relate to the care of orphans and vulnerable children. Such models were also strongly promoted in the post-genocide transitional justice system to rebuild Rwandan society (e.g. through the *gacaca* courts as a means of informal jurisdiction at the grassroots level), and equally taken up in the national social work discourse (see Kalinganire and Rutikanga, 2014).[3] Some of these models, such as *umugoroba w'ababyeyi* (parents' evening forum) and *ubudehe* (community-based poverty reduction) are presented in this volume.

Yet, interactions with social work faculty at the University of Rwanda during the implementation of the PROSOWO project showed that such home-grown solutions had not yet found their way into social work curricula within institutions of higher learning. One argument for not paying much attention to such practices and knowledge might be the lack of scientific study and documentation of these practices. Hence, because there was no authoritative text on such models, they were hardly, if ever, taught and/or discussed in the lecture room. Another argument could be that what is local and traditional is considered common knowledge and can all too often be bypassed until another person, external to the environment and practice, who views it as a novelty, brings it up.

Indigenisation has been inextricably tied up with decolonisation. Proponents argue that the continued adoption of Western theory, philosophy, and models is in fact inseparable from neo-colonialism that transcends all spheres of society rather than simply leaving its marks in education, social work, or social development practice. The adoption of the neoliberal agenda of the International Monetary Fund (IMF) and the World Bank by almost all African countries and other economies of the South, as well as the continued dependence on development aid with all its

---

[3]   Some scholars and human rights professionals caution against the top-down configuration of these 'home-grown solutions' and the concomitant coercion in implementing them at the local level, thus questioning the significance and acceptability of such indigenous approaches (see Straus and Waldorf, 2011). Criticism and resistance in this regard have also been empirically documented on the part of ordinary citizens (Thomson, 2013).

strings attached, serve as examples of a neo-colonial agenda that potentially keeps the countries and peoples of the Global South in subordination to the Global North (Gray, Kreitzer and Mupedziswa, 2014). Gray, Coates and Yellow Bird (2008) actually went to the extent of accusing mainstream social work of being a modernist, Western invention and a means of silencing marginal voices through technology transfer and importing into diverse cultural contexts across the world Western thinking primarily from the UK and the USA. According to these authors, the process has been supported through 'colonizing, Westernizing, globalizing and Americanizing forces' (Gray, Coates and Yellow Bird, 2008, 1).

In light of the need to break free from the shackles of colonial and neo-colonial ideology, influence, and practice, many authors have consistently sustained the debate on indigenisation, most of them focusing on why this is necessary rather than how it should be done, e.g. by providing examples of successful projects on indigenisation. For example, Spaneas (2011), writing on the example of Cyprus, argues that despite the consensus on the [negative] influence of colonial experience and Western theories of modernisation and economic growth, no meaningful attempts have been made to ensure that the profession fits into the social and economic environment in which it operates, thus leading to a lack of fit between traditional social norms and the Western processes of social welfare. This, he further argues, has resulted in changes that do not take into consideration the cultural differences and social norms. This is not different from the situation in Africa.

Spitzer (2017) rightly observes that the heritage of imported theories and concepts from the West is still heavily affecting social work education and practice in the 21st century and that these imported models neither provide sufficient responses to contemporary challenges in society nor do they effectively meet the socio-cultural realities of these contexts. During the Kigali social work conference referred to in the introduction, particular examples were provided where Western models on trauma-based interventions, conceived in largely peaceful countries with an emphasis on individual psychological needs, had failed to realise positive impacts in post-genocide Rwanda (King, 2018). King argues that such interventions 'lacked background information on the cultural, social, historical, and political contexts in which traumatic incidents occurred and from which appropriate interventions could be conceived, assessed and validated.' (26) Similarly, Owusu-Bemba (2003, cited in Spaneas, 2011) attributes difficulties in realising the desired results, such as in this case, to fundamental differences among societies. The author reiterates, as one of the critical differences, the focus on the individual in Western societies as contrasted to collective ideas in African societies. The argument is that in Western societies,

> the individual as unit per se embraces self-knowledge to understand their place and position in the world. This world view perception also guides the individual's

aspirations and shapes the kind of communication with others. However, in collective or communal societies, priority is given to the interdependence, to the obligations towards the community and their role in it, compared to the constituent elements. (Owusu-Bempah, 2003, cited in Spaneas, 2011, 4)

Hence, in the case of Rwanda, genocide survivors could not grasp the essence of individual-focused trauma-informed sessions, and according to King (2018), individuals wondered why they were being separated from their colleagues and being met in secluded rooms. They instead responded better to group models of trauma healing that took into account the collective tendencies of that society.

According to Gray, Coates and Yellow Bird (2008), the hesitation or slowness by social work to acknowledge non-Western and indigenous worldviews, local knowledge, and traditional forms of healing has, in turn, affected its ability to develop and deliver services in an effective, acceptable, and culturally appropriate manner. Such and other considerations have sustained the call for indigenisation of social work in Africa.

A positive trend in this regard is the incorporation of indigenous knowledge in the new global definition of social work that was jointly approved by the International Federation of Social Workers (IFSW) and the International Association of Schools of Social Work (IASSW) in 2014:

> Social work is a practice-based profession and an academic discipline that promotes social change and development, social cohesion, and the empowerment and liberation of people. Principles of social justice, human rights, collective responsibility and respect for diversities are central to social work. Underpinned by theories of social work, social sciences, humanities and indigenous knowledge, social work engages people and structures to address life challenges and enhance wellbeing. (IFSW, 2015, 19)

This revised definition – albeit highly contested – acknowledges that social work is informed not only by specific practice environments and Western theories, but also by indigenous knowledges (IFSW, 2015, 22). For social work in Africa and other countries of the Global South, this step implies an appreciation and encouragement of increased focus on their own cultural values, support systems, and coping strategies (Spitzer, 2018).

A number of difficulties and challenges with indigenising social work have been highlighted in literature. Kreitzer (2013, cited in Gray, Kreitzer and Mupedziswa, 2014), for example, lists the historical challenges in attempts to indigenise social work education as including: the lingering colonial legacy and dependence on Western curricula; social workers' failure to engage in national social development planning; the impact of structural adjustment programmes; lack of indigenous teaching material and outmoded teaching practices; underuse of social research;

lack of public awareness of social work's role in society; and the struggle to reorient the curriculum from case-based remedial social work to community-centred development. Other authors have raised the issue of an African culture – asserting that it is impossible to align social work to culturally relevant ideals since, first of all, culture is dynamic, and secondly, some aspects of culture and tradition can, in fact, contradict the basic principles and ideals of social work and human rights (cf. Kreitzer, in this volume). Kreitzer (2012) contends that the task for Africans is to change the perception of their cultures as negative and Western-dependent, to being a positive contributor to the world as a precursor for social work to be developed from within. Maathai (2009, 168) had referred to these negative perceptions as the demonisation of African culture and traditions that goes back to the colonial period, and which subsequently led to a split life and an identity crisis by and among African peoples.

From an education perspective, indigenisation is also faced with the pressure to train graduates that fit into the global market and context (Osei-Hwedie and Rankopo, 2008). In this regard, indigenisation is mistakenly construed as limiting the global competitiveness of social work graduates. Counter to this argument, Twikirize (2014) contends that indigenisation does not have to imply a total overhaul and rejection of everything considered Western and non-African, but rather to ensure that the ideology, the theories, practice models, and ethical principles are relevant and align well to the context within which social work is practised. Gray and Coates (2008) rightly argue that indigenisation does not have to contradict internationalisation since social work's goals, principles and values remain universal, and, in principle, the profession's call is to solve personal and communal difficulties wherever it is applied.

Conversely, Osei-Hwedie (2002) and Rankopo and Osei-Hwedie (2011) caution that indigenisation should not be equated to adopting the so-called traditional or 'primitive' values but be predicated upon whatever the masses regard to be an authentic expression of themselves. Gray, Kreitzer and Mupedziswa (2014, 112), in defending the enduring legacy of indigenisation, assert that

> if one considers issues of history and location in the world, differences between European and African – and all indigenous – values and beliefs, local relevance, and responsiveness to context to be ethical matters, then it would seem that indigenisation is an ethical imperative which should form part of local formulations of ethical principles, while continuing to be explored, debated and developed.

Indigenous and Innovative Models of Practice

Official definitions of the concept of indigeneity often link it to First Nations or the Indigenous Peoples of North America, Australia, and other mostly industrialised societies that have pockets of original inhabitants of the land in often secluded communities, such as the Aboriginals in Canada and Australia, the Maori of New Zealand, and the Ainu people of Japan. In Africa, the Khoisan of South Africa, the Masaai of Kenya and Tanzania, and the Twa of Rwanda, Burundi and South-western Uganda could fit this classification. According to the United Nations Declaration (2007), Indigenous Peoples are culturally distinct and often possess a history of colonisation or external invasion that threatens their existence. Ibrahima and Mattaini (2017, 5) observe that such a definition of indigeneity is based on the current state of colonisation; disregarding many countries in Africa and Asia that have '"undergone decolonization"', with the assumption that they have achieved self-determination'. Owing to difficulties in reaching a consensual definition of indigeneity, the UN agrees that the most fruitful approach is to identify, rather than define, indigenous peoples (UN, 2007; United Nations Permanent Forum on Indigenous Issues, n.d.). According to Ibrahima and Mattaini (2017), indigenous knowledge emerges from a range of sources embedded in institutions, relationships and rituals, and is a dynamic mix of past tradition and present innovation and is, thus, ever evolving and usually tacit.

Gray, Coates and Yellow Bird (2008) define indigenous social work as being essentially about the development of culturally relevant social work for, with, and by Indigenous Peoples and actually contest the use of the term 'indigenisation' when referring to culturally relevant social work. Walton and Abo El Nasr (1988) prefer to use the term '*authentisation*', which proposes a move away from simply adapting and modifying Western social work theory and practice to instead generate knowledge and practice models from the ground up, drawing on the values, beliefs, customs, and cultural norms of local and indigenous helping practices. Through this way, social work can become genuinely culturally appropriate, relevant, and authentic (Gray, Coates and Yellow Bird, 2008). Gray, Kreitzer and Mupedziswa (2014, 105), referring to Mohale (2010), state that in Africa 'indigenous' is synonymous with 'African' and 'anti-colonial', and 'indigenisation in African social work means Africanisation'.

In consideration of these aforementioned arguments, we use the concept 'indigeneous' in this publication to refer to distinct knowledges, practices and ways of living and doing that have their majority origin within specific local communities. In other words, we do not use it to strictly refer to practices with or for the officially acknowledged Indigenous Peoples. Since most African societies are still mostly organised around ethnic groups, occupying particular regions of a country and characterised by a number of unique cultures and languages, we choose to use the concept of indigeneity to describe the adopted models of problem solving, healing, and helping as well as the local knowledge systems that are associated with such groups, communities, or even countries. Hence, we refer to such practices as the *ikibiri* system and the *bashingantahe* institution in Burundi as systems of community development, leadership, and conflict resolution; the *msaragambo* model of community organising among the Chagga people in Kilimanjaro Region, Tanzania; the *bataka* model of self-help in Western Uganda; and *umugoroba w'ababyeyi* and *ubudehe* in Rwanda, among others. As argued by Ibrahima and Mattaini (2017), developing indigenous approaches to development is linked to indigenous knowledge development, as knowledge is the base for designing interventions and helps to avoid replicating futile programmes. In our case, the underlying endeavour throughout the book is to link such knowledge systems and practices to the social work profession.

As stated before, in countries such as Rwanda, indigenous models of helping, healing, and problem solving have been integrated and mainstreamed into national development plans and constitute the main models of community and social development. Indigenous models do take cognisance of the cultures and practices of producers and consumers of social work interventions as well as of the contexts within which social workers practice. In a previous study under the PROSOWO project (Twikirize et al., 2014), practitioners identified gaps in the extent to which social work education had prepared them for culturally relevant social work. They gave examples of how they sometimes found difficulties in appreciating and integrating local knowledges and practices into their formal work, which sometimes led to a lack of efficacy of services and to subtle conflicts with the target communities. Yet, for practitioners to develop cultural competencies or, as argued by Weaver (1999), to progress from cultural sensitivity to cultural competence and the ability to integrate cultural knowledge and sensitivity with skills for a more effective and culturally appropriate helping processes, requires an understanding of indigenous approaches by social work practitioners. Sillitoe and Marzano (2009, cited in Ibrahima and Mattaini, 2017) acknowledge that incorporating local knowledge and values into the development process (typically dominated by foreign ideas and hierarchies) requires substantial time, efforts and resources, and that this is compounded by the fact that local knowledge is heterogeneous and complex which, according to the authors, is inconvenient for development.

Conversely, we use the concept of 'innovative models' to refer to those hybrid practices that exhibit features of creative use of knowledges and practices, not necessarily linked to any particular origin but which are perceived to effectively and appropriately respond to people's needs and aspirations. According to Dudchenko (2015, cited in Makarov et al., 2017), innovation is a special field of theory and practice, a system of actions on the part of a social subject that is improving the qualities of a socio-cultural object, which allows the agent to acquire the necessary resources and rewards him or her with a positive reputation. Makarov et al.

(2017) contend that innovation processes should be regarded as changes that are implemented after scientific research or discovery, which are qualitatively different from their previous counterpart. Some of the bases of social innovation include changes in the external environment, social problems that cannot be solved through conventional methods, and changes in the demands of a society; and specifically, unresolved social problems which demand new means and regulations in the social sphere (Makarov et al., 2017).

In this book, Luwangula et al. provide an example of *akabondo* (cluster model), an innovative form of community development adopted by World Vision in South-western Uganda to deal with persistent problems of household poverty and deprivation, having observed that their long applied, largely Western approaches were neither cost-effective nor making lasting improvements. Other examples discussed in this volume refer to village savings and loans associations (VSLAs), traditional fostering in Northern Uganda – a hybrid of formal and traditional approaches to foster care in the aftermath of the two-decade armed conflict in this region; as well as the innovative use of mobile telephony in Kenya to change the landscape for social service delivery.

Unravelling Indigenous and Innovative Models through Practice Research

Spitzer (2017) underlines the importance of intensified research, coupled with theory building that aligns social work and social development with cultural concepts and epistemologies in order to identify innovative approaches that work in a given context. In the East African region, a lack of adequate research has been consistently identified as one of the gaps in the bid to indigenise social work. Practice research is particularly critical, since it emphasises bottom-up approaches to knowledge generation. The study that informed most chapters in this book adopted an approach that tended towards practice research to guide the collection and analysis of data about indigenous and innovative models of social work. Uggerhøj (2011, 51) describes practice research as a 'bottom-up knowledge production, or a field of research oriented towards subjects more than objects'. In the *Salisbury Statement* (Salisbury Forum Group, 2011, 5), the following characterisation is provided:

> Practice research involves curiosity about practice. It is about identifying good and promising ways in which to help people; and it is about challenging troubling practice through the critical examination of practice and the development of new ideas in the light of experience. It recognizes that this is best done by practitioners in partnership with researchers, where the latter have as much, if not more, to learn from practitioners as practitioners have to learn from researchers. It is an inclusive approach to professional knowledge that is concerned with understanding

the complexity of practice alongside the commitment to empower, and to realise social justice, through practice.

In this statement, it is further said that 'practice research involves the generation of knowledge of direct relevance to professional practice and therefore will normally involve knowledge generated directly from practice itself in a grounded way' (5). Practice research is thus based on a combination of research methodology, field research, and practical experience (Uggerhøj, 2011). Flyvbjerg (2001, cited in Uggerhøj, 2011, 51) contends that practice research operates via practical rationality based on judgement and experience, with the following key elements being integral to the process:

- Getting close to reality (the research is conducted close to the phenomenon or the group studied and is subject to reactions from the surroundings, and remains close during the phases of data analysis, feedback, and the publication of results);

- Emphasising little things (the focus is on minutiae, where research studies the major in the minor and where small questions often lead to big answers);

- Looking at practice before discourse (discourse analysis is disciplined by the analysis of practice, and research focuses on practical activities and knowledge in everyday situations);

- Studying concrete cases and contexts (research methodically builds on case studies, because practical rationality is best understood through cases; practices are studied in their proper contexts);

- Joining agency and structure (the focus is on both the actor and the structural level; actors and their practices are analysed in relation to structures, and structures in terms of agency); and finally

- Dialoguing with a polyphony of voices (the research is dialogical and includes itself in a polyphony of voices, with no voice claiming final authority).

It is the consideration of these elements that provided the basis for adopting aspects of this approach in studying indigenous and innovative models of social work practice in the East African Community. We ensured close interactions with the people at the grassroots level and let them tell their stories, rather than let our preconceived ideas determine what we were looking for. We tried to decipher the 'major from the minor' – in this case the minor being seen as the routine and sometimes taken-for-granted practices and knowledge from within the communities. In as far as possible, we worked alongside the social workers and community volunteers to better understand the modalities of collecting and interpreting the data.

Key research questions explored include:

- What are the historical and emerging indigenous models and approaches used in helping and problem solving?
- Are these models still considered relevant in contemporary societies?
- Are these models integrated into mainstream social work practice and education?
- Which models are seen as being innovative in the respective East African contexts?
- What are the perceived strengths and gaps in the existing social work curricula with regard to indigenous and innovative models of social work practice?
- What opportunities and challenges do curricula in the respective East African countries present for these models to be delivered to social work students?
- To what extent do practitioners associate with and appreciate the indigenous models of social work?
- What are the missed opportunities associated with delayed adoption or non-adoption of indigenous models of social work?
- What factors influence the (non-)uptake of indigenous and innovative social work models among social work trainers (into the curricula), and practitioners?
- What is the level of documentation and popularisation of the indigenous and innovative social work models?
- Is there any evidence of contextualisation of these models where they are used?

Research Methods and Processes

Studies were conducted in five countries in East Africa, namely Kenya, Uganda, Tanzania, Burundi, and Rwanda, in 2016. The research protocol was jointly developed between the partner institutions of the PROSOWO project and were adapted to the particular contexts of the partner countries. Research teams in the partner countries obtained ethical clearance and research approvals from the respective institutional review boards available in their countries. Research approvals were obtained from the National Council of Scientific Research and Innovation (Kenya), the MildMay Research Ethics Committee (Uganda), the College of Arts and Social Sciences Department of Research and Post-graduate Studies (Rwanda), and the National Commission for Science and Technology (Tanzania). In Burundi, clearance was sought from the Hope Africa University Graduate Research Department as well as from heads of communes.

Qualitative data collection methods were used in all the study sites. In all five countries, participants included community members and social service users, local cultural leaders and community volunteers such as para-social workers, social work practitioners in government and non-governmental organisations, social work educators, social work students, and key informants at the policy level. The rationale for including a multiplicity of participants was to understand indigenous and innovative models from not only the everyday experiences and knowledge of people at the grassroots, but also to include the perspectives of practice, education, and training. Policy-level participants were useful in interrogating the extent of integration or, at least, consideration of these 'home-grown' and innovative models and knowledge systems in social policy-making and analysis. Table 1 shows the summary of participants reached and the data collection methods used.

Table 1: *Study participants, sample and research methods per country*

| Target Group | Methods | Number per country | | | | |
		Burundi	Kenya	Rwanda	Tanzania	Uganda
Community members and service users	Focus group discussions (FDGs)	4	8	8	6	11
Local leaders	Interviews	5	3	5	10	13
	FGDs	0	4	3	0	0
Social work practitioners	Interviews	6	8	19	20	27
Social work educators	Interviews	0	5	2	12	4
	FGDs	0	0	1	0	0
Social work students	FGDs	0	3	0	4	3
Policy makers	Interviews	1	0	2	10	3

Whilst each research team was responsible for their own data analysis, a similar approach was adopted to analyse data, i.e. that of thematic analysis. Emerging themes and sub-themes were identified, based on their level of recurrence within the data collected and in line with the key research questions. Basic socio-demographic data about the respondents were captured in order to facilitate data analysis and interpretation. The most recurrent themes were identified, and then subjected to further analysis.

The indigenous and innovative models presented in this book provide only a few examples of numerous practices and approaches identified and analysed in the course of the study.[4] The analysis and presentation bring out histories and features of the different approaches, institutions, and practices, their current application, as well as their strengths and weaknesses, particularly in view of contemporary human rights discourses around issues such as gender sensitivity, and the linkages and lessons for contemporary social work.

A Guide through the Book

This book is conceptualised within the broad framework of indigenisation and cultural appropriateness – concepts and notions that are critical for effective social work practice and sustainable social development. The underlying pan-African philosophical framework of *ubuntu* permeates all the approaches, practices, and so-called models of helping and problem solving as presented in this book. This *ubuntu* concept and philosophy is elaborated in Chapter 2 by Rodreck Mupedziswa, Morena Rankopo and Lengwe-Katembula Mwansa. The concept of *ubuntu*, a term predicated on the notion of *quid pro quo* – which emphasises a spirit of humanness and sharing – is unpacked with diverse examples from different parts and spheres of life in Africa.

In Chapter 3, Linda Kreitzer discusses culturally relevant curricula for social work as an ethical imperative. She provides a historical contextualisation of the African social work curriculum and highlights some of the current issues concerning culturally relevant social work education and practice as it relates to Africa. The main purpose of this chapter is to enable scholars and researchers in Africa to think about their ethical responsibility for appropriate social work education and practice.

The next set of chapters (4-14) presents discourses and specific indigenous and innovative models from different countries within the East African Community. We start with Rwanda. In Chapter 4, Charles Rutikanga analyses one of the home-grown models for poverty reduction in Rwanda, the *ubudehe* traditional approach. *Ubudehe* is a culture-based social protection system of intra-community cooperation based on collective and individual actions. The chapter demonstrates how, in post-genocide Rwanda, the cultural context was made a strong basis from which home-grown solutions to fulfil needs would emerge and how these culturally owned practices are being adopted to translate sustainable development programmes into practice.

---

[4]   A detailed account of these and other approaches will be published in country-specific reports and publications; see the concluding chapter in this book.

In Chapter 5, Théogène Bangwanubusa, Consolée Uwihangana and Alexandre Hakizamungu present *umugoroba w'ababyeyi* (parents' evening forum), a government-led grassroots model through which men, women, and children participate in promoting better cohabitation of family members to improve their living conditions and to contribute towards sustainable community development.

The next two chapters focus on cases from Tanzania. In Chapter 6, Zena M. Mabeyo and Abigail Kiwelu provide a critical analysis of indigenous and innovative models of problem solving in Tanzania, highlighting their inherent strengths and weaknesses. The application of these approaches is described in relation to social work practice, particularly in problem solving and helping the vulnerable and marginalised groups.

In Chapter 7, Zena M. Mabeyo, Abu Mvungi and William Manyama delve into a deeper analysis of one such model, namely the *msaragambo* model of community organising in Kilimanjaro Region. The *msaragambo* model demonstrates how collective efforts and resources are organised and utilised to help poor individuals, settle disputes, correct behaviour, and care for the elderly, widows, and vulnerable children. The authors argue that the use of this and other culturally based models is evidence that indigenous problem-solving approaches are relevant and effective in specific cultural settings.

Chapters 8-11 present perspectives and case examples from Uganda. Ronald Luwangula, Janestic M. Twikirize, Justus Twesigye and Stanley Kitimbo provide an overview of social work practice and its attempts towards cultural responsiveness. They argue that whilst elements of practice have embraced some indigenous knowledge and practices, social work education has been slow to integrate such knowledge, and yet these indigenous and innovative models of helping promote a developmental social work perspective and, therefore, have important implications for social work's contribution to sustainable development.

In Chapter 9, the same authors elaborate on *bataka* groups, a form of mutual aid approach prevalent in South-western Uganda, which promotes resilience, household wellbeing, and community development.

In Chapter 10, Ronald Luwangula, Janestic M. Twikirize and Justus Twesigye discuss an innovative model of child fostering in post-conflict Northern Uganda. This model, initiated by a group of women at the grassroots level, has features of both traditional and formal aspects of fostering and has been acknowledged and integrated into the formal child protection system in that particular region by both the government and other development partners.

In Chapter 11, Sharlotte Tusasiirwe offers a practical perspective on the everyday challenges of poor and vulnerable older women in rural areas and how they are innovatively using their agency and resources to survive. She argues that social workers working with older people need to listen to the voices of such older women to inform the development of strengths-based interventions.

Two specific indigenous problem-solving mechanisms from Burundi are presented in Chapters 12 and 13 by Susan Muchiri, Jacqueline Murekasenge and Serges Claver Nzisabira. In this conflict-ridden society, the *bashingantahe* cultural institution, made up of eminent wise men, is presented as a leadership ensemble that aims to promote peaceful living through conflict management at different levels of Burundian society, particularly at the grassroots level.

Conversely, the *ikibiri* system refers to activities organised at the community level for public interests, such as building schools and roads and cleaning public places, and it reflects the collective nature of Burundian society as far as community life is concerned. Although these institutions and practices have been weakened through modernisation and globalisation, coupled with large-scale violence and conflict, the authors argue that contemporary social work in Burundi would do well to embrace aspects of these cultural mechanisms for more effective service delivery.

In Chapter 14, Elijah Macharia Ndung'u discusses how mobile telephones are revolutionising the landscape for social work services in Kenya by being innovatively used to improve the design and delivery of social services to the most vulnerable groups, individuals, households, and communities. Beyond ordinary communication, the telephone has become a mini-bank, a mechanism for social protection, and a source of livelihood. At the service level, mobile telephone applications are increasingly adopted by social workers and social development practitioners to monitor services, manage referrals, and provide psycho-social support.

The main thread throughout these chapters is the significance of placing people, culture and context at the centre of social work intervention. The *ubuntu* ideals that mostly reflect the collective nature of African societies are evident in all the models presented. This strengthens the argument to not only acknowledge the need for the integration of indigenous knowledge and practices but to take concrete steps to bring such knowledge into the mainstream. The key message in the concluding chapter is that empirical research on contextual and innovative ways of addressing social problems is a key pillar for social work education, theory formation, practice, and policy. Thus, some essential future research areas in the context of East Africa are expounded.

References

ASASWEI (2017) *Report on the 2017 Social Work Conference Held at OR Tambo Conference Centre from 8-11 October 2017*. South Africa.

Gray M and Coates J (2008) From Indigenization to Cultural Relevance. In: Gray M, Coates J and Yellow Bird M (eds) *Indigenous Social Work around the World: Towards Culturally Relevant Education and Practice*. Aldershot: Ashgate, 13-30.

Gray M and Coates J (2010) 'Indigenization' and Knowledge Development: Extending the Debate. *International Social Work*, 53(5): 613-627.

Gray M, Coates J and Yellow Bird M (2008) Introduction, In: Gray M, Coates J and Yellow Bird M (eds) *Indigenous Social Work around the World. Towards Culturally Relevant Education and Practice*. Aldershot: Ashgate, 1-10.

Gray M, Kreitzer L and Mupedziswa R (2014) The Enduring Relevance of Indigenisation in African Social Work: A Critical Reflection on ASWEA's Legacy. *Ethics and Social Welfare* 8(2): 101-116.

Ibrahima AB and Mattaini MA (2017) Social Work in Africa: Decolonizing Methodologies and Approaches. *International Social Work*. https://doi.org/10.1177/0020872817742702.

International Federation of Social Workers (IFSW) *IFSW's Policies 2015*. Berne: IFSW.

Kalinganire C and Rutikanga C (2015) *The Role of Social Work in Poverty Reduction and the Realisation of Millennium Development Goals in Rwanda*. Kampala. Fountain.

Kalinganire C and Rutikanga C (2014) The Status of Social Work Education and Practice in Rwanda. In: Spitzer H, Twikirize JM and Wairire GG (eds) *Professional Social Work in East Africa. Towards Social Development, Poverty Reduction and Gender Equality*. Kampala: Fountain, 108-120.

King RU (2018) Trauma, Psychosocial Healing and Social Work. Keynote Speech at the International Social Work Conference, 19-22 March 2018, Kigali, Rwanda. In: Spitzer H and Kitimbo S (eds) *Professional Social Work and Sustainable Development in Africa. Conference Programme and Book of Abstracts*. East Africa Centre for Research and Innovation in Social Work, 26.

Kreitzer L (2012) *Social Work in Africa: Exploring Culturally Relevant Education and Practice in Ghana*. Calgary: University of Calgary Press.

Maathai W (2009) *The Challenge for Africa*. London: Arrow Books.

Makarov V, Rostovskaya T, Shimanovskaya Y, Tyapkina T, Kozlovskaya S, Firsov M and Sizikova V (2017) Innovative Models of Social Activity and their Adaptation to Social Work. *Espacios*, 38(43). Available at: http://www.revistaespacios.com/a17v38n43/a17v38n43p30.pdf (accessed 24 May 2018).

Mawere M (2015) Indigenous Knowledge and Public Education in Sub-Saharan Africa. *Africa Spectrum*, 50(2): 57-71.

Mawere M and Awuah-Nyamekye S (2015) (eds) *Between Rhetoric and Reality. The State and Use of Indigenous Knowledge in Post-colonial Africa*. Bamenda: Langaa Research and Publishing CIG.

Mupedziswa R (2001) The Quest for Relevance: Towards a Conceptual Model of Developmental Social Work Education and Training in Africa. *International Social Work*, 44(3): 285-300.

Ndahiro A, Rwagatare J and Nkusi A (2015) *Rwanda. Rebuilding of a Nation*. Kigali: Fountain.

Osei-Hwedie K (1993) The Challenge of Social Work in Africa: Starting the Indigenization Process. *Journal of Social Development in Africa*, 8(1): 19-30.

Osei-Hwedie K (2002) Indigenous Practice – Some Informed Guesses. Self-evident and Possible, *Social Work/Maatskaplike Werk*, 38(4): 311-23.

Osei-Hwedie K and Rankopo MJ (2008) Developing a Culturally Relevant Social Work Education in Africa: The Case of Botswana. In: Gray M, Coates J and Yellow Bird M (eds) *Indigenous Social Work around the World. Towards Culturally Relevant Education and Practice*. Aldershot: Ashgate, 203-218.

Rankopo MJ and Osei-Hwedie K (2011) Globalization and Culturally Relevant Social Work: African Perspectives on Indigenization. *International Social Work*, 54(1): 137-147.

Salisbury Forum Group (2011) The Salisbury Statement. *Social Work and Society*, 9(1): 4-9.

Spaneas S (2011) Social work in Cyprus. The challenge of indigenization. *9th Annual ESPAnet conference: Sustainability and transformation in European Social Policy*, Valencia, 8–10 September. Available at: https://www.academia.edu/879976/Social_Work_in_ Cyprus_The_challenge_of_indigenization. (accessed 24 May 2018).

Spitzer, H (2018) Soziale Arbeit und soziale Entwicklung in Afrika. In: Otto H, Thiersch H, Treptow R and Ziegler H (eds) *Handbuch Soziale Arbeit. Grundlagen der Sozialarbeit und Sozialpädagogik*. Munich: Reinhardt, 1448-1457.

Spitzer H (2017) Social Work in East Africa: A *Mzungu* Perspective. *International Social Work*, 1-14. doi.org/10.1177/0020872817742696.

Spitzer H and Twikirize JM (2014) A Vision for Social Work in East Africa. In: Spitzer H, Twikirize JM and Wairire GG (eds) *Professional Social Work in East Africa. Towards Social Development, Poverty Reduction and Gender Equality*. Kampala: Fountain, 373-84.

Spitzer H, Twikirize JM and Wairire GG (eds) (2014) *Professional Social Work in East Africa: Towards Social Development, Poverty Reduction and Gender Equality*. Kampala: Fountain.

Straus S and Waldorf L (2011) (eds) *Remaking Rwanda: State Building and Human Rights after Mass Violence*. Madison: University of Wisconsin Press.

Thomson S (2013) *Whispering Truth to Power. Everyday Resistance to Reconciliation in Postgenocide Rwanda*. Madison: University of Wisconsin Press.

Twikirize JM (2014) Indigenisation of Social Work in Africa: Debates, Prospects and Challenges. In: Spitzer H, Twikirize JM and Wairire GG (eds) *Professional Social Work in East Africa. Towards Social Development, Poverty Reduction and Gender Equality*. Kampala: Fountain, 75-90.

Twikirize, JM, Spitzer H, Wairire, GG, Mabeyo, ZM and Rutikanga, C (2014) Professional Social Work in East Africa: Empirical Evidence. In: Spitzer H, Twikirize JM and

Wairire GG (eds) *Professional Social Work in East Africa. Towards Social Development, Poverty Reduction and Gender Equality.* Kampala: Fountain, 189-216.

Uggerhøj, L (2011) Theorizing Practice Research in Social Work. *Social Work & Social Sciences Review,* 15(1): 49-73. DOI: 10.1921/095352211X604318.

United Nations Permanent Forum on Indigenous Issues (n.d.). *Indigenous Peoples, Indigenous Voices: Fact Sheet.* Available at: http://www.un.org/esa/socdev/unpfii/documents/5session_factsheet1.pdf. (accessed 21 May 2018).

United Nations (2007) *United Nations Declaration on the Rights of Indigenous Peoples.* United Nations.

Walton RG and Abo El Nasr MM (1988) Indigenization and Authentization in Terms of Social Work in Egypt. *International Social Work,* 31(2): 135-144.

Weaver HN (1999) Indigenous People and the Social Work Profession: Defining Culturally Competent Services. *Social Work,* 44(3): 217–225.

Ubuntu as a Pan-African Philosophical Framework for Social Work in Africa

Rodreck Mupedziswa, Morena Rankopo and Lengwe-Katembula Mwansa

Introduction

There seems to be some consensus among scholars that population segments domiciled in different parts of the world tend to hold different worldviews. The term 'worldview' relates to the 'way a person tends to understand his or her relationship with social institutions, nature, objects, other people and spirituality' (Barker, 1999, 522). It is in the context of this thinking that concepts such as 'Eurocentric' and 'Afrocentric' have gained currency, with people of Eurocentric extraction expected to hold a different worldview from that of those of, say, Afrocentric extraction. Thabede (2008) cites Mazrui (1986) and Mbigi (1997) as both arguing that the philosophical integrity of traditional Africa has survived among continental Africans long enough to render Africans to possess a distinct African ethos. Thus, the essence of the argument is that African people have always viewed phenomena from the vantage point of an African worldview, which is informed by African culture.

Perspectives that are culturally determined include, among others, notions of cause and effect, conceptions of time, values, and ideas (Torrey, 1972). Among these culturally determined perspectives is the notion of *ubuntu*, a theme that shall be the focus of this chapter. The concept of *ubuntu* is considered from the perspective of its potential as a philosophical framework for social work practice in Africa. The purpose of the chapter, therefore, is to push the frontiers of analysis of the concept of *ubuntu* essentially as it relates to social work practice in Africa. While it is a fact that in Africa 'political systems, social structures, economic conditions and cultural practices vary greatly' (Spitzer, 2014, 15), it is equally true that there are certain tenets of social work that cut across the entire continent. Social work is both an art and a science and its knowledge base is eclectic (IFSW, 2017). The paper explores the relationship between social work and the concept of *ubuntu*, with particular focus on its relevance to Africa.

The Philosophical and Conceptual Basis of *Ubuntu*

The concept of *ubuntu* has attracted much attention and even debate in the past decades. Swanson (2007, 53) has referred to this concept as Africa's 'indigenous philosophy of Ubuntu', noting that the term is borne out of the philosophy that community strength comes out of community support, and that dignity and identity are achieved through the values of mutualism, empathy, generosity, and community commitment. This suggests that the concept of *ubuntu* is essentially linked to the notions of cooperation and working together and, in essence, it is imbued in principles that compel individuals and families to care for each other out of moral obligation (Rankopo, Osei-Hwedie and Modie-Moroka, 2007). The idea behind *ubuntu*, Khoza (1994) has argued, is grossly opposed to rugged individualism and its negation of ideas of social groups or community units to the point of depersonalising the individual. In other words, for this concept, emphasis is placed on linking the individual to the collective through brotherhood or sisterhood (Swanson, 2007). In corroborating this contention, Khoza (1994) averred that *ubuntu* (or African humanism, as he calls it) encompasses ideas such as the universal brotherhood of Africans, treating and respecting other people as human beings, and placing great importance on the concept of sharing. Tutu (1999) explained that in African culture, if you wanted to praise someone, you could say '*Yu u nobuntu*', suggesting that the individual is generous, hospitable, friendly, caring and compassionate. Tutu further explained that *ubuntu* suggests that '[m]y humanity is caught up, is inextricably bound up, in yours', further noting that the concept suggests that '[w]e belong in a bundle of life' (Tutu, 1999; Swanson, 2007).

Interestingly, there does not seem to be any broad consensus regarding the origins of this term, although the idea itself has apparently always been engrained in African culture. Thus, while Swanson (2007), for instance, opined that the term '*ubuntu*' is derived from an isiXhosa proverb in Southern Africa that goes '*Umuntungumuntu ngabantu*' (a person is a person through others), Magumbate and Nyanguru (2013), on the other hand, argue that, in fact, the term '*ubuntu*' derived from 'Nguni and Bantu languages of Africa'. Whether the Bantu languages referred to include isiXhosa is not clear. Even so, any debates about the origins of this term aside, there appears to be broad consensus that words that have been associated with the meaning of *ubuntu* have included compassion, solidarity, kindness, caring, generosity, harmony, consensus, hospitality, sympathy, and sharing – among others (Khoza, 1994; Mbigi and Maree, 1995; Mbiti, 1990; Swanson, 2007; Kamwangamalu, 1999). All these concepts seem to suggest that the *ubuntu* philosophy has to do with humanity towards others.

In further elucidating the idea behind this philosophy, Rankopo, Osei-Hwedie and Modie-Moroka (2007) observed that the point of departure of the *ubuntu* principle is that those who are privileged at one point may become vulnerable at another point; hence, the need to support relatives, neighbours, and community members. This suggests that the idea of *ubuntu* is predicated on the *quid pro quo* mantra – which emphasises reciprocity, a spirit of sharing, and a belief that one earns respect by respecting and empowering others. Thus, serving others is perceived as an investment for assistance in the future. Viewed from this angle, *ubuntu* seems to be concerned with the equitable distribution of resources – and thus, to a great extent, also with the promotion of social justice. There seems to be broad consensus that *ubuntu*, and not political expediency, should be the first and most important principle to inspire economic progress, particularly in African countries. And this is where the profession of social work comes in, as will be shown later.

Much of the existing literature tends to suggest that the term '*ubuntu*' has South African roots. However, it is interesting to note that this philosophy is known by several different names in this region. Vernacular terms for *ubuntu* include *bomoto* (Congo); *gimuntu* (Angola); *botho* (Botswana); *umunthu* (Malawi); *vumuntu* (Mozambique); *vumunhu, vhutu* (South Africa); and *humunnhu/ubuthosi* (Zimbabwe) (Magumbate and Nyanguru, 2013; Swanson, 2007; Kamwangamalu, 1999; Khoza, 1994). Southern Africa, however, can never claim monopoly over this concept. In East Africa, for instance, terms used have included *bumuntu* (Tanzania) and *umuntu* (Uganda). Furthermore, Magumbate and Nyanguru (2013, 87) cite Wichtner-Zola (2012) as stating that in Runyakitara, a language spoken by the Banyankore, Banyoro, Batooro and Bakiga of Western Uganda, and also by the Bahaya, Banyambo and others in Northern Tanzania, the term used is *obuntu*. The two authors further explain that in the dialect of Central Uganda, the term *obuntu-bulamu* refers to the same general idea (Magumbate and Nyanguru, 2013).

The philosophy of *ubuntu* promotes teamwork and collaboration, meaning this principle promotes group cohesiveness and group support. Its cornerstone is a deep sense of belonging to a group, be it the extended family, the clan, or the community. This principle further seeks to promote the worth and dignity of all human beings, with an emphasis on self-respect. *Ubuntu* works on the premise that everyone must contribute towards community initiatives and aspirations and, by implication, towards national development. Based on the spirit of *ubuntu*, human service professions like social work are expected to assist their clients to harness their energies and knowledge in the promotion of the goals of social development.

Ubuntu and its General Application in African Contexts

The concept of *ubuntu* has been applied in various spheres of life, including economic, political, and social arenas. Traditionally, in many African countries the office of the chief was responsible for both governmental (administrative) and spiritual functions. As observed by Magumbate and Nyanguru (2013, 96), 'in managing community conflicts, the application of African traditional jurisprudence, leadership and governance is usually helpful and this is espoused in the values of ubuntu. The chief's subjects attained levels of wellbeing through cultural processes that were inculcated at the family and community levels. Thus, the concept of *ubuntu* commenced right at the family level and was reinforced through initiatives that included rituals such as the traditional initiation schools that focused on teaching young people social/life skills that promoted communalism (Ntseane and Solo, 2007). Every task the chief wanted performed for the wellbeing of his tribe had to be done through communalistic systems such as age regiments or classifications of youth, men, and women, depending on the nature of the task. In some tribes, the age regiment also worked in the fields, to produce food that would then be kept in the chief's granary, for use by the needy.

In many parts of Africa, the chief, just like the Biblical Joseph in Egypt, would mobilise households to work in communal fields controlled by the chief and to store the harvest in large granaries for future use. Focusing on the example of Zimbabwe, Magumbate and Nyanguru (2013) noted that this initiative was referred to as *zunde ramambo* (the chief's granary), and it involved members of the community working together to grow food that would be kept by the chief for distribution to the needy. In many instances, the chief had an age regiment whose role was to provide security to the tribe in times of threats or war with neighbouring tribes.

Human relations predicated on the notion of *ubuntu* would be governed by values such as social justice, respect, and dignity (Bloom, 1990). In modern-day Africa, many sitting governments and management structures in private institutions (Karsten and Illa, 2005) take advantage of this and, in the case of governments, in some cases attempt to invoke *ubuntu* to whip up support, or to promote unity and solidarity among the citizenry, with varying degrees of success. *Ubuntu* as a concept or philosophy (as Tutu, 1999 would aver) has been expressed differently by various observers in Africa. The former President of Zambia, Kenneth Kaunda, made reference to what he termed humanism (Kaunda and Morris, 1976) while the late Tanzanian President Mwalimu Julius Nyerere spoke of *ujamaa* (Hyden, 1975). Both concepts, consistent with *ubuntu*, can be understood as ideologies that incorporate various core values and beliefs about the person within the context of a community or family. Such ideologies spell out how persons should interact with others.

In the case of South Africa, for instance, the concept of *ubuntu* was incorporated into the transitional post-apartheid constitution. The epilogue to that country's Interim Constitution of 1993 read, inter alia, 'there is need for understanding but not for vengeance, a need for reparation but not for retaliation, a need for Ubuntu, but not for victimisation' (Gade, 2011). In Kenya, following independence in 1963, President Jomo Kenyatta adopted what he termed *harambee*, a Swahili term that meant 'all pull together'. The motto encouraged Kenyan society to pull the country together to build a new nation, with an emphasis on self-help initiatives, an idea consistent with the *ubuntu* philosophy.

In the case of Botswana, the term *botho* (*ubuntu*) was the guiding principle in the crafting of the country's *Vision 2016* initiative. The document explained that *botho* was a key tenet of African culture, which served as a social contract of mutual respect, responsibility, and accountability by the members of society towards each other. It further noted that the concept defined a process for earning respect by first giving to others, and to gain empowerment by empowering others. Additionally, the philosophy of *botho* encouraged people to applaud rather than resent those who succeed. The *botho* philosophy also disapproved of any form of anti-social, disgraceful, inhuman, and criminal behaviour, while at the same time promoting the idea of social justice for all. The essence of the argument was that the spirit of *botho* ought to be felt in every sphere of life – the home, the community, the education system, and the workplace (Government of Botswana, 1997). It was meant to inspire and to promote social harmony (*kagisano*).

Across Africa, at the household level, community members traditionally were vigilant and every adult instilled discipline at the neighbourhood level. This was done with dignity informed by the *ubuntu* philosophy. Strangers had to be formally introduced to the head of the household who, in turn, would take them to the headmen of the ward and, ultimately, the chief for 'vetting'. This was done to promote the security of members of the community. All elders, both men and women, constituted a council of some sort, based on their seniority at the household level. This group's role was to listen to all cases that were brought before the headman and the chief. There was a communal justice system where customs and traditions were used as standards during customary court proceedings. The concept of *ubuntu* was used to promote social cohesion and participation in community life.

Ubuntu and Community Mobilisation

In the African context in general, principles such as self-determination have greater meaning with regard to the interests and obligations of and towards a group, such as the family or the community, rather than concerning notions of individualism and autonomy. *Ubuntu* is more inclined towards community. Mangaliso (2001, 23) explains that *ubuntu* refers to humaneness, 'a pervasive spirit of caring and community, harmony and hospitality, respect and responsiveness that individuals and groups display for one another'. In traditional African societies, prior to the advent of colonialism, no formal social services were in existence. Therefore, community members were socialised to have a spirit of compassion and care for one another. At the family level, for example, adults and children were socialised to care for vulnerable members of their households. Older children were socialised to care for their younger siblings. Neighbours cared for one another, as did members of the wider community. Such gestures were consistent with the *ubuntu* philosophy.

In sub-Saharan Africa, the extended family system has served as a most effective response, enabling access to support, for any household facing a crisis (Foster, 2007). Traditionally, members of extended families would assist each other socially, economically, psychologically, and financially. The assistance could take many forms, including regular urban-rural and inter-household income transfers. Such gestures were informed by the notion of *ubuntu*, of course. Since the dawn of HIV and AIDS, many households have experienced income stress due to the impact of this pandemic. Consistent with the true *ubuntu* spirit, such people have been able to send their children away to live with relatives (Foster, 2004, 2007; Miller et al., 2006; USAID, 2010). In some instances, relatives even took it upon themselves to send these children to school. Those gestures have largely remained intact, despite the strain brought about by modernisation, industrialisation, and urbanisation.

The extended family network has also been a major source of support for vulnerable children. The fostering of children by aunts, uncles, grandparents and other relatives has been a very common phenomenon. In sub-Saharan Africa today, an estimated 90% of orphaned children in households live with extended family members (Miller et. al., 2006). Working or income-earning households provide several forms of support to needy relatives, such as food, access to education, shelter, clothing, psycho-social support, and other basic needs (Foster, 2004; Miller et al., 2006). Constraints families, and women in particular, have had to grapple with included a lack of income. Even where they have managed to generate an income in the informal sector, the amounts generated have hardly been enough for their own upkeep, let alone for the extra mouths to feed in the persons of the orphaned children joining them. And yet, in most cases, not even a murmur of complaint is heard. The reason for this lies in the fact that their lives were strongly informed by the philosophy of *ubuntu* – which clearly is in their blood.

Inherent in the concept of *ubuntu* is the value of communalism. This relates to the idea that the interests of the individual must be subordinate to those of the collective. Swanson (2007) notes that the *ubuntu* philosophy is predicated on the search for the notion of what she terms 'humble togetherness'. Other terms used to advance this thought include 'living in each other's spirit', which depicts *ubuntu* as an 'organic relationship' between people everywhere such that when people see others, they should recognise themselves (Swanson, 2007, 54). This is consistent with the famous cliché 'I am because we are'. Ideally, this idea is inculcated at the family level, where siblings are socialised to care for and support one another. Children are socialised to treat adults as though they were their own biological parents. Thus, traditionally, children did not only belong to their own biological parents, but to the entire community. The adage 'It takes a village to educate a child' has always been the guiding mantra. The belief that an individual cannot even imagine organising his/her life outside that of the family is well entrenched in many African cultures (Gyekye, 1987; Prinsloo, 1996). This, of course, is based on the notion of *ubuntu*.

In the context of East Africa, in Kenya, among the Kikuyu tribe, for instance, the spirit of *ubuntu* dictates that individuals may not isolate themselves from their relations. Individuals are socialised to believe that their uniqueness as individuals is secondary to their collective existence (Mthembu, 1996). Hence, any given individual is considered a relative by several other people and, as such, has a moral obligation and duty towards them. Thus, traditionally, the spirit of communalism was widely practised across African societies. However, it must be acknowledged that rapid urbanisation and interactions with Western cultures have somewhat eroded the depth of communalistic practices (Mthembu, 1996).

Ubuntu and Volunteerism

The notion of volunteering is consistent with the *ubuntu* philosophy. Flick et al. (2002) have contended that volunteering may be seen as an indicator of how socially healthy and connected a community is. In Africa, a considerable amount of volunteering has happened in the context of the devastating impact of the AIDS pandemic. When the HIV and AIDS epidemic first appeared, many governments found themselves cash-strapped and most of them invoked the spirit of *ubuntu* to appeal to volunteerism through community home-based care and programmes for orphans and vulnerable children (Rankopo et al., 2007). Volunteers often stepped forward to provide comprehensive care services at home and at the community level in order to meet the needs of terminally ill patients, including those living with AIDS and their families (Government of Botswana, 2005).

The driving force behind volunteerism has been the philosophy of *ubuntu*. Individuals and communities have contributed material and non-material goods and services to ensure that fellow community members survived not only as individuals but also as a collective. Focusing on Botswana, for instance, Osei-Hwedie and Bar-On (1999) noted that from planting individual farms, through harvesting, creating and maintaining communal infrastructure such as dams and granaries, many individuals gave their time and energy to voluntary causes. Traditionally, those activities, firmly rooted in the spirit of *ubuntu* (*botho*), ensured that the goals of the community were realised.

Self-help, Hospitality, and *Ubuntu* in Africa

In Africa, there are numerous examples of initiatives that are based on the philosophy of *ubuntu*. Across the continent, many societies have traditionally adopted a raft of non-formal initiatives, anchored in locally arranged social protection measures that are grounded in people's cultural beliefs, norms, and values. Olivier et al. (2008) note that the core values of the non-formal system include self-help, inherent solidarity, reciprocity, contribution obligation, and entitlement; these values are socially and culturally determined. The notion of non-formal social protection relates to self-organised safety-nets based on membership of a particular social group or community that includes family, kinship, age group, neighbourhood or ethnic group. Thus, many African societies have traditionally been used to (informally) caring for their needy community members, and this was obviously driven by the spirit of *ubuntu*.

One profound value driven by the spirit of *ubuntu* that African societies have cherished is that of hospitality. In recent history, perhaps nowhere has the spirit of hospitality shone brighter than during the 1960s through to the 1980s, when large influxes of refugees occurred across the African continent. In the 1960s, Tanzania, for example, took in thousands of Rwandese refugees, going to the extent of granting citizenship to many of them. This prompted one commentator to remark that '[t]he extremely generous and Pan-African attitude of the Tanzanian government in conferring […] citizenship status onto (these) refugees is […] unusual' (Mwase, 1988, 21). Malawi was a recipient of huge numbers of Mozambican refugees in the 1980s and the country handled them with utmost hospitality. As noted by *Refugees Magazine* (1989, 13), 'In Malawi the hospitality of the local population and the response of the authorities (particularly) in the early stages of the (refugee) influx, managed to prevent an emergency situation from occurring'. Zambia, too, provides a good example. According to Mijere (1980, 3), Zambia received Mozambican refugees as brothers, consistent with the local proverb which states that '*Mlendo ndimame sachedwa ku kamuka*' (A visitor is like dew, disappearing quickly).

African hospitality has shone through in many other respects, too. Traditionally, it was not unheard of for someone to seek overnight shelter at a stranger's homestead and to continue the journey the following morning. The common belief in Botswana was that 'no individual should lead a solitary life' (*bana ba motho ga ba latlhane*). This implied that human beings belonged together ('no man is an island') and that the chance meeting of strangers would always lead to new and long-lasting familial or social relationships. When formal education was first introduced by the missionaries, it was common for Batswana children in small villages (with limited school capacity) to do the first three years in their village and then move to another village (where they might live with strangers) to complete their primary education. All these acts of hospitality were made possible through the spirit of *ubuntu*, which swept across the communities like a strong wind.

Ubuntu as a Framework for Social Work in Africa

Over the years, debate has raged over the relevance and appropriateness of social work in Africa, given its Western roots and orientation. A clarion call was sounded on the need to make social work in Africa relevant to the needs of the continent. Suggestions for improvement included the need to indigenise social work (Mupedziswa, 2001; Osei-Hwedie, 1993; Walton and El Nasr, 1988). However, the march towards indigenisation and, therefore, relevance and appropriateness appears to be painstakingly slow. Perhaps adopting the values of *ubuntu* might help expedite the process. Many commentators (e.g. Rankopo and Osei-Hwedie, 2011) have, however, cautioned that embracing the notion of indigenisation of social work in Africa should not be taken to mean that social work must be 'grounded in the so-called traditional or "primitive" values but in whatever the masses regard to be an authentic expression of themselves' (Twikirize, 2014, 86).

A perusal of the relevant literature suggests that there might be a natural relationship between *ubuntu* and aspects of the profession of social work as practised in Africa. This suggests that *ubuntu* has enormous potential to serve as a framework for social work in Africa. There is potential for a perfect fit between social work and *ubuntu*, as the guiding principles of the two are similar. In some countries, attempts have been made to use *ubuntu* as a guiding framework for social work. Magumbate and Nyanguru (2013, 91) noted that the Code of Ethics of Social Workers in Zimbabwe, for example, includes the concept of *ubuntu* in its lines, and that it elaborates on the fact that *ubuntu* means humanness, based on such values as human solidarity, empathy, and human dignity. These values are also key in the profession of social work. The expectation, therefore, is that teachers and practitioners of social work in Africa ought to recognise and adopt the concept of *ubuntu* as a guiding framework for training and application.

The profession of social work shares a great deal of its vision, mission, values, and principles with the concept of *ubuntu*. There is a fundamental recognition that 'an individual is because of another person' (Tutu, 1999) with whom he or she lives. Hence, there is a need to recognise the importance of living in harmony with other people and of sharing the burdens. The philosophy of *ubuntu* holds that problems are solved using a communal approach, which characterises mutual living. The common Igbo and Yoruba (Nigeria) proverb cited earlier ('It takes a whole village to raise a child') means that the extended family and local villagers are expected to help in the upbringing of all children. This proverb reflects the essence of the ecological and family systems theories, which are celebrated in social work (Hardcastle et al., 2004; Bronfenbrenner, 1979; Bowen Center, 2016). Approaches of the *ubuntu* philosophy and social work both adhere to tenets which respect the power of collective action and hence the use of the group and the community as contexts. The postulation that individuals are found in a group or community context defines who they are in relation to others. Hence, solutions to the demands and vicissitudes of life have to be generated in the context of a group or community.

The essence of the concept of community as an organising principle and a context cannot be overemphasised in the process of problem solving as provided for in social work practice. Similarly, the philosophy of *ubuntu* has adopted the ecological notion in explaining its worldview of the human person. It is no coincidence, therefore, that both social work as a profession and *ubuntu* as a philosophy have adopted the concept of community as a context for seeking solutions to social problems. Communities bear 'properties' that potentially include nurturing social conditions such as inclusiveness, protection, security, emotions, economy, culture, social relationships, violence, exclusion, and poverty (Hardcastle et al., 2004). All these properties may help promote conditions that might turn out to be threats and risks to human security. Community practice has become a natural method of social work as it resonates well with the notions of both *ubuntu* and social work.

Social work normally operates at three levels: micro, meso, and macro (Netting, 2012; Netting et al., 2017). On the macro level, social work is associated with services that deal with programmes, policies, non-governmental organisations, civil society, community-based and government institutions. These provide services that aim at helping groups of people in an 'indirect' manner, as opposed to direct practice. The services in this category are broad and assist communities and institutions to bring about change in enabling them to realise their potential. There is emphasis on mutual cooperation, community resilience, empowerment, the common good, the preservation of people's lives, and community-based endeavours. According to Netting (2012), these tenets are backed up by services such as administration, research, supervision, policy development, programme evaluation, and education.

At macro practice level, the 'sub-set' methods of community practice, such as social planning, social action, and community development (which serve as indirect practice-oriented initiatives) take centre stage in an arena of action or interchange (Hardcastle et al., 2004). This operates at the levels of macro- and meso-practice as opposed to micro (or direct) practice. It should be stressed, however, that community practice is not restricted to the macro and meso levels, but can also operate at the direct (micro) level of practice. This usually includes examining the impact of elements of culture and other influences on individuals as they function in larger systems. Most importantly, it is pertinent to acknowledge the utility of the concept of community in both *ubuntu* and social work practice vis-à-vis issues around the problem-solving process, especially with respect to dealing with poverty, isolation, basic human needs, and cooperation.

According to Hardcastle et al. (2004), the problem-solving process starts with thinking about values, culture, norms, and traditions. These all tend to be related in the process of finding solutions to social problems. Osei-Hwedie and Bar-On (1999) appear to concur with this observation when they stress the importance of appreciating clients' culture in social work practice. Social work scholars also tend to agree that many interventions in social work processes apply these elements both in practice and professional activities. The core business, or bedrock and, indeed, foundation of the social work profession, is the promotion of social justice, which, as a concept, is related to the notion of *ubuntu*. Both the principles of social work and the notion of *ubuntu* uphold the value of the individual and of collective human dignity. This shared tenet is considered the founding principle in the daily exchange with individuals, groups, and communities. However, there is also a mutual agreement and understanding that, while human beings are similar, individuals are unique and diverse.

In the delivery of services, for example in the realm of child welfare, social work aims at developing the capacity of parents or guardians as bearers of duty. This is essentially meant to ensure that the child's rights are recognised and upheld to provide a meaningful start in life and to assure a safe passage into adulthood (Maundeni, 2008; Foster, 2007). Besides, children are made to realise their rights and responsibilities as holders of these and to ensure that their voices are heard. The reasoning that children ought to be seen but not to be heard is flawed (Maundeni, 2008) as it falls short of the provisions of *ubuntu*. In both principles of social work and the *ubuntu* philosophy, an attempt is often made to ensure that both the child and parent or guardian are recognised as part of whatever solution is felt suitable. This is why it is plausible to seek internally generated solutions from the community or family.

Ubuntu, as a concept and approach, provides for considerable opportunities for social work   practice in Africa, both in the context of its academic and its practical endeavours. In short, it does provide a framework for social work across the continent. Learners and practitioners alike can develop their competencies, techniques and skills based on the framework of this philosophy. Many interventions for the promotion of human potential at individual, family, group, community and organisational levels, particularly in the context of Pan-Africanism, can be guided by the *ubuntu* philosophy. It is, therefore, pertinent for schools of social work across the continent to incorporate the notion of *ubuntu* into their curricula while practitioners take the opportunity to adopt this philosophy in their daily professional activities.

There appears to be enormous potential for all the three core levels of social work practice (macro, meso, micro) to tap into the concept of *ubuntu*. There is, therefore, a need to fully exploit the commonality between the values of social work and the philosophy of *ubuntu*. The following paragraphs will elaborate on this.

Ubuntu and macro-level social work

Macro-level social work appears to resonate well with the philosophy of *ubuntu* as it reflects the essence of the concepts of community and group, and the belief in the mantra that 'I am my brother's keeper', an idea that happens to be consistent with the provisions of the concept of *ubuntu*. Focusing on the theme of macro-practice, Magumbate and Nyanguru (2013, 95) appear to corroborate the above view when they argue: 'Ubuntu has greater relevance in the application of social work with communities'. The authors give a number of examples in the possible application of the *ubuntu* philosophy in the context of community, including child welfare and jurisprudence. They opine that in traditional African society, repercussions of a crime committed between two people can far extend beyond the two individuals to incorporate not only the family but at times the entire community. There is, therefore, a need to amplify this 'commonness' in all aspects of macro-practice and apply those values and principles that may allow *ubuntu* and values of social work to move (together) to another level.

There is a common belief that human beings have great value and are, hence, worthy of investment. This value will facilitate opportunities to provide services that may effectively serve humans at macro, meso and micro levels. Hence, certain services will be provided to citizens as an integral part of community life. Deliberate efforts, therefore, have to be made to search for indigenous methods and theories that allow for integration of the *ubuntu* philosophy in all social endeavours. According to various observers (Tutu, 1999; Kaunda and Morris, 1976; Hyden, 1975), it must be recognised in the context of Africa that an individual is community-based as opposed to being individualistic. As noted, the definition of *ubuntu* identifies the concept of community as being paramount vis-à-vis that of the individual.

Ubuntu and meso-level social work

The *ubuntu* philosophy potentially also has a critical role to play in social work practices at the meso level. According to Magumbate and Nyanguru (2017, 97), '[g]roups are a key feature of African society', and what binds groups together is the *ubuntu* spirit. A notable challenge, however, as the two authors argue, lies in the fact that in meso-level practice, groups tend to be made up of people from diverse backgrounds who may band together to try and deal with a particular life challenge, something that is inimical to African culture. Even so, the notion of African solidarity suggests cooperation among individuals. Countries such as Burundi are known for emphasising the principle of solidarity. Many other African societies operate on the basis of the motto that 'an injury to one is an injury to all'. Hence there is definitely potential for the use of certain key tenets of the philosophy of *ubuntu* at the meso level.

Ubuntu and micro-level social work

This suggests that the challenge of integration comes in the wake of applying *ubuntu* in the context of direct social work practice, since micro-practice emphasises the essence of an individual. The micro-practice approach and conception differs diametrically from the social work practice at the macro level, which is more consistent with the *ubuntu* philosophy. Micro-level services (such as clinical work) are often referred to as 'one-on-one' because of the emphasis on an individual (Netting et al., 2017). Even so, opportunities for tapping into the philosophy of *ubuntu* do also exist at the micro level of social work practice. *Ubuntu* has several tenets that support the achievement of goals in micro-practice. Magumbate and Nyanguru (2013) argue that in counselling, for example, *ubuntu* values can play a significant role. The values will be useful in working with children in conflict with the law, or with people with disabilities. However, whereas Western values dictate that direct (micro) practice ought to involve counsellor and client on a one-to-one basis in an environment of singular confidentiality, in African culture, however, consistent with the spirit of *ubuntu*, there is a concept termed 'group solidarity'. This means that several Africans can share a confidential piece of information (even in the context of counselling), with none of them divulging this to any 'outsider'. This suggests that counselling in the African context need not be based on the one-to-one stipulation as the textbooks recommend.

Ubuntu and Social Work in Africa: A Critique

The *ubuntu* philosophy has had its fair share of criticisms. Magumbate and Nyanguru (2013) cite Hailey (2008) as questioning the applicability of *ubuntu* across cultures. They argue that *ubuntu* does not seem to have a solid framework, meaning that its central elements cannot be theorised. There are also concerns that this philosophy has the potential to weaken, rather than strengthen, societies as some of the tenets that comprise this theme might make communities docile and overly compliant without the urge to question things. As the authors put it, a major concern is related to the fear that '[t]he weaker tenets of Ubuntu may be used to make Africans submissive and dependent' (Magumbate and Nyanguru, 2013, 98). They add that some authors have argued that, in some instances, rather than weaken society, *ubuntu* might, in fact, make society so united as to create a 'herd' mentality; the authors use the xenophobic attacks experienced in countries such as South Africa as an example of this kind of scenario.

In light of the above criticisms, a number of challenges can be discerned with regard to attempts at integrating the *ubuntu* philosophy into social work practice. According to several observers, social work is generally regarded as an academic discipline and a professional practice which works with individuals, families, groups, and communities in order to enhance social functioning and overall wellbeing (Hardcastle et al., 2004; Crisp et al., 2012; Stefaroi, 2014; IFSW, 2017). Social work operates on the basis of values such as social justice, human rights, individual worth, and uniqueness. However, the profession is also grounded in theories that are drawn from cognate fields. Currently, there are debates about the use of indigenous knowledge in social work practice (Rankopo et al., 2007; Gair, 2016; Gair, Mills and Thompson, 2005; Gale and Bolzan, 2013). Attempts have been made to reignite the discourse on the need for a better appreciation of the thinking and understanding of the worldviews of indigenous peoples. Thus, the argument is that inclusion of indigenous knowledge in social work training and practice in Africa would resonate with the philosophy of *ubuntu*. Most importantly, if the values of social work are to sufficiently resonate with the provisions of *ubuntu* (the argument goes), deliberate efforts will need to be made to incorporate indigenous knowledge systems.

It has also been argued that, while the *ubuntu* philosophy is consistent with the notion of community, which, in turn, is consistent with macro- and meso-practice, the approach may not work well with regard to micro-practice. The services rendered in direct practice help the client directly, and so they tend to target individuals and families. In micro-practice, the focus is on the 'assessment, treatment and prevention' generally of behavioural, psychological, and emotional disturbances. Micro-practice thus provides services to the person because it believes in treating the individual. The method believes that problems are not with the environment but with individuals and families that, therefore, need assistance to improve their life situations. The approach also posits that problems must be defined at the individual or family level and not the community level. This suggests a fundamental departure from the expectations of *ubuntu,* which conceives community as the starting point in the problem-solving process. As noted, *ubuntu* posits that life's problems must be solved from a communal point of view, which considers an individual to be part of the system. This socio-cultural conception makes the direct approach more Eurocentric as opposed to the macro-approach, which is regarded to be more Afrocentric. Thus, overall, while *ubuntu* can be used as a framework for practice at macro and meso levels, there seems to be a disjuncture when it comes to the tenets of social work practice on the micro level.

Conclusion

The values of social work per se, and the philosophy of *ubuntu* in general, seem to have much in common. It seems logical, therefore, that many of the tenets of *ubuntu* ought to be incorporated into social work education and practice in Africa. However, as the critique has shown, there are certain fundamental arguments that seem to negate the integration of *ubuntu* philosophy and the values of social work. Given that *ubuntu* does indeed place a premium on community-based practice (while neglecting the micro-level approach), the question that ought to be asked is this: Going forward, how can the two themes find common ground so that they can co-exist and provide critical services to persons? This is an area for the academics, researchers and practitioners in the field of social work to resolve in the interest of efficient human service delivery.

This challenge provides a solemn invitation to all concerned to try to find compelling arguments to bring the 'two sides' together with a view to helping create an environment towards realising relevance and appropriateness in social work practice in Africa. Perhaps the need to improve the human condition will provide enough impetus and, thus, an opportunity for social work practitioners to seek new frontiers in knowledge and practice as the current situation dictates. There is a need for the crafting of new thinking and new, more appropriate theories that can further effectively offer viable and adequate solutions to the emerging problems of the 21st century. Indeed, there is a need to search for new theories and practice paradigms that will adequately respond to the factors present in modern-day society in various contexts. In fact, it would be too much to expect of theories of yesteryear to offer hope for solutions to issues of globalisation, violence, and poverty, which are predominant today. The use of the *ubuntu* philosophy as a framework for social work may indeed be a theme that appeals in the context of these pressing challenges.

References

Barker, RL (1999) *The Social Work Dictionary*. Washington, DC: NASW Press.

Bloom, M (1990) *Introduction to the Drama of Social Work*. Itasca: F.E. Peacock Publisher.

Botswana Institute for Development Policy Analysis (1997) *A Study of Poverty and Poverty Alleviation in Botswana*. Gaborone: MFDP.

Bowen Center (2016) *Eight Concepts. Family Systems Theory*. Available at: http://www.thebowencenter.org/theory/eight-concepts/ (accessed 13 March 2018).

Bronfenbrenner, U (1979) *The Ecology of Human Development*. Harvard University Press.

Crisp, BR and Beddoe L (2012) *Promoting Health and Well-Being in Social Work Education*. London: Routledge.

Dembow J and Phenyo C (2006) *Culture and Customs of Botswana*. London: Greenwood Press.

Flick M, Bittman M and Doyle J (2002) *The Community's Most Valuable [Hidden] Asset – Volunteering in Australia*. Sydney: University of New South Wales (Social Policy Research Centre).

Foster G (2004) Safety Nets for Children Affected by HIV/AIDS in Southern Africa. In: Pharoah R (ed) *A Generation at Risk? HIV/AIDS, Vulnerable Children and Security in Southern Africa*. Pretoria, Cape Town: Institute of Security Studies (ISS), 65-92.

Foster G (2007) Under the Radar: Community Safety Nets for AIDS-Affected Households in Sub-Saharan Africa. *AIDS Care*, 19, (Supplement 1): 54-63.

Gade, BN (2011) The Historical Written Discourse on Ubuntu. *South African Journal of Philosophy*, 30(3): 303-329.

Gair S (2016) Critical Reflections on Teaching Challenging Content: Do Some Students Shoot the (White) Messenger? *Reflective Practice*, 17(5): 592-604.

Gair S, Miles D and Thomson J (2005) Reconciling Indigenous and Non-Indigenous Knowledge. *Journal of Social Work Education*, 41(2): 179-190.

Gale F and Bolzan N (2013) Social Resilience: Challenging Neo-Colonial Thinking and Practices around 'Risk'. *Journal of Youth Studies*, 16(2): 257-271.

Government of Botswana (1997) *A Long Term Vision for Botswana*. Gaborone: Presidential Task Group for the Long Term Vision for Botswana.

Government of Botswana (2005) *Community Home Based Care Programme Guidelines*. Department of Social Services & Ministry of Local Government: Gaborone: Ministry of Local Government.

Gray CC (2001) *Afrocentric Thought and Praxis: An Intellectual History*. Trenton NJ: Africa World Press.

Gyekye K (1987) *An Essay on African Philosophical Thought: The Akan Scheme*. Cambridge: Cambridge University Press.

Hardcastle DA, Powers PR and Wenocur S (2004) *Community Practice: Theories and Skills for Social Workers*. 2nd ed. Oxford University Press

Hyden G (1975) Ujamaa, Villagisation and Rural Development in Tanzania. *ODI Review*, (1): 53-72.

International Federation of Social Workers (IFSW) (2017) Global Definition of Social of Social Work. Available at: http://ifsw.org/get-involved/global-definition-of-social-work (accessed 13 March 2018).

Kamwangamalu NM (1999) Ubuntu in South Africa: A Sociolinguistic Perspective to a Pan-African Concept. *Critical Arts Journal*, 13(2): 24-42.

Karsten L and Illa H (2005) Ubuntu as a Key African Management Concept: Contextual Background and Practical Insights for Knowledge Application. *Journal of Managerial Psychology*, 20(7): 607-620.

Kaunda KD and Morris C (1976) *A Humanist in Africa*. London/Letchworth: The Garden City Press.

Khoza RJ (1994) *Ubuntu Botho. Vumunhu Vhuthu. African Humanism*. Discussion Paper. Johannesburg: Ekhaya.

Magumbate J and Nyanguru A (2013) Exploring African Philosophy: The Value of Ubuntu in Social Work. *African Journal of Social Work*, 3(1): 82-100.

Mangaliso M (2001) Building Competitive Advantage from Ubuntu: Management Lessons from South Africa. *Academy of Management Executive*, 15(3): 23-34.

Maundeni T (2008) The Silent Survivors of Divorce: A Quest for Comprehensive and Inclusive Strategies for Botswana. In: Maundeni T, Levers LL and Jacques G (eds) *Changing Family Systems: A Global Perspective*. Gaborone: Bay Publishing, 146-164.

Mbigi L and Maree J (1995) *Ubuntu: The Spirit of African Transformation Management*. Randburg: Knowledge Resources.

Mbigi L (1997) *Ubuntu: The African Dream in Management*. Randburg: Knowledge Resources.

Mbiti JS (1990) *African Religions and Philosophy*. Johannesburg: Heinemann.

Mijere N (1998) Refugees' and Local Communities' Attitudes to Refugee Settlements: The Case of Zambia. Paper presented at ASAUK Conference, Sept 14-16 1998. Cambridge: Cambridge University.

Miller C, Gruskin S, Subramanian S, Rajaraman D, and Heymann S (2006) Orphan Care in Botswana's Working Households: Growing Responsibilities in the Absence of Adequate Support. *American Journal of Public Health*, (96): 1429-1435.

Mthembu, D (1996) African Values: Discovering Indigenous Roots of Management. In: Lessem R and Nussbaum B (eds) *Sawubona Africa: Embracing Four Worlds in South African Management*. Sandton: Zebra Press, 215-226.

Mupedziswa R (2001) The Quest for Relevance: Towards a Conceptual Model of Developmental Social Work Education and Training in Africa. *International Social Work*, 44(3): 285-300.

Mwase N (1998) Namibian Refugee Situation: Past, Present and Future. Paper Presented at ASAUK Conference, Sept 14-16 1998. Cambridge: Cambridge University.

Netting, FE (2012) Social *Work Macro Practice*. Boston, MA: Pearson Education.

Netting FE, Kettner PM, McMurty SL and Thomas ML (2017) *Social Work Macro Practice*. 6th ed. Boston, MA: Pearson Education.

Ntseane D and Solo K (2007) *Social Security and Social Protection in Botswana*. Gaborone: Bay Publishing.

Olivier M, Kaseke E and Mpedi, LG (2008) Informal Social Security in Southern Africa: Developing a Framework for Policy Intervention. Paper Prepared for Presentation at the International Conference on Social Security Organised by the National Department of Social Department, South Africa, 10-14 March 2008, Cape Town.

Osei-Hwedie K (1993) The Challenge of Social Work in Africa: Starting the Indigenisation Process. *Journal of Social Development in Africa*, 8(1): 19-30.

Osei-Hwedie, K and Bar-On A (1999) Sub-Saharan Africa: Community-driven Social Policies. In: Morales-Gomez D (ed) *Transformational Social Policies: The New Development Challenges of Globalisation*. Ottawa: International Development Research Centre, 89-116.

Prinsloo E (1996) The Ubuntu Style of Participatory Management. In: Malherbe JG (ed) *Decolonizing the Mind: Proceedings of the Second Colloquium on African Philosophy*. Pretoria: UNISA Research Unit for African Philosophy, 112-127.

Rankopo M, Osei-Hwedie K and Modie-Moroka T (2007) Issues in Service Volunteerism in Botswana. In: Patel L and Mupedziswa R (eds) *Research Partnerships Build the Service Field in Africa*. Special Issue of JSDA and Social Work Practitioner-Researcher, 24-39.

Rankopo MJ and Osei-Hwedie K (2011) Globalization and Culturally Relevant Social Work Practice: African Perspectives on Indigenization. *International Social Work*, 54(1): 13-147.

Refugees Magazine (1989) Ukwimi: A New Model of Integration.

Schapera I (1938) *A Handbook of Tswana Law and Custom*. Oxfordshire: James Currey.

Schapera I (1970) *A Handbook of Tswana Law and Custom*. London: Frank Cass.

Spitzer H (2014) Social Work in African Contexts: A Cross-Cultural Reflection on Theory and Practice. In: Spitzer H, Twikirize JM and Wairire GG (eds) *Professional Social Work in East Africa. Towards Social Development, Poverty Reduction and Gender Equality*. Kampala: Fountain, 15-28.

Stefaroi P (2014) *Humane & Spiritual Qualities of the Professional in Humanistic Social Work – The Third Way in Theory and Practice*. Charleston: Createspace.

Swanson DM (2007) Ubuntu: An African Contribution to (Re) Search for/with a 'Humble Togetherness'. *Journal of Contemporary Issues in Education*, 2(2): 53-67.

Thabede D (2008) The African Worldview as the Basis of Practice in the Helping Professions. *Social Work/Maatskaplike Werk*, 44(3): 223-245.

Thupayagale C and Rampa M (2005) Volunteerism in Botswana: Survey Report. Presented at the Workshop on Extent, Scope and Pattern of Volunteering in Nigeria and Botswana. 2-3 November 2005.

Torrey EF (1972) *Witchdoctors and Psychiatrists: The Common Roots of Psychotherapy and its Future*. New Jersey: Jason Aronson.

Tutu D (1999) *No Future without Forgiveness*. London: Random House.

Twikirize J.M. (2014) Indigenisation of Social Work in Africa: Debates, Prospects and Challenges. In: Spitzer H, Twikirize JM and Wairire GG (eds) *Professional Social Work in East Africa. Towards Social Development, Poverty Reduction and Gender Equality*. Kampala: Fountain, 75-90.

United States Agency for International Development (USAID) (2010) *Assessing the Implementation of Botswana's Program for Orphans and Vulnerable Children*. Washington, DC: USAID.

Walton R and El Nasr M (1988) Indigenization and Authentization in Terms of Social Work in Egypt. *International Social Work*, 31(2): 135-144.

3

Culturally Relevant Curriculum for Social Work: An Ethical Imperative for our Time

Linda Kreitzer

Introduction

Social work in Africa has made great strides over the past 20 years. The issue of culturally relevant social work education and practice has received increased attention in research and writing from African and non-African academics and practitioners. For me, Dr James Midgley's (1981) book on *Professional Imperialism* challenged my perspective on how social work education and practice was exported to African countries, how a Western curriculum was accepted by Africans, and how this relates to my own understanding of the influences of colonisation, westernisation, and globalisation in this process. My PhD work on this topic can be read in the book *Social Work in Africa: Exploring Culturally Relevant Education and Practice in Ghana* (Kreitzer, 2012). After having finished my PhD, I was informed of conference proceedings from the Association of Social Work Education in Africa (ASWEA), an African social work association that was active from 1973 to 1989, with its secretariat in Ethiopia. Supported by the Association of Schools of Social Work in Africa (ASSWA) and the International Association of Schools of Social Work (IASSW), I could find, copy, and print these proceedings for distribution to universities during conferences in Africa. This six-volume set is accessible on-line for social work academics, teachers, and practitioners to use in the classroom, for research, or in social service agencies (Wits University, n.d.). These documents represent almost 20 years of social work history through conference proceedings, speeches, directories of social service agencies, and academic social work/community development training institutions. In particular, the debate concerning the relevance of Western social work curricula in African countries can be seen in many of the proceedings. I mention these documents as I will refer to them throughout this chapter. A brief summary of the contents of the documents can be found in Gray, Coates and Yellow Bird (2013).

This debate continues today. A recent example is the Association of Schools of Social Work in Africa's (ASSWA) conference in South Africa whose theme was *Rethinking Social Work in Africa: Decoloniality and Indigenous Knowledge in Education and Practice* (ASASWEI, 2017). Culturally appropriate social work education and practice is an ethical issue that continues to challenge social workers and educators in light of colonisation, westernisation, and globalisation which, in turn, impact the way our clients are treated. It is an ethical imperative that social workers have the goal of ensuring they receive the best possible service. Ethics is concerned with addressing what is morally right and wrong (Dictionary, 2017), and the ethical issue of what kind of social work is appropriate for Africa is an imperative for today. A new path towards an appropriate social work curriculum and practice is emerging and is changing the face of social work in Africa today. The mind-set is changing slowly, as colonised people gain confidence in their own understanding of social work and realise that African social work academics, writers, and practitioners can be creative and revolutionary. As the late Maathai (2009, 20) states:

> All Africa must change the mind-set that affects many colonized peoples everywhere. They must believe in themselves again; that they are capable of clearing their own path and forging their own identity; that they have a right to be governed with justice, accountability, and transparency; that they can honour and practise their cultures and make them relevant to today's needs; and that they no longer need to be indebted – financially, intellectually and spiritually – to those who once governed them. They must rise up and walk.

This chapter highlights some of the current issues concerning culturally relevant social work education and practice as it relates to Africa. It is hoped that this discussion will enable others to think about their ethical responsibility for appropriate social work education and practice, think creatively about the content they teach in class and their teaching styles, and how they practise it in their communities. I will begin with a historical contextualisation of the African social work curriculum. Then I will outline cultural issues in relation to education and practice and point out some challenges to creating culturally relevant social work practice. This will be followed by an outlook on potential roads ahead. I will conclude with a story.

Historical Context of the African Social Work Curriculum

In Africa, before colonisation, there were social systems through which the more vulnerable in society were supported. 'Africa was probably more democratic than most other parts of the world, including Europe' (Tandon 1996, 296). In West Africa, the kinship system supported the running of society (Nukunya, 1992). Not all pre-colonial cultural practices were beneficial to everyone; in fact, the more vulnerable people were negatively affected owing to cultural practices. Examples of this are the contested views around female genital mutilation and health issues surrounding this practice, child brides, the disabled (being killed owing to lack of ability or believing that the impediment is a punishment from the ancestors; see Ross, 2008), the *trokosi* system in Ghana (daughters given to priests to appease the ancestors), and witch hunts based on traditional beliefs. Many of these practices negatively targeted women and children. When African countries were colonised, colonial empires transported their social services with little understanding of traditional ways and how these mainly Western remedial services would adversely affect traditional culture and ways of life. After colonisation, the community development movement took hold through the likes of Kwame Nkrumah and Julius Nyerere, a movement much more conducive to the African collectivist society. However, for many countries, the colonial remedial structures took hold and still exist today.

In the 1960s, the United Nations encouraged well established social work programmes to come to Africa owing to the challenges created by independence. These programmes were transported with the assumption, by both Western and non-Western countries, that the Western social work curriculum could be successfully imported to the African setting (Kendall, 1995). This also happened in other parts of the world; for example, in Latin America (Wilson and Whitmore, 2000). Missionary groups and charities also came to Africa, often with a hidden motive to Christianise and civilise Africans (Ife, 2007). The first social work programme in Africa was established at the University of Cape Town, South Africa, in 1924 (Healy, 2008). In the 1970s, the Association of Social Work Education in Africa was created with one of its main goals being to bring social work education together all over Africa to create a common curriculum and to discuss the validity of the Western social work curriculum in Africa (ASWEA, 1986). The secretariat was located in Ethiopia. I will quote from two of their documents to help readers understand that the topic of an African social work curriculum was alive and well in the 1970s. Dr Mumenka (as cited in ASWEA, 1974, 32), an African who strongly advocated broad-based training for social workers and saw the importance of interdisciplinary work, stated the following:

> In my opinion, the time has come for serious and critical re-examination of social work training in Africa. [...] 20th century Africa expects social work to be creative and revolutionary. In the context of the inter-disciplinary approach [...] social workers should be able to make a positive contribution as members of inter-disciplinary development teams. [...] However, it is again necessary to reiterate my earlier concern that unless the profession of social work is prepared to take a new path, social workers will for a long time to come remain ineffective in developing countries.

Dr Murapa, general rapporteur for the ASWEA conference, stated the following:

> African instructors, being from the most part products of western education, have
> proved either incapable or unwilling to engage in extensive and creative revision of
> the existing textbooks, curricula and approaches to make them relevant to the social
> and other developmental problems and aspirations in Africa. (ASWEA, 1977, 32)

The re-visioning of social work teaching and practice is taking place today. African
social work conferences are debating this issue, academics are writing about
culturally relevant social work interventions that have worked for them and social
development is embraced by social work educators and practitioners concerned
with effective social work interventions in Africa. So, what is a culturally relevant
social work curriculum?

A Culturally Relevant Curriculum for Social Work

I once asked a group of social workers in Canada what they would come up with
if we deleted our present curriculum and created a new curriculum. Where would
they begin? Who would be involved? What would the result be? Is the task daunting
to them? Is there a sense of freedom to be creative and revolutionary? Does this
produce fear? The result was mixed, with some feeling refreshed and excited about
the possibility while others found it daunting and fearful. So, what does a culturally
relevant social work curriculum mean and how would one go about creating this
kind of education?

What is culture?

Since the writing of my own research, I have come to see culture as more complex
than I first thought. So, what is culture? According to UNESCO (1982, 1), the
definition of culture is: 'The whole complex of distinctive spiritual, material,
intellectual and emotional features that characterise a society or social groups. [I]
t includes modes of life, the fundamental rights of human beings, value systems,
traditions and beliefs.' Culture is not static nor monolithic (cf. Ife, 2007, 79). Culture
is one of the main issues concerning the social work curriculum and societal change.
It involves the past, present, and future and can be positive and negative. It is learnt
behaviour from thousands of years of adaptation and will continue to change
and evolve. For countries in Africa, there are many different indigenous groups
with different languages and traditions. For example, in Kenya alone, there are 42
ethnicities, each containing several sub-groups (cf. Wairire, 2014). So how do you
create a culturally relevant social work curriculum in such a diverse country? This
begs the questions: Is there a set of values and beliefs that binds together different
African cultures? Some African writers believe there is: 1) Ani's (2007) critique
of European cultural thought and behaviour, comparing African thought and
behaviour in the areas of cultural structuring and thought, religion and ideology, the

power of symbols, self-image, image of others, rhetoric and behaviour, intracultural behaviour, behaviour towards others, progress of ideology and universalism; 2) Asante's (2003) writings about the concept of Afrocentricity, defined by him as 'a mode of thought and action in which the centrality of African interests, values, and perspectives predominate. Regarding theory, it is the placing of African people in the centre of analysis of African phenomena' (2); and 3) Wiredu's (2004) edited book on African philosophy. Exploring the history of African philosophy 'ancient, medieval, modern and contemporary…that have been written in such a way as to be reflective, enlightening and useful to students and scholars' (xix), the 47 chapters delve deeply into African philosophy.

Historically, European philosophy has been taught in African universities. This has driven and still drives a particular understanding of the world, and the African's place in the world. If one brings these concepts to a practical level, we all live in an age of neo-liberalism. This age is characterised by the survival of the fittest, competition as the norm, blaming the victim for their own troubles, privatising services with less government intervention and, above all, a system that is driven by the market, with economics as the most important equation in everything we do. To go further, an African perspective may, like many indigenous cultures, embrace collectivism and spirituality, view relationships as central, and favour a more holistic view of the world while deconstructing the Western understanding of the world by language usage, economic exploitation, and objectivism, many of which came from colonisation and continue today. Ani (2007, 82) gives an example:

> The African metaphysic, the Native American and Oceanic 'majority cultures' (it is safe to generalize here), all presuppose a fundamental unity of reality based on the organic interrelatedness of being; all refuse to objectify nature and insist on the essential spirituality of a true cosmos.

A more specific example is the conflict between modern science and traditional practices. Ross (2008) speaks about the difference between modern medicine and African beliefs concerning healing with natural resources – stemming from the spiritual and land concepts in South Africa – as an ethical dilemma for social workers. Relating this to social work education and practice, Van Wyck and Higgs (2007, 62) see the importance of African philosophy to social work education and this can be started in the classroom: 'African philosophy should be able to respond to the problems and human conditions in modern Africa. It should also clarify concepts, beliefs and values that we hold, use and live by, through sustained discussion and dialogue.' These authors caution that there is not one universal African philosophy, but these can be different depending on culture (Kreitzer, 2012, 147).

In looking at these different worldviews, there should be an acceptance of a hybrid of the understanding of the world. What parts of the African worldview should social work education look to for more appropriate practice and research? Have African philosophies and worldviews been critiqued in classrooms in relation to the African context, the international definition of social work, our ethical principles and European thought? The importance now given to social development theory and appreciative inquiry in research is a way of bringing African social work practice into line with a holistic African understanding of how to practically address social issues in African cultures.

Definition of 'relevant'

According to the Oxford Dictionary (2017), relevant means 'appropriate to the current time, period or circumstances; of contemporary interest [...] closely connected to or appropriate to what is being done or considered' (para. 1). It addresses social issues that are important for the time. It is an established fact that social work in Africa has had a colonial history, and a continuing debate about changing social work education and practice to be more appropriate to the African context is ethically necessary, so that African social workers can provide services that service users can relate to and feel comfortable with. This means that African social workers, through education and practice, are continually re-inventing services and service delivery that reflect the current trends which are appropriate to each country's needs and which support the international values of social work and human rights. Both the South African concept of *ubuntu* (humanity to others – 'I am what I am because of who we all are' [Ubuntu, 2018]) and *vyamas* ('members with common needs join hands and find ways and means to collectively deal with their needs'), an integral part of Kenyan culture, are being written about and used in social work practices in both countries (on *ubuntu*, cf. Sewpaul, 2008; for *vyamas*, cf. Wairire, 2014, 101). Relevant social work combines traditional thinking with modern ideas to provide services relevant to a particular culture.

Combining worldviews

In putting these two worldviews together, a culturally relevant social work curriculum should address social issues of the time that are relevant to the cultures of the country. In practice, this implies culturally appropriate interventions that address contemporary social work issues and that support positive change in that country. It also involves the continuing evaluation of cultural practices in light of international, regional, and national polices.

International, regional, and national policies and concepts

The cornerstones of creating culturally relevant social work curricula and practices come from policies at different levels. International policies include the UN Universal Declaration on Human Rights (UN, 1948) and the UN Declaration of the Rights of Indigenous Peoples (UN, 2007). Regional polices include the African (Banjul) Charter on Human and Peoples' Rights and, of course, each country's constitution. Important international social work policies include the Global Definition of Social Work (IASSW, 2014) and Ethical Principles of Social Work (IFSW, 2012). Particular attention should be paid to the concept of social justice. These instruments will be briefly expounded below.

Universal Declaration on Human Rights: This declaration, which is non-binding, declares that

> Everyone is entitled to all the rights and freedoms set forth in this Declaration, without distinction of any kind, such as race, colour, sex, language, religion, political or other opinion, national or social origin, property, birth or other status. Furthermore, no distinction shall be made on the basis of the political, jurisdictional or international status of the country or territory to which a person belongs, whether it be independent, trust, non-self-governing or under any other limitation of sovereignty. (UN, 1948, Article 1)

Unfortunately, not all countries adhere to this declaration, which causes tension for social workers who practise from a human rights' perspective and find themselves in direct conflict with national policies which may not be in accordance with this declaration.

Declaration on the Rights of Indigenous Peoples: This most recent UN Declaration (2007), to which African countries are signatories, states that

> [i]ndigenous peoples have the right to the full enjoyment, as a collective or as individuals, of all human rights and fundamental freedoms as recognized in the Charter of the United Nations, the Universal Declaration of Human Rights and international human rights law. (UN, 2017, para. 1)

This declaration challenges an individualistic Western perspective in the areas of land and treaties, collective rights, terminology (peoples vs populations), and self determination.

African Charter on Human Rights: This Pan-African instrument is 'intended to promote and protect human rights and basic freedoms in the African continent' (Organisation of African Unity, 1981, para. 1). Not only does it respect individual rights but it, like the Declaration of the Rights of Indigenous Peoples, recognises collective and group rights, which are so important to African societies.

International Definition of Social Work: The International Association of Schools of Social Work (IASSW) and the International Federation of Social Workers (IFSW) have defined social work as follows:

> Social work is a practice-based profession and an academic discipline that promotes social change and development, social cohesion, and the empowerment and liberation of people. Principles of social justice, human rights, collective

responsibility and respect for diversities are central to social work. Underpinned by theories of social work, social sciences, humanities and indigenous knowledge, social work engages people and structures to address life challenges and enhance wellbeing. (IASSW, 2014, 1)

The Statement of Ethical Principles includes the principles of human rights and human dignity, as well as social justice:

> Social work is based on respect for the inherent worth and dignity of all people, and the rights that follow from this. Social workers should uphold and defend each person's physical, psychological, emotional and spiritual integrity and wellbeing. (IFSW, 2012, para. 4.1)

The document says that '[s]ocial workers have a responsibility to promote social justice, in relation to society generally, and in relation to the people with whom they work' (para. 4.2). Social justice is one of the most important concepts of social work and separates us from many other professions. In order to work towards social justice and ethical practice we need to educate social workers to work at all levels of society. In other words, without working with people at the grassroots cultural level, any social policy that is enacted will not be successful. If we work at the grassroots level to change unhealthy cultural practices, we will not be successful without the support of social policy. An example for this issue is female genital mutilation. In Ghana, it is illegal to engage in this cultural practice, but it continues because work at the grassroots level was not sufficient in order to install an alternative and safer practice that could be established with the people. Social workers are agents of change at the micro, meso, macro and chrono levels, and this is part of what culturally appropriate social work practice and training is all about. One of the recommendations from my PhD work was to encourage the Institute of African Studies to engage in co-teaching with social work educators so that social work interventions and theories could be critically examined in relation to cultural practices.

To sum up, African social work education and practice should take into consideration these policies and instruments as ideal goals to guide them in knowledge and skills.

The Ethical Imperative to Teach a Culturally Relevant Social Work Curriculum

Ethics deals with values relating to human conduct, with respect to the right and wrong of certain actions, and to the good and bad of the motives and ends of such actions (Dictionary 2010, para. 4). In social work, our personal and professional ethics can conflict as well as work well together. Social workers have an important ethical role to play in supporting 'human dignity, equality and freedoms from discrimination' (Wairire, 2014, 94). It is essential that social workers have a self-awareness to understand where some of their personal values clash with professional values. Below are some possible conflicting political and professional values with regard to the clash of ethics, culture, and poverty.

Poverty is a huge issue on the African continent. Neo-liberal economics continues to widen the gap between the rich and the poor, with many countries still under structural adjustment programmes that advocate less government spending. As social workers, we are advocates for people who live in poverty and act to empower them to work towards a life that is free from poverty.

Marginalisation of certain groups is another huge issue. The Universal Declaration on Human Rights declares that each person has universal human rights, and yet countries in Africa uphold the British colonial anti-homosexuality laws, and the LGBTQ[5] communities continue to be persecuted for their sexual orientation. Persons with albinism continue to suffer from stigma and discrimination, particularly in the education system, and suffer from physical violence and subsequent impunity, with no repercussions for the perpetrators. Xenophobia continues to be rampant in many parts of Africa, putting migrants from other parts of Africa under the risk of harm.

These and other important social issues should be critically discussed in social work classrooms in order to look for ways to move forward for a more inclusive society. Linda Smith (2008, 371) from South Africa stated: 'To achieve social change, social work education thus needs to critically engage with post-colonial and post-apartheid socio-political realities of inequality, oppression, racism and cultural hegemony, and facilitate critical conscientization.' Social work is a political profession and we are often asked to challenge cultural practices and policies, which can be uncomfortable. But for social workers, it is an ethical imperative to address oppression and discrimination. A colleague of mine has as her email motto: *Put your humanity before your fear.* This is what we are called to do as social workers and our social work education should teach these skills of advocacy, challenging the status quo with humility, patience, and boldness.

Applying Culturally Relevant Social Work

How then is culturally relevant social work education and practice applied at the local level? The following paragraphs discuss some key elements towards achieving this process.

Education

It is increasingly accepted that African social work education begins from a perspective of social development theory. This has been considered by African

---

[5]   This acronym refers to lesbian, gay, bisexual, transgender, and queer people.

scholars as the most appropriate approach to economic and social development for Africa (Gray, 2005; Sewpaul and Lombard, 2004). Secondly, the curriculum needs to address current social issues relevant to the specific contexts and to Africans' self-understanding of the history of their continent and, more importantly, of the introduction and expansion of social work in Africa. Not only does African social work education need to address contemporary social work issues; other important issues, including the profession's education system in relation to colonialism, westernisation, and globalisation, the type of curriculum needed today, ethical issues around practice, and the use of African interventions to support practice, should also be included.

Personal and professional values

Education should challenge students' own values, biases, and prejudices concerning the way they view others. Self-awareness, along with social work skills, encourages ethical practice.

Research methods

It is generally recognised that most of Africa has a history of collective societies in which oral history has been handed down through the generations. And yet, in relation to research, more collective-orientated methodologies, like those of qualitative research, are rarely encouraged. Participatory action research (Fals Borda, 2001) and appreciative inquiry (Watkins, Mohr and Kelly, 2011) are examples of research methods that encourage citizen participation in understanding issues in communities as well as identifying culturally relevant interventions that the community sees as a way forward. Quantitative research is considered more 'scientific' than qualitative research and this comes from the Western, positivist, and colonialist mind-set. In other parts of the world, indigenous peoples are using research methods that are better suited for their collective communities and that, for example, regard ceremony just as important in research (Smith, 2012; Wilson, 2008).

Culturally appropriate interventions

The idea of creating social work interventions that are integrated with cultural practices is being considered more and more by African social work scholars and practitioners. Osei-Hwedie and Jacques (2007), Gray, Coates and Yellow Bird (2008), Gray, Coates, Yellow Bird and Hetherington (2013), Butterfield and Abye (2013), Spitzer, Twikirize and Wairire (2014), Noble, Strauss and Littlechild (2014) are all edited books with chapters devoted to African interventions that work. Kreitzer's (2012) book on culturally relevant education and practice in Ghana and Okraku's (2017) PhD on Liberian female child soldiers add to this knowledge base. Over the years, other books and journal articles have moved this issue forward. In fact, one of the earliest ideas around culturally appropriate social work education was documented in ASWEA (1974), where social workers in Mali used a traditional approach to find out what kind of social work education was needed in their context. More recent books and journal articles include Laird (2003), Patel (2005), Coates, Gray and Hetherington (2006), Earle (2008), Kabeera and Sewpaul (2008), Sewpaul (2008), Ellis, Devereux and White (2009), Gray and Coates (2010), Kreitzer and Jou (2010), Mwanza (2010), Engelbrecht and Kasiram (2012), Groch, Gerdes, Segal and Groch (2012), Lombard, Kemp, Viljoen-Toet and Booyzen (2012), Ochen, Jones and McAuley (2010), Patel, Kasckc and Midgley (2012), Roestenburg and Oliphant (2012), Olaore and Drolet (2016), Spitzer (2017) and Ibrahima and Mattaini (2018), to name a few. These have written on social work interventions that work in Africa, examining positive local cultural interventions that enhance the wellbeing of the individual, community, and country, as well as on the challenges in creating culturally relevant social work education and practice. As has been stated on many occasions, colonial empires brought their social services agencies, mainly remedial, to these countries, and these organisations continue to function. Social work education should critically look at the relevance of these governmental and non-governmental organisations to analyse their current usefulness.

African articles and books

For many years, very few African social work scholars were writing about social work in Africa. Today, there is an increase in writing and this allows for the use of African social work articles and books in the classroom, instead of relying on Western articles and books. Southern Africa leads the way in social work articles and books but now articles are coming from West, Central and East Africa as well. Chinua Achebe once said: 'There is that great proverb – that until the lions have their own historians, the history of the hunt will always glorify the hunter…Once I realised that, I had to be a writer' (African Heritage, n.d.). Sharing knowledge is crucial for continuing the growth of the profession in Africa. In Ghana, Anansi is a storyteller and sometimes a trickster and this is a story that concerns the importance of sharing knowledge:

> There is a story of Anansi who was given all the wisdom in the world in a clay pot by the Lion King. Anansi had to promise to share this wisdom with all the world. Of course, Anansi said yes and took the pot home. At home Anansi looked into the pot and saw depths of wisdom he did not know about. He decided not to share the wisdom with anyone else. So, he put all the knowledge in the world into a pot, hung the pot around his neck and climbed up a coconut tree so that nobody else could have access to that knowledge. He had hung the pot right in front of him, so he had some difficulty in climbing the tree. His son, Ntikuma, stood by, watching Anansi climb the tree with difficulty. He suggested to his father to put

the pot of knowledge on his back for that would facilitate the climbing. Anansi did not like being told by a child what to do but did so anyway and found the climbing to be easier that way. However, he slipped, and the pot smashed down to the ground and all of the wisdom in the pot flew to all parts of the world. People collected the wisdom and shared it with friends and family. The point of the story: Nobody can claim to know everything and so must be open and ready to acquire new knowledge. Sharing knowledge is what makes a person wise. (Farfaria, 2018, 1)

Appropriate field education

Field education is an important part of social work education. Field education may look very different in African countries due to the fact that there are still many rural areas. In the 1970s, the emphasis on group and community work was important to social workers (ASWEA, 1974, Doc. 6). In Ghana, we found that students of social work at university had no experience of living in rural areas and, therefore, one month of field education in rural areas, often without running water and electricity, was a difficult but good experience for them. Gray and Simpson (1998) looked at community-based student units whereby a 'group of four students go into a community, for months at a time and work alongside the community in identifying developmental needs and local resources with full community participation' (as cited in Kreitzer, 2012, 153). Gray et al. (2017) conducted a recent study on field education in South and Eastern Africa and looked at whether social development was reflected in fieldwork education. It seems that social development is the foundation for fieldwork education. Some of the critical issues around field education are, for example: the length of time of an assignment in the field; the lack of trained supervisors; the lack of choice of assignment; or problems regarding the integration of theory and practice.

In the classroom

Vishanthie Sewpaul, former president of the Association of Schools of Social Work in Africa and an African social work scholar, once said that she tells her students on the first day of class that 'from now on, we will practise social work in the classroom'. That means that the ethical principles will be adhered to, including the acceptance of all students, independent of their ethnicity, sexual orientation, class, gender, ability, etc. An inclusive and safe environment is also highly relevant to a culturally relevant curriculum. Issues in social work can be very contentious when students with different sets of values, developed from their ancestors, their family, from social media, friends, academic articles, etc. come together. It is, therefore, essential that the classroom is a safe place to discuss different viewpoints in such a way that different or opposite perspectives are respected. For example, if an LGBTQ student was part of a class where many students would not advocate gay rights, would that student feel safe or would they stay silent for fear of retribution?

Or would another student from a different part of Africa and with a different ethnic background, labelled as a refugee, feel safe in a classroom? It is the professor's and students' responsibility to create a safe place for all to share. Ndura (2006, 98) speaks to this issue:

> Educational programs should develop awareness of and appreciation for people from different ethnic groups and their experiences. As they acquire empathic ability, individuals would also learn to respect and value the humanity that unites their diverse ethnic groups and understand that such unity is a major prerequisite for local, national, and regional lasting peace as well as individual prosperity. Most of all, these programs would enhance participants' awareness of and appreciation for the increasing and unavoidable inter-ethnic interdependence that is engrained in the very fabric of African history, traditions and customs.

This involves a change in the style of teaching in social work classrooms. Generally, speaking from my experience in Ghana, the professor gives an hour-long lecture in which students take down notes, word for word, of what was taught. The student is expected to share this knowledge in an exam. This type of system reflects a colonial mentality of the professor knowing everything and the student knowing nothing, which does not incorporate the knowledge, skills and experiences of the student. Freire (2000) describes this kind of education as the banking method in which the professor gives the knowledge, the students take it in and deposit the information in the exam. He describes this type of learning as oppressive:

> Knowledge is a gift bestowed by those who consider themselves knowledgeable upon those whom they consider to know (sic!) nothing. Projecting an absolute ignorance onto others, a characteristic of the ideology of oppression, negates education and knowledge as processes of inquiry. The teacher presents himself to his students as their necessary opposite; by considering their ignorance absolute, he justifies his own existence. The students [...] accept their ignorance as justifying the teacher's existence...never realizing that they educate the teacher as well. (Freire, 2007, 72)

Lecturing is fine but having a balance of open discussion, group work, sharing different ideas with each other, role playing, etc. creates an opportunity for students to critically think about issues right in the classroom. If created in a safe environment, it supports the building of relationships with all peoples of the world. I believe that teacher training is needed to change the mind-set of professors in relation to teaching. This was highlighted in ASWEA (Doc. 9, 1975), which challenged professors in the areas of '1) relationships between teachers and students; 2) use of case studies; 3) use of role play in the classroom; 4) using media for developing ideas; and 5) planning the teaching process' (Kreitzer, 2012, 23).

Appropriate language and local documents

Finally, language and using local documents have been an ongoing issue in African social work education. Using language that fits within the African context for titles of classes would be a start. For example, in Canada, indigenous social work professors might use the term 'other ways of knowing', instead of research methods, to reflect that there are other ways of knowledge gathering and understanding the world besides the Eurocentric beliefs. A critique of the language used in course outlines would be a good faculty team exercise. Using local or continental case studies is crucial. This may seem to be potentially problematic at the moment but, in the future, as African social work textbooks are written, case studies will emerge. I found in my work that African social work students were rather tired of using North American and European case studies and then adapting them to the African setting. Why should they have to do this?

The above are suggestions for creating a more culturally relevant African social work curriculum. What are the challenges and barriers to this process?

Challenges to Creating a Culturally Relevant Social Work Curriculum

There are challenges to creating culturally relevant social work education and practice, and this can be seen by how long it has taken for this idea to evolve and move forward in Africa. Our own cultural practices, religious beliefs and cultural values, our consideration of Western knowledge as the best knowledge, the brain drain of social workers to the West, a lack of time, low pay and resources, a lack of writing, and a lack of commitment to regular evaluations of the curriculum all play a part in creating barriers for this to take place. These issues will be discussed in more detail below.

Our own cultural practices

There are cultural practices that can be oppressive to citizens in any country. Social workers need to critically look at those traditions and practices to see if they are destructive to people's everyday lives and if they work against human rights. If so, the social worker as a change agent can challenge these practices, always working from the bottom up. Policy decisions that start from the top (government) can often be ineffective if local people are not convinced of a need to change or have no alternative to replace the practice. Working with leaders of communities is very important. A case in point and a poignant example can be seen with a community in Madagascar. Traditionally, twins were considered in a negative light and were often killed after birth owing to traditional beliefs, until the wife of the community leader became pregnant with twins. After that, traditional thinking about twins was changed from a negative to a positive outcome. All countries have laws that do not fully adhere to the human rights instruments set out by the United Nations, and these should be discussed in social work classrooms.

Our own religions and cultural values

Sometimes our religious beliefs and our own upbringing can hinder us from practising in an ethical manner that aligns with our international and national social work values and ethics as well as with human rights instruments. Part of social work training is to challenge students concerning their own beliefs, and when there is no reconciliation and understanding, the appropriate response to such ethical dilemmas needs to be addressed.

Western knowledge is the best knowledge

This idea is very much engrained in colonised countries and it takes a long time to come out from under its spell. Said (1991, 8-9) speaks of his own experience with Western education:

> There was a tremendous spiritual wound felt by many of us because of the sustained presence in our midst of domineering foreigners who taught us to respect distant norms and values more than our own. Our culture was felt to be of a lower grade, perhaps even congenitally inferior and something of which to be ashamed.

Ndura (2006, 93) agrees:

> What did we learn from this lesson that was imported from our colonial master? [W]e learned that the White man was the supreme symbol of civilization. We learned to accept the superiority of the White man and his products and the inferiority of Blacks and their products. We learned that our worth was determined by our closeness to the White man's ideals and way of life. We learned to be ashamed of our ancestors, our customs, our history and ourselves.

A balance between Western social work education and practice with Africa-specific education is important here. For a more radical approach, a whole new social work curriculum specific to Africa could be created with Western cultures learning from this re-creation.

Brain drain of social workers to the West

Connected with the idea of a culturally relevant social work curriculum in African countries is the situation of social work students who want to go to the Western world to practise social work and, therefore, would prefer a Western curriculum to help them on their way (Engelbrecht, 2006). Western countries also encourage this by advertising jobs which often, in the end, do not pay well and prove to be difficult and not what the person taking the job expected. If African social work is going to continue to grow and develop, African trained social workers need to stay in Africa to develop the profession and strengthen it. The lure of going westwards continues to be strong as is the idea that when one gets to the Western world, things will be that much better. Many find, however, that once they are in Europe, the US or Canada, life is not easy, and most trained social workers need to take additional training in order to practise.

Lack of resources

One of the reasons for wanting to go abroad to practise is that social workers in many parts of Africa are not paid well and working conditions can be harsh. Also, resources can be scarce, and this challenges social workers to work effectively with a paucity of resources to draw upon.

Lack of writing

When I first came to Ghana in 1994 and was there facilitating my research in 2002, I found little use for African social work writings in the course outlines. This was partly due to the inaccessibility of these articles via the library or the Internet. Also, at the time, other than in South Africa, many African social work academics were not writing about their research. This is changing now, and it is encouraging to see so many journal articles and books concerning social work education and practice in Africa being published. Access to Internet journal articles has helped tremendously and it is hoped that course outlines will reflect this trend.

Commitment to a regular evaluation of the curriculum

A commitment to evaluate the curriculum on a regular basis is important. Ideally, a participatory action research evaluation approach would be beneficial, drawing information about the relevance of social work education and practice from professors, past and present students, community leaders, and staff from social welfare agencies, non-governmental and international social welfare organisations, as well as service users. When looking at curriculum evaluation and considering voices from the list above, it is important to evaluate in light of the international policies of the United Nations, the African Charter and the international social work organisations. Finally, a critique of theories and practices of social work in light of African philosophy, history, and traditional practices could be incorporated in the classroom.

Conclusion

Social work in Africa is growing and, in some countries, is now recognised as an important profession in terms of the many avenues through which it can affect change in society. It is an ethical imperative that a social work curriculum teach from an ethical, human rights perspective that is inclusive of diversity, cultural shifts, values, and traditions and that is inclusive of all human beings. This curriculum should include past historical events that influenced the emergence of social work in

Africa. This demands a continual evaluation of values and beliefs at the individual, community, and national levels. Ross (2008, 392) further comments on this from a South African context:

> South African social workers need to revisit the issue of formulating African models of social work practice that do not rely exclusively on British, European or American models but which draw on indigenous best practices, knowledge and culture from the African continent. We need to understand, appreciate and engage the cosmological, ontological and epistemological differences that separate Euro-American and African medical and cultural practices.

At the core of social work practice is the building of relationships with diverse peoples. So much homophobia, xenophobia, and other phobias are due to seeing people as objects to berate and oppress. There are many tensions in the world today that challenge our own beliefs and values and, therefore, we feel uncomfortable in dealing with these conflicts. But social work is about inclusion and confronting oppression and discrimination, and this starts in the classroom.

Teaching techniques that encourage critical thinking, group discussions, and a safe place to share views that others may not agree with give future social workers the skills to address oppression and discrimination in a respectful way. Van Wyk and Higgs (2007, 70) explain their ideas about the role academia should play in today's African context.

> The African university has to provide a service to the continent and its people. The African continent is immense, not only in terms of its size, but more important, with respect to the cultural, linguistic and ethnic diversity that characterizes the people who live in its various parts. The challenge that awaits the African university is to improve the quality of the lives of all those who inhabit this continent.

If universities can shift in their thinking, this will have an enormous effect in Africa. The increase in writing about culturally appropriate social work interventions is encouraging and can be part of any classroom whereby students are challenged to develop their own innovative interventions that reflect their society and that are ethical and positive, and that uphold human rights. They also have the opportunity to critique cultural practices that are oppressive to people in society and to work to replace these cultural practices with alternatives that are in line with human rights.

I end with an African story to challenge social work practitioners and academics when critiquing social work education and practice in Africa:

Do You Want Adapted Shoes or New Shoes?

> Mecca was a very fortunate West African man. He had a job that drew envy from his fellow villagers. He worked for a White man who was very generous. Indeed, the White boss was so nice to Mecca that he gave him a special gift: a pair of used shoes. Mecca was very excited. This was his very first pair of shoes. The shoes had a

little problem, though. They were too tight to fit Mecca's untamed feet. But he was still determined to wear them. So, he drilled holes in the corners of the shoes such that his pinky toes would stick out as he walked. He was very proud. He marched through the village showing off his new acquisition to friends and neighbours and praising the White man for his infinite goodness. (Ndura 2006, 92-93)

Do we want to continue to walk around with a used social work curriculum from another world that is very distant from African culture, do we want to take the good bits of the shoes and make our own, or do we want to throw the old shoes away and make completely new ones designed for the African context?

References

African Heritage (n.d.). *Chinua Achebe in His Own Words*. Available at: https://afrolegends. com/2013/03/22/chinua-achebe-in-his-own-words/ (accessed 8 April 2018).

Ani M (2007) *Yurugu: An African-Centered Critique of European Cultural Thought and Behavior*. Washington, DC: Nkonimfo.

Asante MK (2003) *Afrocentricity: The Theory of Social Change (revised and expanded)*. Chicago: African American Images.

ASASWEI (2017) *Report on the 2017 Social Work Conference Held at OR Tambo Conference Centre from 8-11 October 2017*. South Africa.

ASWEA (1986*) Association for Social Work Education in Africa*. Addis Ababa: ASWEA.

ASWEA (1974) *Relationship Between Social Work Education and National Social Development*, Doc. # 6. Addis Ababa: ASWEA.

ASWEA (1977) *The Role of Social Development Education in Africa's Struggle for Political and Economic Independence, Doc. # 12*. Addis Ababa: ASWEA.

Butterfield AK and Abye T (2013) *Social Development and Social Work: Learning from Africa*. New York: Routledge.

Coates J, Gray M and Hetherington T (2006) An 'Ecospiritual' Perspective: Finally, a Place for Indigenous Approaches. *British Journal of Social Work*, 36(3): 381-399.

Dictionary (2017) Ethics. Available at: http://www.dictionary.com/browse/ethics (accessed 8 April 2018).

Earle N (2008). *Social Work in Social Change. The Profession and Education of Social Workers in South Africa*. Cape Town: HSRC.

Ellis F, Devereux S and White P (2009) *Social Protection in Africa*. Cheltenham: Edward Elgar.

Engelbrecht, LK (2006) Plumbing the Brain Drain of South African Social Workers Migrating to the UK: Challenges for Social Service Providers. *Social Work/Maatskaplike Werk*, 42(2): 127-146.

Engelbrecht C and Kasiram MI (2012) The Role of *Ubuntu* in Families Living with Mental Illness in the Community. *South African Family Practice*, 54(5): 441-446.

Fals Borda O (2001) Participatory Action Research in Social Theory: Origins and Challenges. In: Reason P and Bradbury H (eds) *Handbook of Action Research*. Thousand Oaks: Sage, 27-37.

Farfaria (2018) *Anansi and the Pot of Wisdom*. Available at: https://www.farfaria.com/ anansi-and-the-pot-of-wisdom (accessed 8 April 2018).

Freire P (2007) *Pedagogy of the Oppressed*. 30th ed. New York: Continuum.

Gray M (2005) Dilemmas of International Social Work: Paradoxical Processes in Indigenisation, Universalism and Imperialism. *International Journal of Social Welfare*, 14(3): 231-238.

Gray M and Coates J (2010) 'Indigenization' and Knowledge Development: Extending the Debate. *International Social Work*, 53(5): 613-627.

Gray M, Coates J and Yellow Bird M (2008) *Indigenous Social Work Around the World*. Burlington: Ashgate.

Gray M, Coates J, Yellow Bird M and Hetherington T (2013) *Decolonizing Social Work*. Burlington: Ashgate.

Gray M, Agllias K, Mupedziswa R and Mugumbate J (2017) The Expansion of Developmental Social Work in Southern and East Africa: Opportunities and Challenges for Social Work Field Programmes. *International Social Work*. Available at: https://doi. org/10.1177/0020872817695399 (accessed 8 April 2018).

Groch K, Gerdes KE, Segal EA and Groch M (2012) The Grassroots Londolozi Model of African Development: Social Empathy in Action. *Journal of Community Practice*, 20(1-2): 154-77.

Healy LM (2008) *International Social Work*. 2nd ed. New York: Oxford University Press.

IASSW (2014) *Global Definition of Social Work*. Available at: https://www.iassw-aiets.org/ global-definition-of-social-work-review-of-the-global-definition/ (accessed 8 April 2018).

Ibrahima AB and Mattaini MA (2018) Social Work in Africa: Decolonizing Methodologies and Approaches. *International Social Work*. Available at: https://doi. org/10.1177/0020872817742702 (accessed 8 April 2018).

Ife J (2007) *The New International Agendas: What Role for Social Work*. Inaugural Hokenstad International Social Work Lecture, San Francisco, 6 November 2007. Available at: http://ifsw.org/news/the-new-international-agendas-what-role-for-social-work/ (accessed 8 April 2018).

IFSW (2012). *Statement of Ethical Principles.* Available at: http://ifsw.org/policies/statement-of-ethical-principles/ (accessed 8 April 2018).

Kabeera B and Sewpaul V (2008) Genocide and its Aftermath. *International Social Work*, 51(3): 324-336.

Kendall KA (1995) Foreword. In: Watts TD, Elliott D and Mayadays NS (eds) *International Handbook on Social Work Education.* Westport, CT: Greenwood.

Kreitzer L and Jou MK (2010) Social Work with Victims of Genocide: The Alternatives to Violence Project (AVP) in Rwanda. *International Social Work*, 53(1): 73-86.

Kreitzer L (2012) *Social Work in Africa: Exploring Culturally Relevant Education and Practice in Ghana.* Calgary: University of Calgary Press.

Kreitzer L (2013) Decolonizing Social Work Education in Africa: A Historical Perspective. In: Gray M, Coates J and Hetherington T (eds) *Decolonizing Social Work.* Farnham: Ashgate.

Laird S (2003) Evaluating Social Work Outcomes in Sub-Saharan Africa. *Qualitative Social Work*, 2(3): 251-270.

Lombard A, Kemp M, Viljoen-Toet N and Booyzen M (2012) An Integrated Developmental Model for Poverty Reduction in South Africa: An NGO's Perspective. *Journal of Community Practice*, 20(1-2): 178-195.

Maathai W (2009) *The Challenge for Africa.* New York: Pantheon.

Midgley J (1981) *Professional Imperialism: Social Work in the Third World.* London: Heinemann.

Mwanza LKJ (2010) Challenges Facing Social Work Education in Africa. *International Social Work*, 53(1): 129-136.

Ndura E (2006) Western Education and African Cultural Identity in the Great Lakes Region of Africa: A Case of Failed Globalization. *Peace & Change*, 31(1): 90-101.

Noble C, Strauss H, and Littlechild B (2014) *Global Social Work: Crossing Boundaries, Blurring Boundaries.* Sydney: University of Sydney.

Nukunya GK (1992) *Tradition and Change in Ghana: An Introduction to Sociology.* Accra: University of Ghana.

Ochen EA, Jones AD and McAuley JW (2012) Formerly Abducted Child Mothers in Northern Uganda: A Critique of Modern Structures for Child Protection and Reintegration. *Journal of Community Practice*, 20(1-2): 89-111.

Okraku O (2017) *Resilience and Coping Strategies of Liberian Former Girl Child Soldiers Living in Ghana.* Doctoral Dissertation. University of Alberta, Canada. Available at: https://era.library.ualberta.ca/items/1d8fb157-8c3d-47ed-81ec-f22fd4249b9c/view/ef4dc29c-6165-4c1d-84f5-70e6abb2a004/Okraku_Olive_2017-7_PhD.pdf (accessed 8 April 2018).

Olaore AY and Drolet J (2016) Indigenous Knowledge, Beliefs, and Cultural Practices for Children and Families in Nigeria. *Journal of Ethnic & Cultural Diversity in Social Work*, 26(3): 254-270.

Organisation of African Unity (1981) *African (Banjul) Charter on Human and People's Rights*. Available at: http://www.achpr.org/files/instruments/achpr/banjul_charter.pdf (accessed 8 April 2018).

Osei-Hwedie K and Jacques G (2007) *Indigenising Social Work in Africa*. Accra: Ghana Universities Press.

Oxford Dictionary (2017) *Relevant*. Available at: https://en.oxforddictionaries.com/definition/relevant (accessed 8 April 2018).

Patel L (2005) *Social Welfare and Social Development*. Cape Town: Oxford University Press.

Patel L, Kaseke E and Midgley J (2012) Indigenous Welfare and Community-Based Social Development: Lessons from African Innovations. *Journal of Community Practice*, 20(1-2): 12-31.

Patel L (2014) Social Workers Shaping Welfare Policy in South Africa: The White Paper for Social Welfare and Lessons for Policy Practice. *CSD Perspectives* 14-23. Available at: https://csd.wustl.edu/publications/documents/p14-23.pdf (accessed 8 April 2018).

Roestenburg W and Oliphant E (2012) Community-Based Juvenile Offender Programs in South Africa: Lessons Learned. *Journal of Community Practice*, 20(1-2): 32-51.

Ross E (2008) The Intersection of Cultural Practices and Ethics in a Rights-based Society: Implications for Social Work. *International Social Work*, 51(3): 384-395.

Said E (1991) Identity, Authority and Freedom: The Potentate and the Traveller. *Transition*, 54: 4-18.

Sewpaul V and Lombard A (2004) Social Work Education, Training and Standards in Africa. *Social Work Education*, 23(5): 537 554.

Sewpaul V (2008) Community Intervention and Social Activism. In: Barnard A, Horner N and Wild J (eds) *The Value Base of Social Work and Social Care: An Active Learning Handbook*. Berkshire: Open University.

Smith L (2008) South African Social Work Education: Critical Imperative for Social Change in the Post-Apartheid and Post-Colonial World. *International Social Work*, 51(3): 371-383.

Smith LT (2012) *Decolonizing Methodologies: Research and Indigenous Peoples*. 2nd ed. London: Zed.

Spitzer H (2017) Social Work in East Africa: A *Mzungu* Perspective. *International Social Work*. Available at: http://journals.sagepub.com/doi/full/10.1177/0020872817742696 (accessed 8 April 2018).

Spitzer H, Twikirize JM and Wairire GG (2014) *Professional Social Work in East Africa: Towards Social Development, Poverty Reduction and Gender Equality*. Kampala: Fountain.

Tandon Y (1996) Reclaiming Africa's Agenda: Good Governance and the Role of NGOs in the African Context. *Australian Journal of International Affairs*, 50(3): 293-303.

Ubuntu (2018) *The Ubuntu Story*. Available at: https://www.ubuntu.com/about/about-ubuntu_(accessed 8 April 2018).

UN (1948) *Universal Declaration on Human Rights*. Available at: http://www.un.org/en/universal-declaration-human-rights/ (accessed 8 April 2018).

UN (2007) *UN Declaration on the Rights of Indigenous Peoples*. Available at: http://www.un.org/esa/socdev/unpfii/documents/DRIPS_en.pdf (accessed 8 April 2018).

UNESCO (1982) *Mexico City Declaration on Cultural Policies*. World Conference on Cultural Policies, Mexico City, 26 July to 6 August 1982. Available at: http://www.wwcd.org (accessed 8 April 3018).

Van Wyck B and Higgs P (2007) A Call for an African University: A Critical Reflection. *Higher Education Policy*, 20: 61-71.

Wairire GG (2014) The State of Social Work Education and Practice in Kenya. In: Spitzer H, Twikirize JM and Wairire GG (eds) *Professional Social Work in East Africa: Towards Social Development, Poverty Reduction and Gender Equality*. Kampala: Fountain, 93-107.

Watkins JM, Mohr B and Kelly R (2011) *Appreciative Inquiry: Change at the Speed of Imagination*. 2nd ed. San Francisco: Pfeiffer.

Wilson MG and Whitmore E (2000) *Seeds of Fire*. Winnipeg: Fernwood.

Wilson S (2008) *Research is Ceremony*. Winnipeg: Fernwood.

Wiredu K (2004) *A Companion to African Philosophy*. Oxford: Blackwell.

Wits University (n.d.). *ASWEA Documents*. Available at: http://www.historicalpapers.wits.ac.za/?inventory/U/collections&c=AG3303/R/9014 (accessed 8 April 2018).

Yeneabat M and Butterfield A (2012) "We Can't Eat a Road:" Asset-Based Community Development and the Gedam Sefer Community Partnership in Ethiopia. *Journal of Community Practice*, 20(1-2): 134-153.

4

A Social Work Analysis of Home-grown Solutions and Poverty Reduction in Rwanda: The Traditional Approach of *Ubudehe*

Charles Rutikanga

Introduction

As part of the effort to reconstruct Rwanda and nurture a shared national identity after the 1994 genocide, the Government of Rwanda has drawn on aspects of Rwandan culture and traditional practices. Therefore, the cultural context was made a strong basis from which home-grown solutions to fulfil needs would emerge. After the genocide, these solutions were understood as culturally owned practices aimed to translate sustainable development programmes into practice. In addition to contributing valuable inputs to Rwanda's reconstruction and development, home-grown solutions came together with insightful approaches that successfully mobilise citizens' participation towards their own development (Ndahiro, Rwagatara and Nkusi, 2015).

Under the framework of the PROSOWO project (*Professional Social Work in East Africa*), an empirical study on indigenous and innovative models of social work practice was undertaken. Field data was collected on traditional/indigenous approaches from different categories of informants through focus group discussions (FGDs) and personal interviews. Initial findings established that development programmes in place are informed by cultural practices and are more or less similar to social work models of helping individuals, families, and communities. This chapter will focus on the traditional approach of *ubudehe*.

Ubedehe: **An Overview**

Ubudehe is a social protection system of intra-community cooperation rooted in Rwandan culture and based on collective and individual actions. The programme has been designed based on the traditional Rwandan practice of collective work (OSSREA, 2006). *Ubudehe* is a traditional Rwandan practice and cultural value of working together to solve problems; the approach can be compared to *ikibiri* in Burundi, *msaragambo* among the Chagga ethnic group in north-western Tanzania, or *bulungi bwansi* and *gwanga mujje* in the Buganda kingdom in Uganda. In Kenya, this approach can be related to *harambee* and *chamas*, where community members put their resources and efforts together to help one another.

As argued by Habiyonizcye and Mugunga (2012), the word *ubudehe* describes the practice of preparing the fields before it rains and the planting season starts. A group of households would join together to dig their fields, acting collectively to share the burden of the work and to make sure that everyone is ready in time for the planting season. What should be noted here is that *ubudehe* was not only limited to agricultural activities, but also extended to other activities that needed support from many people.

The *ubudehe* concept is very inclusive, covering men, women, and all social groups, including the most marginalised community members. It also extends to those who are very poor or incapacitated so that they, too, can participate in the collective action. After the group completed their fields, they moved on to the fields of those who had not been able to participate directly. A successful harvest was then celebrated with *umuganura* (a celebration of the harvest, a day that is still celebrated in Rwanda on every first Friday of August) made from collecting contributions from everyone's first harvest (Republic of Rwanda, 2003).

The innovative use of neo-traditional cultural institutions as operational tools to support the implementation of the country's poverty reduction and development strategies was born out of the national dialogue known as *umushikirano* which took place in *Urugwiro*, the President's office. Habiyonizeye and Mugunga (2012) contend that it was during these dialogue meetings that *ubudehe* (collective action to reduce poverty), *gacaca* (informal conflict settlement arrangements), *imihigo* (competitive performance contracts and accountability mechanisms), *itorero* (cultural mentoring and leadership training) and *umuganda* (communal work), and others were first presented as practical ways of overcoming the immense challenges faced by Rwanda at the turn of the century (Habiyonizeye and Mugunga, 2012).

All the traditional approaches mentioned above were re-introduced after the 1994 genocide to help in the reconstruction of the country after the atrocities, which left around one million people dead, three million refugees, ten thousand people in prison on genocide-related charges, a large number of widows and orphans, as well as leaving the country in a state of extreme poverty (OSSREA, 2006). The *ubudehe* approach was re-introduced to address rural poverty through community action, creating empowerment and participatory democracy (European Commission, 2006). What should be mentioned here is that *ubudehe* features in a number of national programmes, strategies and policies related to economic development and poverty reduction. Some of these strategies include the Economic Development and Poverty Reduction Strategy (1 and 2), Vision 2020 *Umurenge*, community development policy, health insurance scheme, and others.

In re-introducing the traditional approach of *ubudehe*, the Government of Rwanda believed that the complexity and specific nature of poverty at household level do not mean that there are no solutions or that these solutions have to be complicated. This implies that 'outsiders' cannot design those solutions for the affected people but that they themselves must do so. There is sometimes a tendency to underestimate the abilities of illiterate peasants to analyse what is going on around them and their ability to implement solutions (Republic of Rwanda, 2003 and 2009). The same understanding is also shared by developmental social work, where it is believed that social action and systems advocacy engage citizens in understanding and building power and using it to advocate and negotiate for the interests of the community that later on contribute to the improved quality of life of all community members (Lombard, 2014).

The key part of the *ubudehe* approach was to re-build the social capital, the relationships and interdependencies that were destroyed during the civil war that started in 1990 and the 1994 genocide. Implementing change is about people's ability to transform their own lives, and, where necessary, with support from others. The Government of Rwanda believed that local government institutions have a vital role to play in facilitating people to do things by themselves (Republic of Rwanda, 2003). The *ubudehe* was set up as part of the Participatory Poverty Assessment (PPA). The overarching goal of the PPA is 'to help community members and some poor households create their own problem-solving experiences' (Republic of Rwanda 2003, *ubudehe* to fight poverty, concept note, 5). As such, information gathered at the cell level[6] by the community members helped to understand people's experience of poverty and was integrated into the final Poverty Reduction Strategy Paper (PRSP 2002-2006). The following principles were used to guide the PPA and the Poverty Reduction Strategy: enhancing local problem-solving experience; ensuring participation of all actors; enabling affected individuals to participate; protecting the 'action-experience-knowledge-new action' cycle of all nationals (Republic of

---

[6]   A cell, also known as *akagali* in Kinyarwanda, is the second lowest unit of the local authority administrative units, followed by a village known as *umudugudu*, which is the lowest unit. Cells make a sector, and sectors make districts.

Rwanda, 2009). In supporting people's participation in their own development, Easterly (2006) asserts that, in the use of foreign aid, the poor have little power to hold anyone accountable for meeting their needs. To their credit, the World Bank and the International Monitory Fund now show some awareness of this problem by respecting some choices of the poor and insisting on their participation in development-related activities (Easterly, 2006).

Ubudehe and Developmental Social Work

From a developmental social work perspective, Lombard (2014), citing Mbeki (2009), argues that developmental social work should emphasise giving the voice to the people to engage in and influence their own development. The same author further points out that citizens need institutions that facilitate cooperation and leadership to make such institutions function and deliver on the citizens' expectations (Lombard, 2014). This shows how social workers are very important in providing a leadership role to approaches and programmes that are citizen-oriented, such as *ubudehe*. In a study carried out about the role of social work in poverty reduction and the realisation of the Millennium Development Goals (MDGs) in Rwanda, Kalinganire and Rutikanga (2015) explain that social workers in Rwanda play multiple roles towards the country's development and poverty reduction. Such roles include the mobilisation and sensitisation of masses; advocacy and networking for the good of the client at different levels; planning, monitoring and evaluating of development- and poverty reduction-related projects; education and providing training in various aspects of development and poverty reduction.

Since the *ubudehe* approach is crosscutting in many development and poverty reduction programmes in Rwanda, social workers play these roles not at the *ubudehe* approach level alone but in multiple development and poverty reduction programmes. It can also be argued that the *ubudehe* approach and those used in developmental social work are inseparable. For example, *ubudehe* is about citizen participation, advocacy and citizen mobilisation for collective action, empowerment, and the struggle for the equality of life for all. This is not different from the intentions and approaches of developmental social work as argued by Lombard (2014), where she contends that social work intervention is relevant to advocacy for the poor and the most vulnerable. This advocacy intends to build capacities and promote participation and empowerment, which leads to the promotion of social equality and human rights (Lombard, 2014). It is in the same sense that *ubudehe* advocates for the poor and the most vulnerable members of the community, where they are given support of different kinds that may include, but is not limited to, housing, health insurance, domestic animals, and direct support in the form of money.

The philosophy behind the *ubudehe* approach is to increase the level of institutional problem-solving capacities at the local level by citizens and the local government. It seeks to put into operation the principles of citizens' participation through local collective action. The word *ubudehe* was selected to present a quick mental image of people working together; action to solve the problems of local people, by local people, for local people; with support from local governments, NGOs, local resources, and donors. It sets out to strengthen democratic processes and governance, starting from the people's aspirations, their abilities, and traditions (Republic of Rwanda, 2009).

The *ubudehe* process seeks to create deliberate opportunities for people at the cell level to interact with one another, to share worldviews, and to create institutions of their own which assign duties, benefits, responsibility and authority. It is through such processes of local interaction for mutual benefit that trust between individuals increases, and reciprocal relationships grow. The assumption made is that strong social capital creates high trust, communication within a group, and opportunities for economic co-operative formation. If such a group faces a conflict situation, it will attempt to resolve the conflict through local institutional means, without resorting to violence. Consequently, the *ubudehe* process, through encouraging local collective action, is also building a foundation for reducing vulnerability and the potential for divisionism and conflict (Republic of Rwanda, 2009).

Ubudehe in Numbers

Ubudehe is targeted at the village (*umudugudu*), which is the lowest level of administrative units in Rwanda, composed of about 100 to 150 households; it is small enough to foster collective action. In Rwanda, there are 14,744 *imidugudu* (villages), and targeting this level is part of a broader attempt to increase community-level participation in governance and development (Habiyonizeye and Mugunga, 2012). The *ubudehe* programme was implemented in phases. The pilot phase was conducted in 2001-2002 in Butare (currently in the South Province). Based on the good results recorded during the pilot phase, a first phase, scaling up the programme countrywide, was initiated for the period 2005-2006. The second phase (current) started in 2007 and is still ongoing (RGB, 2014). From 2007, each selected village received a grant of 600 euro every year to finance projects of their own choice, based on their priorities and needs, without the influence of any local authorities. Prior to this, each village selects persons to be trained in the village needs assessment. Mupenzi (2014) estimates that, in Rwanda today, there are 20,000 trained *ubudehe* facilitators and each village has been involved in a planning exercise. This involves the collection of information at the village level through the *ubudehe* methodology, which, in turn, informs district development plans (Mupenzi, 2014). The same exercises involve identifying one individual or a household in each village every year that is in great need. The identified individual or family is given a loan equivalent to 60 euro – about 60,000 Rwandan francs (RWF) – which is repayable with no interest (European Commission, 2006). The period of paying out the individual loan depends on the nature of projects and it might also be determined by the village council with some flexibility. Given its positive results, in 2008, *ubudehe* won a prestigious United Nations Public Service Award for the best managed and implemented development programme (United Nations, 2008) and it was also appreciated by the European Commission for involving citizens in their own development (European Commission, 2006).

Traditional *Ubudehe* versus Contemporary *Ubudehe*

As stated earlier, the practice was not only limited to farming but also involved other activities that required support from many people, and these included, but were not limited to, collecting construction materials such as poles and grass for roofing a house. The one who was helped through *ubudehe* was supposed to prepare local beer to give to people after work; this beer was commonly known as *inzoga y'ubudehe* (the beer of *ubudehe*). While that beer was consumed, the people reserved one drinking pipe, which was called *umuheha w'umwami*, literally translated as 'the pipe of the King'. This pipe was not for the actual King but for the king's people (*Rubanda*). This reserved pipe was for whoever would come even if he or she did not participate in the *ubudehe* activity of that day; he or she was just invited for the drink.

Like many other traditional approaches in Africa and Rwanda in particular, *ubudehe* was also affected during the colonisation period, when new approaches like a cash-based transfer economy was introduced. This weakened the practice as some members of the community were able to pay others to do work for them. In the same vein, Kreitzer (2012) argues that traditional social systems and previously established mechanisms for social development were broken down with the colonisation of Africa, since they were considered inferior, primitive, and less important as defined by European colonial discourse. Kreitzer further points out that most African universities were established according to a European model and many Africans were trained in Western universities. On their return, some were given teaching positions in their countries' universities, while these universities were using models and methods studied in Western universities. She continues to argue that this process promoted dependence upon Western written materials and often undermined local knowledge and expertise (Kreitzer, 2012; see also Rankopo and Osei-Hwedie, 2011). However, while this trend occurred across Rwanda, in some places, *ubudehe* was still practised until the 1980s and even the 1990s under other names, such as *guhingirana* (helping each other to dig), *gufashanya* (helping each other), *gutabarana* (helping each other in emergency situations), and others. Community members continued to help one another in different activities that required support from many people, but it was based upon individual or household requests. The practice continued to foster solidarity, social cohesion, mutual respect, and trust (Republic of Rwanda, 2009).

The contemporary *ubudehe* was re-considered through a series of meetings of political, social, legal, and religious leaders between 1998 and 1999 known as the *Urugwiro* debates, as mentioned above. These gatherings discussed the most pressing issues concerning national reconstruction after the 1994 genocide. The contemporary *ubudehe* approach utilises two levels of developmental social work intervention – the micro level, targeting individuals and families, and the macro level, which targets the community. Other important aspects of *ubudehe* today include its promotion of democracy, participatory development, unity and reconciliation, local solutions to local problems, and the empowering of all communities across Rwanda. The approach has its roots in the Participatory Poverty Assessment (PPA) whereby citizens would self-identify as poor or otherwise, according to a set of criteria. The objective was to help community groups and poor households create their own problem-solving strategies (Republic of Rwanda, 2003).

Current Conceptualisations of *Ubudehe*

In this study, the research was interested in understanding the views of study participants regarding the *ubudehe* concept. Participants provided the following explanations:

- The *ubudehe* is a government programme that aims at boosting the social welfare of Rwandese citizens, based on their own capacity and participation (Rugarama, Fumbwe and Kaniga, FGDs). *Ubudehe* is a programme where the government gives direct support in the form of money to the poor people for self-development and getting out of poverty. With the funds provided, they may decide to buy domestic animals like cows and goats depending on the amount of money given to them (Mutete, FGD).

- *Ubudehe* is a programme that is used to establish categories of people in order to determine who may receive direct governmental support (Mutete, FGD).

- *Ubudehe*, which, in the past, was called *igiterankuba* in Musanze Region, is one of the approaches that are being used for community development today (Musanze, FGD).

- *Ubudehe* is a popular traditional practice which today has been transformed into a programme that is used for socio-economic development with a major focus on poverty reduction (Rugarama, FGD).

The contemporary *ubudehe* has the following objectives:

- To assist people in classifying the level and type of poverty that exists in their community and to reach a common understanding of this classification;
- To help communities define their developmental priorities;
- To bring communities together to discuss and decide upon the most effective and efficient ways to achieve poverty reduction and to define their developmental priorities; and
- To help communities establish ways of funding their developmental plans at group and individual levels.

The *Ubudehe* Process

Community members collectively draw a social map on the ground, using local materials, which is later copied onto a piece of cloth for the community to keep as a tool for future planning. This map details every household's location, their social category, type of shelter, all social and economic infrastructure and landmarks in the village, such as water points, schools, shops, roads, bridges, health centres, etc. This exercise ensures that every family is acknowledged and represented in the process, and that no one is excluded and everyone's needs are better identified. At the end, community members share their understanding of poverty, its causes, and consequences (RGB, 2014). The *ubudehe* approach operates at the community and household levels. Assisted by the *ubudehe* facilitators or trainers, the community-level intervention is described as follows:

- Determine the poverty profile as perceived by the people themselves;
- Determine the causes and consequences of poverty;
- Draw up the social map of the cell, which includes the names of household heads, their social category (different categories are again decided by the people themselves), their developmental infrastructure, and the roofing material of each household.
- Identify and analyse the problems facing their community and determine a priority problem to be addressed; and
- Plan the activities and relative means needed to address the prioritised problem through a collective action plan (*ubudehe*).

After this process, the funds are provided by the Local Administrative Entities Development Agency (LODA), which is currently responsible for the implementation of the *ubudehe* programme and is supervised by the Ministry of Local Government

(MINALOC) (RGB, 2014). There is also intervention at the household level. The community identifies a particularly poor household. Then, trainers and facilitators visit the household where a participatory approach is supposed to be used to make the household address the challenge of fighting poverty. The *ubudehe* concept paper (Republic of Rwanda, 2003) outlines the procedure as follows:

- Determine their coping strategies throughout the year (seasonality);
- Analyse these strategies in order to develop a strategy favourable to the promotion and improvement of the living conditions within the household (preference scoring);
- Plan activities and a necessary budget to be able to execute the developed strategy;
- A pertinence test is then carried out by wise men in the cells (*Inyangamugayo*) to make sure that the developed strategy is appropriate and will be of good use to the household; and
- The household members finally accept and sign for the funds that are accorded to them. They agree that the funds supporting the execution of their strategy will have a rotating character.

The Socio-Economic Impact of the *Ubudehe* Programme

Different evaluations carried out on the impact of *ubudehe* have highlighted its achievements and impact towards contributing to poverty reduction at community and household levels (Niringiye and Ayebale, 2012). An evaluation carried out by the European Commission on Rural Poverty Reduction established that the *ubudehe* programme has contributed greatly to improvement in access to health services, education, shelter, food, and social cohesion. It further adds that the level of beneficiaries' participation in decision-making processes is also significant (European Union, 2009). In the same regard, Mupenzi has praised the programme for directly engaging citizens in their own development (Mupenzi, 2014). In terms of social impact, a poverty analysis of *ubudehe* also found that the *ubudehe* programme creates a mechanism for grassroots communities' empowerment, whereby communities have the opportunity to improve both their quality of life and their social cohesion (OSSREA, 2006, 7).

Regarding the access to health care, the assessment carried out by the Rwanda Governance Board (RGB) in 2014 indicates that health access increased from 40.6% to 75.4% owing to the *ubudehe* programme, and participation in health insurance, known as 'Mutuelle de Santé', increased from 81.8% to 97.1%. The same assessment further established that *ubudehe* has contributed to improvements in access to education, shelter, and food. In terms of the economic impact, the assessment confirmed the developed capacities of individuals and households for income generation, the capacity to reimburse the loans received from the programme, and allowing more community members to get the loan and develop themselves (RGB, 2014).

Niringiye and Ayebale (2012) also lauded the way in which *ubudehe* has brought communities together for collective action, based on their own priorities. The provision of a bank account to each community has enabled thousands of community-led actions, such as purchasing livestock, undertaking agricultural activities, building clean water facilities, classrooms, terraces, health centres, as well as silos for storing agricultural produce. In 2006-2007, 9,000 communities undertook projects through *ubudehe* and in 2007-2008, that number rose to 15,000. The year 2010 saw over 55,000 collective actions taken by communities with the assistance of 30,000 *ubudehe* facilitators. At least 1.4 million people (20% of the population) have been direct beneficiaries of *ubudehe*. Between 2005 and 2008, around 50,000 people were trained in *ubudehe* concepts. Regarding the impact of *ubudehe*, an evaluation carried out by European Union has shown that about 95% of the sampled population confirmed that their incomes had improved; within that percentage, about 71% reported that their income had doubled and 22% considered that their income had more than tripled (Niringiye and Ayebale, 2012).

Contribution of *Ubudehe* to Poverty Reduction: Perspectives from the Grassroots

Poverty reduction is a primary priority of the Government of Rwanda. One of the astonishing effects of the 1994 genocide was extreme poverty among Rwandese. Infrastructures such as schools, hospitals, roads, and bridges were seriously damaged or completely destroyed. The agricultural sector, once considered the backbone of the country's economy, was significantly affected. Therefore, it was important for the Government of Rwanda, which took over after the genocide, to put in place different programmes that would help to reconstruct the country and enable sustainable development (Republic of Rwanda, 2003). One of the foremost poverty reduction programmes that the government introduced was *ubudehe*. Some empirical evidence of our study is presented below, both in terms of the success of the *ubudehe* programme as well as with regard to some critical comments raised by study participants.

Ubudehe and community infrastructure development

In different sectors where the research was conducted, many respondents revealed that the *ubudehe* programme facilitated the construction or the renovation of different community infrastructures, such as roads, water sources and water pipelines, schools, local authority offices, health centres or health posts, bridges, etc. The same was also emphasised by the assessment carried by out by RGB on home-grown solutions (RGB, 2014).

Supporting the above assertion, in Musanze District, Northern Province of Rwanda, one of the participants in the FGD revealed that they managed to construct the Cyivugiza cell offices in Kivuruga Sector that also shared offices with a health post; this office was also constructed with the support provided by the *ubudehe* programme as well as through citizens' direct contributions.

> We managed to construct the offices of our cell on our own and we are very proud of this big achievement which we could not have achieved without the *ubudehe* support, plus our little contributions.

The projects have been made possible through a combination of a national grant to each village as well as local contributions from community members. The local contribution can be in cash or kind. It was revealed by respondents that some community members give their contribution in kind by providing the required manpower to the project, while others contribute financially to the construction of those infrastructures. When a project benefits more than one village they all combine their efforts and resources to solve the problem. Projects of this nature included the construction of schools, water sources, health centres and health posts, roads, and bridges that benefit the participating villages.

In other parts of the country like Kigali, where water is a major problem in some parts of the city, the *ubudehe* programme facilitated the construction of water tanks and the payment for water trucks that bring water to communities at a nominal fee, compared to what each individual would pay for the same quantity of water. On this, respondents reiterated the official literature on *ubudehe* regarding the distinctiveness of projects at the village level, attributable to the principle of self-determination that has been espoused through the approach.

While explaining the community infrastructure development in Rugarama, Gatsibo District, one of the FGD respondents said:

> Before the *ubudehe* programme came to our village, we were using unsafe water which we used to fetch from swamps and unsafe sources. But with the funds provided by the *ubudehe* programme, together with our own contributions, we managed to get safe drinking water in our village. This has solved the problem of spending much time collecting water from long distances and the problem of using unsafe water was also solved.

Ubudehe and poverty reduction at household and individual levels

Apart from community development and the renovation of community infrastructures, the *ubudehe* programmes also target very poor individuals in different villages. The poor people and poor families are given a loan of 60,000 RWF to execute projects of their choice. The most common types of income-generating activities financed by the *ubudehe* programme from the different places where the data was collected included: crops and livestock farming, non-agricultural projects such as small-scale trade (mostly retail), handicrafts, and tailoring. While agriculture-based projects were mostly implemented in rural areas, trading was more common in urban and semi-urban contexts. This component of the *ubudehe* programme, which helps the poorest people and their families to come out of poverty, was introduced in 2007. The beneficiaries of *ubudehe* loans are mostly from the first and second category of the programme (see below). In 2014, the Local Administrative Entities Development Agency (LODA) created new *ubudehe* categories. Under the programme, households are placed into categories based on their socio-economic status, their level of property in terms of land and other belongings, and what the families' breadwinners do to earn a living. The categories are as follows:

- Category 1: Families that do not own a house and can hardly afford basic needs.

- Category 2: Those who have a dwelling of their own or are able to rent one but rarely get full-time jobs.

- Category 3: Those who have a job and farmers who go beyond subsistence farming to produce a surplus which can be sold. The latter also includes those with small and medium enterprises who can provide employment to a larger number of people.

- Category 4: Those who own large-scale businesses, individuals working with international organisations and industries, as well as public servants. (Republic of Rwanda 2015)

In our study it was mentioned that people usually choose projects depending on their capacities to execute them. Some beneficiaries of the above-mentioned categories are given cows from either the *ubudehe* programme or from other projects that give people cows like *girinka munyarwanda* (one cow per family). Other beneficiaries are given goats or pigs, depending on their capacities to look after them. Regarding cattle farming, participants said that it has multiple benefits, especially providing milk for the household and having a surplus for sale to generate income for the household. Another benefit of cattle farming is that it also provides organic manure for fertilising people's gardens, as many of them practise subsistence farming for their livelihoods.

In many areas where the *ubudehe* programme operates, citizens have the problem of infertile soil that needs to be fertilised before they can grow anything. Those who do not have cows or other domestic animals to provide this kind of manure have to buy it, usually at a rather high cost. This explains why many consider livestock farming as important to them. The study participants also mentioned that the offspring of the animals provided by the *ubudehe* project, be it cows, goats or other livestock, would often be given to another needy individual or family that, in turn, would share the offspring of these animals with others. Owing to this rotational approach, the project can have a multiplier effect, specifically building trust and friendship among the individuals and families exchanging and sharing these animals.

An FGD member in Fumbwe Sector, Rwamagana District reflected on how *ubudehe* support through loans had changed his and his family's lives.

> I am one of those who benefitted from an *ubudehe* loan of 60,000 RWF when it was started in our sector in 2010. When I got that money, I added the little money I had saved and bought a pregnant cow at 76,000 RWF. The cow gave birth to a bull calf after a few months. When the calf had grown up, I sold it at 75,000 and paid my loan, respecting the agreed time to pay it back. The cow gave birth to another calf and, after some time, I decided to sell it, together with its calf, and bought land for farming at 300,000 RWF [equivalent to approximately 300 euro], as the lack of land was my major problem. After selling that cow for an understandable purpose, the community members decided to give me another cow through the *ubudehe* programme. The new cow is now pregnant with one month to go before it gives birth. From the time I received the *ubudehe* loan, my life and the life of my family has improved. I now have enough land for cultivation where I grow enough food for my family. I am now able to buy health insurance for all my family members, which was not easy before, pay school fees, and buy other school-related materials for my children. I also managed to enlarge the size of my house by adding more iron sheets. Apart from the above, I was able to organise two weddings for my daughters. All the above was made possible due to the support provided by the *ubudehe* programme.

Other beneficiaries of *ubudehe* loans, especially those living in urban or semi-urban centres, use them to improve or carry out new business activities. The businesses mentioned included: selling second-hand clothes or vegetables; operating small retail shops; and improving existing tailoring, motorcycle, and bicycle workshops. An Executive Secretary in Huye District had this to say:

> For the poor people who received support of 60,000 RWF, it helped them to start up small businesses or other activities that can help them to generate incomes through trade, mostly by selling second-hand clothes, or vegetables, or establishing other small retail businesses. From the time they were given those loans, many beneficiaries' economic situations and standards of living have gone up compared to before they received those loans, and they have moved up from poverty remarkably.

However, some of the participants also criticised local authorities for not following up on those who are given the *ubudehe* loans to pay them back and to extend loans to other needy community members. While elaborating on the danger of not paying back loans on time, several respondents commented that some beneficiaries thought that they were given free money, since nobody was reminding them to pay back. Another issue raised regarding these loans was that the beneficiaries are not provided with the necessary training to boost their capacities to use their loans properly. This was highlighted as the major cause of making losses and failing to pay back. These outcomes contradict the intended results when giving out these loans. In some places, the situation of the poor worsens, as they are forced to pay back and are left with nothing after that. Because of the pressure put on them to pay back, some sell their remaining property while others decide to run away from their villages.

Direct support to the most vulnerable people

Through *ubudehe*, the poor from the first category in the *ubudehe* classification (see above) who are able to work are helped by local authorities to find employment within their communities or in the nearby communities. In our study in was stated that the most common activities where these people usually find a job are the so-called public works, such as road construction, the preparation of radical terraces, the construction of schools, health centres, and water sources or water pipelines. For one day of work, from seven a.m. to 12 p.m., they are paid around 1,000 RWF, which is equivalent to one euro. During the study, some local leaders explained that they also negotiate with employers to allow people to work for only a half-day so that, in the evening, they can get time to engage in other development-related activities for their households.

Another component of *ubudehe* is what is known as direct support or emergency fund (*Inkunga y'ingoboka*). The direct support targets families in the first category of *ubudehe*, a household with no working family members; these include households headed by children, very old or physically disabled people. These families receive monthly financial support, depending on the size of the family. For example, a family with only one household member is given 7,500 RWF; two are given 12,000 RWF; three get 15,000 RWF; four get 18,000 RWF, etc. The bigger the family, the more the financial support awarded.

The *ubudehe* programme also helps the most vulnerable people in the community to acquire shelter. Community members, either through *ubudehe* or *umuganda* (communal work), come together, make bricks, or gather other construction materials to construct the house. The *ubudehe* funds are then used to buy iron sheets and other required construction materials which the individual or the family cannot afford.

Another non-material benefit of the *ubudehe* programme is that it has facilitated people to work together, which, in turn, promotes unity and reconciliation, aspects that were seriously damaged by the 1994 genocide. *Ubudehe* brings people together, without discrimination of any kind, and promotes the participation of everyone in the village.

The Role of Social Workers in the Implementation of the *Ubudehe* Programme

The *ubuhehe* programme has three major components: 1. Supporting villages, poor households' and individuals' projects; 2. The *ubudehe* categorisation (*ibyiciro by'ubudehe*); and 3. The provision of livestock to poor families, which is currently managed by the *girinka* programme. With these different components of *ubudehe*, independently of how well they are known or understood, social workers play the following key roles at different levels of programme implementation (based on our study findings):

- Advocating for poor individuals and families in need of help; the identified individuals and families receive direct support from the government social welfare department or from non-governmental agencies.

- Participating in the provision of technical support to communities during the selection of sustainable projects to be financially supported by the *ubudehe* programme.

- Linking individuals, families, and communities in need of help in order to complement the *ubudehe* support and community resources.

- Mobilising and sensitising communities to participate in the *ubudehe* programme activities and assurance of proper use of the programme funds.

- Fighting against injustices, in cases where funds are given to individuals or families that are not eligible to receive support.

- Actively participating in the planning, implementation, and follow-up of individual, family, and village projects under the *ubudehe* programme.

- Participating in *ubudehe* committees to influence the betterment of the programme beneficiaries.

- Category 3: Those who have a job and farmers who go beyond subsistence farming to produce a surplus which can be sold. The latter also includes those with small and medium enterprises who can provide employment to a larger number of people.

- Working with the local government to identify where programme funds might be misused.

- Regularly visiting families under the programme for quick graduation from one *ubudehe* category to the other, which is the major aim of the programme in its support of individuals and families.
- Active involvement in the *ubudehe* categorisation process, as these categories are the basis for social welfare service provision.

Challenges of the *Ubudehe* Approach

From a critical point of view, regardless of all the programme's achievements credited to *ubudehe*, there are also a number of challenges that require attention in order to ensure future progress. In all the sites of the study, participants raised concerns about how households were put into the *ubudehe* categories, accusing their local leaders of manipulating the information provided by the community members. Conversely, some village members preferred to be classified into lower poverty levels as a way to receive support from social security programmes, such as health insurance, *girinka*, and other programmes that target the poor by using the *ubudehe* categorisation as a basis.

What should be noted concerning this categorisation is that the support for expenses such as tuition fees for students' higher education, students' upkeep fees, and contributions to health insurance are determined by the *ubudehe* category to which one belongs. It is a problem for students from poor families to cover their tuition fees and living expenses, since only students from families that are grouped in the first and second categories receive a waiver for tuition and receive support to cover their living expenses. If a family is put in a category that does not reflect its economic status, this will have a negative implication for their children at the time they want to enrol in public universities. A 'wrong' categorisation will also affect the contributions towards health insurance fees, as different categories receive differing amounts of support. The assessment of home-grown solutions also raised concerns regarding the unrealistic categorisation of families into *ubudehe* categories; hence, a review and potential correction of these categories was recommended (see also RGB, 2014). As a result of this inappropriate categorisation or owing to changes made concerning their family's grouping into a particular *ubudehe* category, some students failed to complete their university studies and several families found it impossible to cover their health insurance premiums. To overcome this, respondents recommended that the assignment of *ubudehe* categories on the basis of household poverty levels should take place publicly with all community members present and should be validated by the village itself. Additionally, the outcome of this process should be respected by the local leaders.

According to the guideline of the *ubudehe* categorisation, community members who are not satisfied with the category they were put in are given a chance to complain and appeal in the first instance at the sector level, and if the respective community members remain discontented with the decision, they can appeal in the second instance to the district level. The final level of appeal is the office of the Ombudsman at the central government level. For ordinary community members, especially those from rural areas, this appeal process will be complicated as it involves high travel costs. Therefore, some would decide against filing complaints in spite of their dissatisfaction.

Another challenge mentioned by research participants was that the funds allocated to some community projects, even considering the added contributions of community members would, in some cases, not be enough to complete the planned activity. Moreover, the loans given to individuals and/or households were also partly considered to be insufficient. Respondents recommended that the loan amount be doubled (from 60,000 to 120,000 RWF). The same concern was raised by the Rwanda Governance Board assessment for the home-grown solutions, when the board stated that the loans given to individuals and households to reduce poverty is too little to speed up the beneficiaries' graduation from one poverty level to another one and to make a tangible difference in the lives of the beneficiaries (RGB, 2014). Respondents in our study recommended that funding should be increased, and each village project should be considered as unique in terms of funding.

At the household level, it was also observed during the field study that some beneficiaries struggled to manage the funds or loans they had received. There were some households that had spent the money on things other than their project, or that had sold the livestock they had had received. Similar concerns were raised by the Rwanda Governance Board's assessment (RGB, 2014), which highlighted challenges of limited capacity and knowledge regarding project planning and implementation on the part of the beneficiaries (30%) and projects that are not well designed (22.3%), two factors that might be contributing to the failure of individual and household projects.

Conclusion

Since its re-introduction in 2001, the *ubudehe* approach has contributed to poverty reduction in Rwanda in different aspects that range from community infrastructure development and improved income at individual and family levels. Owing to the *ubudehe* approach, some poor and vulnerable individuals have managed to get their own decent shelters. At the macro level, the *ubudehe* financial support has helped communities to construct and renovate different infrastructures, such as roads, bridges, schools, health centres and health posts, water sources and water pipelines. In some places, community electrification was made possible and, in many parts of the country, construction of local authority offices, especially the ones at the cell level, was facilitated.

The uniqueness of the *ubudehe* approach is that it facilitates the full participation of citizens in their own development where community members decide on which project to take up using the *ubudehe* fund plus their own contributions. Citizens' participation through the *ubudehe* approach also facilitates empowerment and enhancement of people's capacities, as most of the activities are conducted in a collective way where the citizens learn from each other. The approach also boosts the sense of ownership among community members, which results in the infrastructures constructed by the *ubudehe* approach being highly valued and respected. In a nutshell, the *ubudehe* traditional approach has significantly contributed to poverty reduction among individuals and communities in Rwanda, notwithstanding the existing challenges in its administration.

In our study it has become evident that social work professionals play significant roles in the whole *ubudehe* process, mostly in rural communities. Key activities include the identification of individual, family, and community needs; the planning, implementing, and supervision of the *ubudehe* activities; the advocacy for poor individuals, families, and communities; linking them to opportunities; providing technical support; and sensitising community members and mobilising them to participate in the collective activities undertaken via the *ubudehe* approach. This is consistent with the same sense in which Rwomire and Raditlhokwa (1996) see social work roles in this sphere as planning, organising, supervising, advocating, counselling, administrating, and evaluating a programme. In *ubudehe*, social workers help individuals, families, and communities to find solutions to their problems by themselves before asking for external support. With an optimistic view, Rwomire and Raditlhokwa (1996, quoting Khinduka, 1971) recommend that developing countries constructively engage social work in the planning and the implementation of significant structural changes in order to improve their socio-economic development. They also call on social workers to unite and develop a collective, coherent, and strong voice to articulate their roles and interests and to boost their reputation and status if they are to contribute meaningfully to development-related programmes such as *ubudehe*.

References

Ashish S (2011) The Paradox of "Hidden" Democracy in Rwanda: The Citizens Experience of Ubudehe. DPhil Thesis. Department of International Development, Oxford University, Wolfson College.

Easterly WR (2006) *The White Man's Burden: Why the West's Efforts to Aid the Rest Have Done So Much Ill and So Little Good.* New York: Penguin.

European Commission (2006) European Commission Address at the Ubudehe Seminar Kigali, 4 September 2006. Available at: http://www.rwandapedia.rw/rw/cmis/properties?id=workspace%3A//SpacesStore/e4bd570c-0259-45e4-bd74-5926b63ae8d1 (accessed 09 October 2017).

European Union (2009) Evaluation Report of the Decentralized Programme for Rural Poverty Reduction (DPRPR - 9th EDF). Kigali.

Ezeanya C (2015) Home-Grown and Grassroots-Based Strategies for Determining Inequality towards Policy Action Rwanda's Ubudehe Approach in Perspective. Helsinki: UNU-WIDER. (WIDER Working Paper No. 2015/008).

Habiyonizeye AY and Mugunga JC (2012) *A Case Study of Citizen Engagement in Fostering Democratic Governance in Rwanda.* Conference Paper, International Conference on Democratic Governance: Challenges in Africa and Asia August 8-9, 2012. Available at: https://ameppa.org/wp-content/uploads/2018/02/citizen-engagement-in-rwanda.pdf (accessed 14 June 2018).

Kalinganire C and Rutikanga C (2014) Social Development as the Privileged Model for Social Work Practice in Post-Genocide Rwanda. In: Spitzer H, Twikirize JM and Wairire GG (eds) *Professional Social Work in East Africa. Towards Social Development, Poverty Reduction and Gender Equality.* Kampala: Fountain, 232-244.

Kalinganire C and Rutikanga C (2015) *The Role of Social Work in Poverty Reduction and the Realisation of Millennium Development Goals in Rwanda.* Kampala: Fountain.

Kreitzer L (2012) *Social Work in Africa: Exploring Culturally Relevant Education and Practice in Ghana.* Calgary: University of Calgary Press.

Lombard A (2014) A Developmental Perspective in Social Work: Theory and Practice. In: Spitzer H, Twikirize JM and Wairire GG (eds) *Professional Social Work in East Africa. Towards Social Development, Poverty Reduction and Gender Equality.* Kampala: Fountain, 43-55.

Mupenzi A (2014) *Interventions against Poverty in Rwanda: A Case Study of Ubudehe in Gatsibo District, Eastern Province, Rwanda.* Igarss 2014. doi:10.1007/s13398-014-0173-7.2

Ndahiro A, Rwagatare J and Nkusi A (2015). *Rwanda: Rebuilding of a Nation.* Kigali: Fountain.

Niringiye A and Ayebale C (2012) Impact Evaluation of the Ubudehe Programme in Rwanda: An Examination of the Sustainability of the Ubudehe Programme. *Journal of Sustainable Development in Africa,* 14(3): 141-154.

OSSREA (2006) *Economic Development Poverty Reduction Strategy, Poverty Analysis of Ubudehe.* Draft Report.

Rankopo MJ and Osei-Hwedie K (2011) Globalization and Culturally Relevant Social Work: African Perspectives on Indigenization. *International Social Work,* 54(1): 137-147.

Republic of Rwanda (2015) *Community-Led Ubudehe Categorisation Kicks Off.* Available at: http://www.gov.rw/news_detail/?tx_ttnews%5Btt_news%5D =1054&cHash=a315a8b0054e76f9c699f05ce24d3eb8 (accessed 07 February 2018).

Republic of Rwanda (2003) *Ubudehe for Poverty Reduction.* Policy Rationale. Kigali: Ministry of Local Government.

Republic of Rwanda (2009) *Ubudehe mu Kurwanya Ubukene.* Concept Note. Kigali: Ministry of Local Government.

Rwanda Governance Board (RGB) (2014) *Fostering Good Governance for Sustainable Development: The Assessment of the Impact of Home Grown Initiatives.* Kigali: Rwanda Governance Board.

Rwomire A and Raditlhokwa L (1996) Social Work in Africa: Issues and Challenges. *Journal of Social Development in Africa*, II (2): 5-19.

United Nations (2008) *2008 United Nations Public Service Day and Awards Ceremony*, 23 June 2008. New York. Available at: https://publicadministration.un.org/en/2008unpsa. (Accessed 23 March 2018).

Umugoroba w'Ababyeyi: An Innovative Social Work Approach to Socio-Economic Wellbeing in Rwanda

Consolée Uwihangana, Alexandre Hakizamungu and Théogène Bangwanubusa

Introduction

In its drive to search for home-grown and innovative solutions to a number of social problems, Rwanda has initiated a programme locally known as *umugoroba w'ababyeyi* (literally, parents' evening forum). The programme is mainly rooted in the social and cultural context of Rwanda and is geared towards the socio-economic wellbeing of the population. *Umugoroba w'ababyeyi* started after the 1994 genocide and mainly operates at the village level (the lowest administrative entity in Rwanda). It occurs when women and men come together to search for enabling conditions for the harmonious cohabitation of family members. At its inception, the *umugoroba w'ababyeyi* initiative was assigned an objective of improving family relationships and living conditions, on the one hand, and of enabling sustainable development, on the other hand (Republic of Rwanda, 2014).

Umugoroba w'ababyeyi evolved from the women's evening forum (*akagoroba k'abagore*), which gained momentum in 2010 as an opportunity for women to discuss and attempt to address various challenges they were facing. The event typically took place in the evening when the women were somewhat free of their daily household duties. As days went by, the event became popular to such an extent that the Government of Rwanda, via the Ministry of Gender and Family Promotion, proposed that it should become more inclusive by integrating men. Thus, what started as a women's evening forum changed into a parents' evening forum (Republic of Rwanda, 2014).

According to the Republic of Rwanda (2014), *umugoroba w'ababyeyi* came into being as a way to specifically help fight domestic violence and attempt to settle family conflicts at the grassroots level but also inculcate the promotion of family values, hygiene, family planning, children's rights, and gender equality.

Theoretical Framework

For the purpose of this research, the concept of *umugoroba w'ababyeyi* will be analysed via the lens of empowerment theory. In this approach, empowerment is defined as the ways in which people could gain control over their lives in order to achieve their interests as a group, and a method by which social workers enhance the power of vulnerable people (Adams, 2003). According to empowerment theory, people are considered as being capable of taking a lead towards a positive change in problem-solving processes. Conceptually, empowerment is taken as 'a method of enhancing interpersonal and/or political capacity of the individuals so that they are able to participate in the improvement of their situation' (Askheim, 2003, 3).

For the social work profession, the aim of empowering clients is to offer them the possibility to take part in the process of improving their lives by valuing their abilities and strengths. This turns empowerment into a process whereby the social worker intervenes with the client in order to minimise the powerlessness created by stigmatisation (Dalrymple and Burke, 2006).

Midgley raises important points that characterise the developmental perspective in social work. Among them are social change and development, the use of strengths, empowerment and capacity development, self-determination, client participation, commitment to equality, and social justice (Midgley, 2010 quoted in Lombard, 2014). Once people have that capacity, they are able to participate in, work towards, and achieve social change and development (ibid.). This perspective is suitable in Rwanda, mainly to tackle poverty and other related issues. Social workers, as agents of change, play a significant role in this process.

According to Kalinganire and Rutikanga (2015, 47), social work practitioners carry out activities related to the mobilisation and organisation of families to embrace socio-economic development. With this approach, the family level is the starting point. For Lombard (2014, 50), such an approach focuses mainly on qualitative changes happening in people's lives in connection with the improvement of the wellbeing of every individual in society. Such changes enable people to reach their full potential. In Rwanda, this approach can be applied at different layers of local government, with *umugoroba w'ababyeyi* being one of these platforms.

So far, no study has been conducted on the role of *umugoroba w'ababyeyi* in the promotion of the socio-economic wellbeing of local communities. Thus, this research was designed with the aim to explore how different local communities organise and practise *umugoroba w'ababyeyi* and how it contributes to their wellbeing.

Locations, Target Groups and Research Methods, and Data Analysis

The research was carried out in nine selected districts of Rwanda. The choice of these districts was motivated by the fact that they represent all five provinces of Rwanda, namely North, South, East, West, and Kigali City. In Kigali City, the districts of Kicukiro, Gasabo and Nyarugenge were chosen. In the Southern Province, only Huye District was included in the research. In the Eastern Province, Rwamagana and Gatsibo Districts were selected. In the Northern Province, Gicumbi and Musanze Districts were chosen, while in the Western Province, Rusizi District was selected.

The participants involved in this research were ordinary people at the community level, several employees at the district level, and social work academics chosen from three institutions of higher learning in Rwanda. In total, 28 participants were selected, including five local leaders, 19 social work practitioners, two social work educators, and two key informants – both directors of social protection at the district level. To identify the ordinary people to take part in the research, the snowball sampling technique was used. This means that the researchers contacted the authorities at the district level and these helped the researchers to reach out, step by step, to the right people. The targeted employees at the district level were the directors of social protection, those in charge of gender and family promotion, directors of good governance, those in charge of the civic education academy (*umutahira*), and social work practitioners.

To collect the data, FGDs with ordinary people and academics were used, while individual interviews were used with other respondents. All the data collected were qualitative in nature. FGDs as well as individual interviews revolved around three important areas, namely: how local communities were practising *umugoroba w'ababyeyi* (e.g. the frequency of events of *umugoroba w'ababyeyi*; the categories and the number of people attending; the roles played by those attending; as well as record-keeping and reporting mechanisms), which problems or issues are discussed in *umugoroba w'ababyeyi*, and what people considered as gains and/or challenges of *umugoroba w'ababyeyi*.

FGDs and interviews were conducted, audio-recorded, and transcribed in the local language – Kinyarwanda – but later translated into English for analysis purposes. The responses were first thematically analysed by arranging them according to the following main areas underpinning this research: the organisation and practice of *umugoroba w'ababyeyi*; the topics discussed in these fora; the gains from these meetings; and challenges of the concept. The next step was for the researchers to familiarise themselves with the responses by reading and rereading them until they could identify themes and sub-themes from the given responses. These themes and sub-themes were identified by means of similarities, differences, contradictions, and omissions which emerged from the respondents' answers. Finally, as an illustration of the identified themes and sub-themes, some responses were directly quoted.

Organisation and Practice of *Umugoroba w'Ababyeyi*

Umugoroba w'ababyeyi is a state-led programme. It has the political support it requires to be properly implemented nationwide. At the level of each village, elected representatives have a clear mandate to mobilise citizens to participate in the fora. To be effective enough, *umugoroba w'ababyeyi* was assigned clear responsibilities (Republic of Rwanda, 2013). First, it was designed to instruct the youth, both boys and girls, about the values of Rwandan culture, on sex education, and on preparations for marriage. Second, it was expected to enable the young people to share testimonies and learn from one another how to solve problems arising at family level. Third, it was mandated to discuss at length the government socio-economic development programmes. Fourth, it was meant as a forum where parents and children who had been made victims of violence or conflict were actively listened to before participants could assist these victims. Fifth, the forum was set to help parents improve on their children's education and, at the same time, exchange ideas on harmonious coexistence among them. Finally, it was supposed to be an appropriate platform to encourage families to visit each other with a view to socialising and preventing eventual conflicts.

From the empirical study, we noted that *umugoroba w'ababyeyi* is generally organised once a month in many parts of the country. However, when there is a crucial issue to be discussed, an ad hoc forum can be convened in order to specifically discuss and settle that particular issue. Another finding was that, even though *umugoroba w'ababyeyi* is intended for both women and men of all ages, the main participants are women.

The researchers further observed that *umugoroba w'ababyeyi* tends to be formally convened and chaired by the chief of the village while the minutes-taker and record-keeper is the representative of the National Women's Council at the village level. In almost all *umugoroba w'ababyeyi* events observed, the chair is the only one to elaborate on the agenda of the event, depending on the issues reported to him or her and the weight given to the issues. In few cases, the chair of *umugoroba w'ababyeyi* and the minutes-taker could be chosen from the people present, thus going against the prevailing norm.

In general terms, each *umugoroba w'ababyeyi* event lasts between two and three hours but surprisingly, it does not necessarily take place in the evening, as its name suggests. Everything depends on the nature and urgency of the reported issue.

Issues Discussed in *Umugoroba w'Ababyeyi*

From both the discussions held with the participants and their field observations, the researchers noted that the issues discussed during *umugoroba w'ababyeyi* events were as varied as circumstances could allow. The issues ranged from cultural and health education to developing the culture of savings and promoting the socio-economic wellbeing of the neediest.

Education of children on cultural values

During *umugoroba w'ababyeyi* events, the education of children on cultural values was given a large amount of time. Asked about the reason behind that, one social worker in Rusizi District had this to say: 'We give more time to the cultural education of children so that they grow up as responsible and respectful people.' To emphasise the same point, an *umutahira* from Rusizi District said:

> There are similarities to what was done in our traditional culture during traditional entertainments (*ibitaramo*, *itorero*, and *urugerero*). Participants could dance, share beer and food, and talk about Rwandan values.

In addition, a participant of an *umugoroba w'ababyeyi* event highlighted:

> During *umugoroba w'ababyeyi* with our children, we remind them of the importance of cultural values in shaping their future.

Education on how to develop the culture of savings and entrepreneurship

The participation in some *umugoroba w'ababyeyi* events showed that parents are keen on educating the young people about how to develop the culture of savings and how to become entrepreneurs. To illustrate this, one female parent in Tumba Sector, Huye District, commented:

> We have opened bank accounts for our children in the local branch of SACCO [Savings and Credit Cooperative] and we make savings for them on a monthly basis. So, when they start secondary school, they can buy school materials for themselves from the savings we have made for them.

Another lady attending the event explained how she developed as an entrepreneur:

> I took a training course on knitting. After that, I stayed home because I had no capital to start a business. By attending the *umugoroba w'ababyeyi* forum, I was given an opportunity to talk about my plans. My presence at the *umugoroba w'ababyeyi* forum prompted the attendees to enlist me among those to receive an *ubudehe* [community-based social protection] credit package. Eventually, I got that package and started my own business of knitting. I sell the clothes I have sown to one secondary school and I can make monthly savings which will enable me to secure a loan from a SACCO and expand my business.

Importance of formal and health education

Formal schooling is another point commonly discussed during *umugoroba w'ababyeyi* events, where attendees exchange ideas about the parents' responsibility to guide and inspire children and the youth to attend school as well as about measures to increase school retention. In the course of the interview with the director of social protection in Ngoma Sector, Huye District, the issue was touched upon in the following terms:

> Problems like school children dropping out of school and ending up on the street are discussed openly and tentative solutions are devised. Probably as a result of that, the rate of dropouts is decreasing.

During *umugoroba w'ababyeyi* forums, other issues pertaining to education at large are discussed, such as sex education, drug and alcohol abuse among the youth, as well as HIV/AIDS. Depending on the setting, the young people can be invited to attend the *umugoroba w'ababyeyi* event. The importance of having the young people in the parents' forum was stressed by one social worker in Gihundwe Sector, Rusizi District, as follows: 'Young people, especially girls, are educated on the dangers of early and unwanted pregnancies.' To support that statement, but in a more nuanced manner, one participant in *umugoroba w'ababyeyi* in Tumba Sector, Huye District, clarified that

> …while talking about health-related matters such as reproductive health, HIV/ AIDS, hygiene and sanitation, […] with the young people, it helps to decide first on their age group so that they obtain proper and relevant information.

Gains from *Umugoroba w'Ababyeyi* Events

The following sections illustrate improvements in the lives of the population by participating in *umugoroba w'ababyeyi*. The examples therein provide useful links to key social work approaches.

Umugoroba w'ababyeyi as an empowering approach in social work

In the course of FGDs and interviews, empowerment turned out to be a concept used in *umugoroba w'ababyeyi* events to counter the issues related to discrimination, marginalisation, and domination. To illustrate this, one civil servant in charge of social affairs in Ngoma Sector, Huye District revealed that *umugoroba w'ababyeyi* 'helps create friendship, familiarity, and a sense of solidarity among those who frequently attend.'

The information from the data demonstrates that male and female members of *umugoroba w'ababyeyi* are empowered to take decisions to develop themselves, to solve their problems, and to achieve sustainable development, as illustrated by an FGD participant:

Of course, the committee cooperates with the leadership committee at the village level so that information is shared faster. The head of the village shares and discusses all government policies planned at the village level where they can even decide the numbers of people to enrol in the Vision 2020 *Umurenge* Programme to get support.

Demonstrating what she had gained in an *umugoroba w'ababyeyi* event, one participant in an FGD held in Tumba Sector, Huye District, argued that '*umugoroba w'ababyeyi* has been an opportunity for community members to open up their minds, increase empathy, and widen their hearts to support their colleagues in need.' The case of *umugoroba w'ababyeyi* shows how, at the village level, parents meet to discuss the problems impeding their socio-economic development and come up with solutions. This is what Sen (1999) called 'development as freedom', to mean that in the absence of freedom, no one can expect development. One participant narrated this:

> This lady's house [pointing a finger at her] was destroyed by rain. In our meeting, the president of our forum told us that we have to help her, that there was no reason to go and beg at the sector or the district office. We collected money, bought trees, made dry-mud bricks and we re-built her house.

As it stands, strong concern for others and empathy are tangible feelings that characterise members. This is reflected in how they assist each other:

> For instance, one member of *umugoroba w'ababyeyi* [touching another member's shoulders] gave birth and we had planned to visit her. Our president reminded us that it is our responsibility to bring her a gift. We bought an *igitenge* [African loin cloth] and food items. When she went for vaccination, she was well clothed like other women who have husbands; you understand that we supported her. When someone passes away, we buy a coffin and are in charge of all burial expenses.

Umugoroba w'ababyeyi as a problem-solving approach

Socio-economic problems affect communities and families in all parts of the world, and Rwanda is no exception. In Rwanda, local and innovative programmes are put in place in order to tackle problems affecting specific populations. Being the smallest social unit and the foundation of society, the family plays an important role in the development of each nation. Because of this, the family needs due attention and care so that it may fulfil its role in the socialisation of children. Empirically, this can also be documented. The director of good governance in Rusizi District, for example, disclosed the following: 'We sensitise people to address their families' problems according to the traditional culture of problem solving under the influence of *umugoroba w'ababyeyi*.'

The family offers multi-dimensional opportunities which justify ways in which it deserves protection. Uwihangana (2014, 30) considered the family as 'the custodian of morals and traditional values recognised by the community.' This statement gives relevance to the importance of culture and traditions as having roots in the concept of the family. Basing on this thinking, the same source suggests that '[c]ulture and tradition play a central role in the lives of most Africans. To entrust the family the custody of these values means that the family is also valued and cherished' (Uwihangana, 2014, 30). Thus, the family needs to be saved from any harm that could prevent it from accomplishing its tasks.

The following statement during an FGD illustrates this:

> It's our responsibility to solve people's problems with reference to the ways of Rwandan culture. There is a programme named *umugoroba w'ababyeyi* […] Here, people meet and discuss their family problems, including those of their children, and find solutions together.

In the particular setting of Rwanda, *umugoroba w'ababyeyi* was initiated with a view to protecting the family. In addition, such a protection of the family has various implications for the country's development. There is ample testimony to support this assumption.

A local leader in charge of social protection delivered one such testimony which can be taken as an illustration of how family conflicts are resolved. It reads as follows:

> Last time we received five families living in harmony and 15 families living in conflicting situations. The five families gave out their testimonies on how they solved their problems; hopefully, those in conflict learnt and will take a decision to change and restore peace in their families.

These remarks make it clear that members of *umugoroba w'ababyeyi* feel concerned for the living conditions of their fellows and are ready to contribute to achieving a common good.

Definitely, in order to achieve positive relationships, a change in the thinking and the conduct of people is needed. *Umugoroba w'ababyeyi* members contribute to that important aspect. It was noted that conflicts sometimes arise because the parties involved do not know how to handle problems or how to behave in a conflicting situation. *Umugoroba w'ababyeyi* offers an opportunity to remedy such situations. A participant in this forum put it thus:

> When there are conflicts between spouses, we invite the husband and his wife; we talk to them in order to know the causes of the conflict. Whoever is responsible for the conflict is encouraged to ask for forgiveness, the other one is encouraged to forgive, and we encourage them to start afresh and set objectives for the future. A committee is elected that will do follow-up consultations until everything is sorted out.

In addition to the above, another participant said:

> Sometimes, we learn that a woman comes home late in the night. We will advise her to change her negative behaviour, while we advise the men to abstain from bandit behaviour.

In general, *umugoroba w'ababyeyi* plays an important role in safeguarding harmonious relationships among family members, on the one hand, and in creating strong relationships among neighbours, on the other. When people live in harmony and are united, they are strong enough to work together to achieve socio-economic development.

Umugoroba w'ababyeyi as a developmental social work approach

Umugoroba w'ababyeyi is considered to be a community-based programme likely to support state strategies aimed at citizens' empowerment, participation, and development. To this end, participants revealed that they are happy to be aware of government development programmes, which enables them to know where to turn in order to improve their socio-economic situations. An illustration of this fact is taken from a female participant in an FGD who said:

> I had a plot of land for rice growing but due to poor production, I was unable to pay for the rent to the cooperative. When local leaders were choosing beneficiaries of the *ubudehe* programme, my fellows supported me to get the loan; I was able to get back the plot and to pay back the loan.

An addition to the above, another lady stated:

> For poverty issues, there are government programmes for poverty reduction but there are other ways of assisting each other by individual contributions. For instance, if we are thirty and everyone contributes 200 RWF [20 euro-cent], we will be able to buy clothes for someone who is in need or we can buy livestock for the poorest person.

Umugoroba w'ababyeyi is also characterised by advocacy and information sharing. Participants advocate for their colleagues who need support from the local government. Thus, being together in *umugoroba w'ababyeyi* is an opportunity to know one another, be aware of each other's strengths and weaknesses, to know who is able to work or not, and to be able to support one another by sharing the available resources for the benefit of the entire community. This is corroborated by the director of social protection in Ngoma Sector, Huye District, who said:

> Members of *umugoroba w'ababyeyi* collect money and give it to a person as capital or they buy livestock for farming. Sometimes, the representative of *umugoroba w'ababyeyi* can approach local leaders and ask them to include a person in need on the list of beneficiaries of development programmes [if they fulfil the criteria].

A participant of the FGD added another important statement, referring to a fellow participant who was poor:

> Y [name of women] is able to work and courageous but had no financial means. As they [local leaders and the population] were selecting someone who was able to work but with financial issues, she got the money from the *ubudehe* programme, because we knew she was honest, hardworking, and needed financial support.

From this, it is clear that working together opens doors for other opportunities, both at the individual and the community levels. Members of *umugoroba w'ababyeyi* who are eligible for government programmes for poverty reduction easily get support through the forum and are easily monitored regarding the proper use of the support received. Furthermore, the benefits are shared. The following testimony illustrates the situation:

> The *girinka* programme allows sharing cows in the community. When the cow has a calf, the latter is donated to another selected beneficiary and so on and so forth, and at the end of the day, many people have cows and their family situation improves.

In Rwandan culture, owning a cow is a sign of wealth; the family that has it can attend to different economic problems, as the following explanation shows:

> The cow from *girinka* helps to solve family-related problems. There is no malnutrition because we get milk, we sell the milk to have money for school materials and attend to other needs, and there is an increase in agricultural productivity thanks to the cow dung. We have a kitchen garden and are able to prepare a balanced diet.

The information from the data clearly demonstrates that members of *umugoroba w'ababyeyi* are happy about how their living conditions have improved through the forum. Family and community relationships are strengthened, solidarity and mutual support are promoted, and economic gains and benefits are achieved through poverty reduction programmes such as the 'one cow per poor family' programme (*girinka*). Others receive loans from saving and credit cooperatives or are supported through poverty reduction programmes such as *ubudehe* and Vision 2020 *Umurenge*.

Challenges Encountered in *Umugoroba w'Ababyeyi* Events

Despite its visible advantages, the information from the field data revealed that there are challenges hindering the success of *umugoroba w'ababyeyi* activities, such as low turnouts of men, and a lack of both follow-up and of financial means to implement some initiatives.

Low turnout of men in umugoroba w'ababyeyi events

From field observations, it was noted that one of the biggest challenges faced by *umugoroba w'ababyeyi* events is the low turnout of men. To illustrate this, during one *umugoroba w'ababyeyi* event held in Tumba Sector, Huye District, only three men were present, while 17 women were in attendance. As one civil servant in charge of gender and family promotion in Nyarugenge District confirmed, this tendency is very similar both in rural and in urban areas.

Lack of information sharing, monitoring, and follow-up

Another challenge faced by *umugoroba w'ababyeyi* is related to a lack of information sharing between the attendees and the local administration. In FGDs with social workers in Rusizi District, they revealed that it was not always easy for local government employees to monitor and follow up on what happened in every *umugoroba w'ababyeyi* event in their administrative entities, owing to their multiple duties. Moreover, there was the problem of transport and limited number of staff to do the job.

Insufficient financial capacity

Umugoroba w'ababyeyi offers an opportunity for its participants to learn to work and to start small income-generating activities to improve their economic situation. Some have already started but they revealed that when they want to take further steps, they are often constrained by insufficient financial capacities. As an illustration, a participant in an FGD disclosed the following:

> The challenges that we have are insufficient financial capacities because if you start a business as you progress you have new ideas and you realise that you have insufficient financial capacities.... Once in this forum, we decided to start a project for tailoring and knitting. An expert in business planning studied the project and found that the required capital would be 20,000,000 RWF [20,000 euro]. Our savings were not enough, and we could not find any other support. We have ideas, but money is a problem.

The challenges outlined above clearly reveal that there is a need to review the organisation, implementation, and follow-up of *umugoroba w'ababyeyi* activities.

Discussion and Recommendations

Umugoroba w'ababyeyi was one aspect of the collected data through an empirical study on indigenous and innovative models of social work in Rwanda which attracted our attention. This attention was raised, on the one hand, by what respondents witnessed to have changed in their lives both socially and economically and, on the other hand, by the fact that no research had yet been done on this important home-grown initiative, as is the case with *ubudehe, girinka, umuganda,* and many others.

Kalinganire and Rutikanga (2014, 234) are correct in stating that social workers in Rwanda play facilitative roles by mobilising members to take part in their own development. The authors (2014, 235) further say that, to promote the participation of citizens in their own development, the Government of Rwanda chose to devise an innovative use of neo-traditional cultural institutions as operational tools to support the implementation of the country's poverty reduction programmes. These local approaches serve as frameworks for social work interventions towards poverty reduction.

Considering the three levels of social work practice, i.e. the micro, meso, and macro levels, it was revealed that *umugoroba w'ababyeyi* is applicable to all these levels in the sense that it can solve problems at the individual, family, community, and society levels. At the micro level, the forum is tackling problems of the individual participant and of families, but also starts from the individual's and family's strengths to improve their status. Meso-level social work practice focuses on formal groups of beneficiaries working together in small arrangements to find solutions to their problems and also highlights the role of community members in the development of their community. At the macro level, *umugoroba w'ababyeyi* is one of the government's initiatives to implement national policies and programmes for the socio-economic development of the population.

In the framework of this research, *umugoroba w'ababyeyi* is considered as an innovative social work approach. It started as *akagoroba k'abagore* (a women's forum, as a reference to what used to be done in the past) but it expanded its reach to include couples in the same neighbourhood and, at some point, also addressed children. It is innovative in the sense that participants do not only discuss women's issues and marriage-related problems but also address contemporary social and economic issues, such as parenting, gender, domestic violence, drug abuse, sanitation, nutrition and family planning, cooperatives, credit and savings, poverty reduction and development programmes, education of the youth on cultural values, reproductive health, marriage, and other subjects pertaining to young people.

It is good that these topics are discussed but it is also important to question the relevance of the information which is shared and the conclusions that are reached. In our study, we observed that sometimes the staff in charge of social protection who have a duty to follow up the activities of *umugoroba w'ababyeyi* were not available at the time of the meeting. This was mainly due to a big workload. In many cases, no other staff from the local government or another expert on a given topic was available to facilitate dialogue during the gatherings. That is why an evaluation of the outcomes of the *umugoroba w'ababyeyi* is needed to make the forum more interesting and instructive.

This research was guided by empowerment theory and by developmental social work perspectives. The analysis demonstrated that not all the outcomes that are desired by the above-mentioned theoretical frameworks are achieved, such as, for example, equality and social justice. This is because, in some parts of the country, participants may miss opportunities since they do not have sufficient information, they may not be empowered enough to fight for their rights, or simply because no professional is available to advocate for them.

The challenges mentioned show that efforts must be put into the mobilisation and sensitisation of the population, especially of men; setting up clear guidelines on monitoring and follow-up of the implementation of the programme's activities; strengthening communication and reporting mechanisms; and assigning staff in charge of the programme who can work closely with the committees of *umugoroba w'ababyeyi* at the grassroots level for setting the agenda and taking care of organisational matters.

The low turnout is due, in some cases, to the fact that there is no clear organisation, and people are discouraged from attending, thinking that it is a waste of time. That is why social work professionals are needed to put to use their organising, mobilising, and facilitating skills and knowledge in order to sustain the positive gains of *umugoroba w'ababyeyi* and to improve its outcomes in the future.

As social work is a new profession in Rwanda, not many social workers are employed in local government to monitor the implementation of home-grown initiatives, *umugoroba w'ababyeyi* included. This is one of the reasons for the occasionally unsuccessful implementation of *umugoroba w'ababyeyi* activities, as shown by the present study. There are principles, guidelines, and approaches specific to social work practice in addressing social problems. If the practice does not follow proper guidelines, the outcomes cannot be fully achieved. Putting in place social programmes is good, but having the right people in the right place, first for the conception and then for the implementation, is necessary and important for the success of all socio-economic programmes.

One of the recommendations of the present research is to hire professional social workers in local government who will contribute their expertise in the conception, implementation, monitoring, and evaluation of programmes and activities, aiming at the wellbeing of the population. Social workers' uniqueness lies in their practice giving a voice to their clients and, thus, contributing to bringing about positive change in the communities.

Conclusion

For successful results in the future, it is of paramount importance that the social work profession be recognised and given its place and value in the socio-economic development process of the country. Second, there is a need for close collaboration between social work practitioners, policy makers, and social work educators and researchers so as to build a strong synergy for the success of home-grown initiatives, in general, and of *umugoroba w'ababyeyi* activities, in particular. Third, social workers need to be strong enough to influence social policies and programmes to achieve sustainable social change. For this to happen, social workers should be knowledgeable about the contexts they are working in (Lombard, 2014). Especially in Africa, social work has to find its own unique way of training and practice to become an influential force for change (Kreitzer, 2012).

References

Adams R (2003) *Social Work and Empowerment*. 3rd ed. Basingstoke: Palgrave Macmillan.

Askheim OP (2003) Empowerment as Guidance for Professional Social Work: An Act of Balancing on a Slack Rope. *European Journal of Social Work*, 6(3): 229-240.

Dalrymple J and Burke B (2006) *Anti-Oppressive Practice: Social Care and Law*. Maidenhead: Open University Press.

International Federation of Social Workers (IFSW) (2014) Global Definition of Social Work. Available at: http://ifsw.org/get-involved/global-definition-of-social-work/ (accessed 10 July 2017).

Kalinganire C and Rutikanga C (2015) *The Role of Social Work in Poverty Reduction and the Realisation of Millennium Development Goals in Rwanda*. Kampala: Fountain.

Kalinganire C and Rutikanga C (2014) Social Development as the Privileged Model for Social Work Practice in Post-Genocide Rwanda. In: Spitzer H, Twikirize JM and Wairire GG (eds) *Professional Social Work in East Africa: Towards Social Development, Poverty Reduction and Gender Equality*. Kampala: Fountain, 232-244.

Kreitzer L (2012) *Social Work in Africa: Exploring Culturally Relevant Education and Practice in Ghana*. Calgary: University of Calgary Press.

Lombard A (2014) A Developmental Perspective in Social Work Theory and Practice. In: Spitzer H, Twikirize JM and Wairire GG (eds) *Professional Social Work in East Africa: Towards Social Development, Poverty Reduction and Gender Equality*. Kampala: Fountain, 43-55.

Republic of Rwanda (2013) *Umugoroba w'Ababyeyi*. Kigali: Inama y'Igihugu y'Abagore.

Republic of Rwanda (2014). *Umugoroba W'ababyeyi Strategy*. Kigali: Ministry of Gender and Family Promotion.

Sen A (1999) *Development as Freedom*. Oxford: Oxford University Press.

Uwihangana C (2014) *Women's Rights and the Wellbeing of the Rwandan Family*. Master's Thesis. University of Gothenburg. Available at: https://gupea.ub.gu.se/bitstream/2077/36131/1/gupea_2077_36131_1.pdf (accessed 20 March 2018).

Indigenous and Innovative Models of Problem Solving in Tanzania: Strengths and Obstacles for their Adoption

Zena M. Mabeyo and Abigail Kiwelu

Introduction

Social work training, research, and practice have to play dual roles. There has to be a focus on local realities while, at the same time, taking into account the adaptation of international standards (Kebede, 2014). Rankopo and Osei-Hwedie (2011) also posit that social work education and practice that consider multiple perspectives and cultural explanations of social reality are more relevant than those that seek to transcend all cultures. This underscores the importance of indigenous and local knowledge in social work practice. In recognition of the importance of local and culturally relevant models and approaches to helping, there has been a growing debate about indigenisation of the social work profession in Africa. The debates, as broadly explained by Twikirize (2014), revolve around the need for a deliberate reorientation of social work from its historical individualistic and remedial nature that has proven ineffective in addressing the underlying problems in Africa. Core arguments point to the need for orienting the profession to focus on structures, institutions, and systems that greatly affect the wellbeing of individuals and communities. Therefore, the advocated change (indigenisation) is based on the varied nature of and contexts in which social problems are manifested in Africa as opposed to the West. However, in pursuit of the indigenisation of the profession, scholars, practitioners, and policy makers have been cautioned not to conceive the process as an attempt to do away with whatever is foreign, neither should they keep lamenting about the inappropriateness of social work theory as handed down from the West. Rather, they, together with those they work with, need to identify what is positive from either side and develop locally appropriate practices (Twikirize, 2014).

The study upon which this chapter is based is an attempt to contribute to this indigenisation discourse.

It is worth noting that in the indigenisation process, there has been a general consensus that the process in Africa has to do with the adoption of a developmental approach to social work as well as with the generation of and respect for indigenous helping processes through culturally relevant practices (Twikirize, 2014). Contrary to this, social work practice and education in Tanzania and other East African countries have continuously and consistently been recipients of externally baked practice and models. According to the findings of studies done in East Africa as analysed by Twikirize et al. (2014), there is a high level of reliance on social work reference materials produced in Europe and other Western countries, thus underscoring gaps in indigenisation and contextualisation of social work in the region. For instance, based on the findings of a study conducted in Tanzania by Mabeyo, Ndung'u and Riedl (2014), a significant number (85.7%) of the 99 social work students included in the study affirmed that they mostly used textbooks from Europe and other developed countries as their reference materials. These findings are in support of arguments raised by Kreitzer (2012) that, despite the reality that African countries have rich cultural and ancient histories, much of it is forgotten and remains unacknowledged by the world today. The profession has been heavily relying on theories, models, approaches, and literature developed and imported from the West in what Twikirize (2014, 76) has termed a 'wholesale' manner of colonialism. To date, local cultural knowledge systems and traditional indigenous approaches have not permeated the social work teaching and practice domains despite their indisputable relevance and applicability in solving the social, economic, and behavioural problems facing African societies. Empirical evidence from studies conducted in Kenya (Wairire et al., 2014), Rwanda (Kalinganire and Rutikanga, 2015), Tanzania (Mabeyo, Ndung'u and Riedl, 2014), and Uganda (Twikirize et al., 2013) confirmed that social work education and practice are not adequately informed by locally generated knowledge and evidence. The Western models have constituted the blueprints and a dominant discourse in the discipline. Hence, for over six decades of practice and training in social work, social workers in East Africa have regrettably maintained the status quo of the profession by pioneering the implementation of the traditional conventional methods developed to respond to local and generalised problems that were predominant in the West.

To bridge the gap explained above, this article presents some distinctive indigenous and innovative models of problem solving in Tanzania. It presents an overview of the study on these indigenous and innovative models conducted in Tanzania; the rationale of indigenisation of social work in Tanzania; and indigenous models and approaches of care for the elderly, children, orphaned children, and widows. It also presents and describes the application of conflict resolution approaches through *washenga* (i.e. dowry negotiators) and local leaders called *wachili;* a community organisation approach known as *msaragambo;* and the use of village community banks for the economic empowerment of people. The application of these approaches is described in relation to social work practice, particularly in problem solving and helping the vulnerable and marginalised groups. Strengths and obstacles affecting the application of these indigenous models in the face of conventional social work practices and the modernised context are also presented.

The Empirical Study

A study on indigenous and innovative models of social work practice was conducted in Tanzania in 2016 (see Mabeyo and Mvungi, 2019). It aimed at the identification, description, and documentation of a number of indigenous and innovative models and approaches of an inherently Tanzanian nature in order to promote their application as well as to increase the visibility of African knowledge and practice systems within the broader scientific body of knowledge.

It was conducted in three regions, namely Dar es Salaam, Kilimanjaro, and Mara Regions, which were purposely selected based on their distinctive characteristics. While Dar es Salaam is the largest urbanised and metropolitan area, with a mixed population structure, many governmental and non-governmental agencies, as well as social work training institutions, Mara Region is less urban and shows a high incidence of female genital mutilation (FGM) and child marriage as well as pronounced acts of violence against women. Kilimanjaro is the region that has historically recorded quite a large number of cooperative societies, as well as savings and credit societies. We were, therefore, interested in learning about the methods, theories, and approaches adopted in communal and cooperative service provision. Although it is also true for other regions, in Kilimanjaro women carry a significant portion of the workload. As a result, the number of day care and other centres caring for children is also high.

Focus group discussions and interviews were the main methods used to gather data from study participants, who included community members/service users, students, local leaders, eminent social workers, and social work educators. A total of 10 FGDs (four with students and six with service users/clients) were conducted. In-depth interviews with 10 local leaders, 20 social workers, 12 social work educators, and 10 policy makers (some of them social workers) were also conducted. This study was particularly interested in the following issues and questions: Which inherently indigenous and innovative models of problem solving are being applied in Tanzania? How are such models affected by the processes of modernisation and social change? How are they integrated into social work education and training? To what extent are these models and approaches combined with modern, Western-based models of social work in both practice and training settings? How effective are these models in addressing massive problems of poverty, vulnerability, and social exclusion?

Why Indigenous Social Work in Tanzania?

Despite the fact that social work has a common purpose, namely the goal and aim of alleviating human suffering through addressing issues of vulnerability and marginalisation and promoting social change, the approaches employed to achieve this global goal differ from context to context, depending on the nature of the prevailing problems and their priority (Twikirize, 2014). Thus, in the context of the current social problems in Tanzania, as opposed to those that existed in 1947 when the profession was first introduced, there is urgent need to identify locally and contextually relevant approaches. Another reason is that not all problems can be solved by using Western methods, as elucidated by a 38-year-old male social worker from Kilimanjaro when asked to state why indigenisation is important.

> It is difficult to apply modern methods to every problem. For example, it is not easy to use modern social work models on marital conflicts. If we strictly use laws to resolve these conflicts, we cannot provide services to people on time but create enmity.

A social worker from Dar es Salaam, while responding to the same question, stated:

> The indigenous approaches are important because what we learn in class does not work with some clients in the field. Also, there were good traditional approaches used in the past for socialising children that can still be used today for the best interest of the child, for instance storytelling.

The above response indicates that there are local problem-solving models that exist and can offer better solutions to clients' problems, as compared to conventional Western approaches and methods used by social workers. However, these rich experiences do not feature in social work literature. As Spitzer (2014, 15) observes, social work in Africa has unique characteristics and specific ways of dealing with social problems which are sometimes very different from how social work is seen in the context of industrialised societies. Spitzer (ibid.) further argues that one feature of social work in African countries is its struggle for appropriateness by overcoming the legacy of imported, Western-based models of intervention which are too often unsuitable with regard to the distinctiveness and complexity of African cultures. Thus, Tanzania, being a country that has been entrapped by over-reliance on Western models, urgently needs to identify, acknowledge, revitalise, and profile the local and indigenous realities of helping and problem solving with a view of mainstreaming them into social work practice and training.

However, we caution here that due to the ethnic diversity of Tanzania, the models presented in this chapter cannot be generalised. Efforts to identify and document other culturally specific models are encouraged. These efforts are backed up by ideas put forth by Kebede (2014). While referring to the Ethiopian situation and analysing the interface between the indigenisation and internationalisation of social work, Kebede observed that it is important to adapt international experiences, research outcomes, theoretical perspectives, and models of practice to the social, cultural, political, and economic contexts of the specific countries.

However, he cautioned that in a country like Ethiopia

> …where over 80 % of the society is living in rural areas and in very poor conditions, and where there are long-held values and traditions which may be specific to Ethiopian societies…, indigenous social work perspectives and training models are of paramount importance. (Kebede, 2014, 164)

Tanzania is not an exception to the above scenario. It is home to more than 130 cultural groupings and has a pervasive income poverty. Obviously, there are diversified, long-held, and useful cultural values and traditions of handling and addressing different problems that ought to be respected and brought to the surface for reference and use alongside other conventional models.

The scope, nature, and magnitude of social problems facing clients who seek help from social workers in Tanzania are different from those in the West. Pervasive poverty and gender-based violence are the major problems faced by social work clients (Mabeyo, Ndung'u and Riedl, 2014). Thus, addressing the challenges posed by poverty requires a multi-dimensional approach that may include, among others, harnessing the cultural and locally relevant approaches of helping and problem solving.

Prior to the inception of the social work profession, African societies (Tanzania inclusive) had traditional and cultural ways of helping and problem solving. These ways and systems of help were weakened through colonialism and modernisation (Twikirize, 2014), and the gap in service provision was filled through the introduction of the profession. Despite the practice of social work for more than six decades, the local and traditional ways of helping have not entirely been pushed aside. No efforts have been made to align the profession with local needs, problems, and cultures, and this can be attributed to the Eurocentric training of local social work professionals. This reality justifies the need for the consideration of reactivating and mainstreaming culturally appropriate indigenous approaches.

Overview of Indigenous and Innovative Approaches: For Elderly Persons, Children, Orphans, and Widows

In writing this part, we have been challenged and inspired by the views raised by Spitzer (2014), who argued that in East Africa there exists a wide range of social theories, traditional philosophies, and ethics that could be integrated into social work theory, education, and practice. He cited and explained the principles of *ujamaa* in Tanzania and *harambee* in Kenya and elaborated on how these culturally relevant thoughts and approaches could be combined with elements of developmental social work and applied at different societal levels.

A recent study by Mabeyo and Mvungi (2019) confirmed that there are different approaches and practices that have existed in Tanzanian communities that could be combined with conventional approaches of the social work profession in order to facilitate social change as confirmed by a participant:

> Indigenous ways of helping each other have existed in our communities for ages. However, these models are taking different shapes across time and space. Some have either been maintained, improved, or abandoned because of their competition with the modern ways of service provision to the community. (Social worker at remand home, Moshi)

Despite the existence of such approaches, the findings of the study indicate that indigenous models are less popular in urban settings as compared to innovative models. This was due to structural factors. The disruption of the urban social fabric makes it difficult for its members to use indigenous, culturally specific approaches of problem solving. For instance, it was stated by a local leader in Dar es Salaam that in rural areas, when a man dies and the widow is incapable of supporting the family, the community, through the local leaders, would help her to the extent of even constructing a house for her. This support ends when she becomes able to support herself or is remarried. However, the support is impracticable in urban settings owing to the mixed nature of the population and the non-existence of such 'local leaders'; hence, widowed women in similar situations would turn to institutional and government help in case of difficulties. They would consult local government and council leaders who refer them to higher government authorities.

It was also learnt that the models differed in various work settings. For instance, the majority of social workers employed in the public sectors applied less of the innovative approaches as compared to those employed in private and non-governmental organisations. Moreover, it was observed that there are problems that attract the application of new innovative models and approaches more than others. For instance, there were many innovative practices focused at addressing the problem of HIV and AIDS, particularly in supporting orphans and the most vulnerable children. It was also learnt that there was a difficulty of applying indigenous models to specific groups of people, such as youths in Tarime, because they consider these approaches outdated.

Approaches for Elderly Care

In this section, an attempt is made to describe the approaches that were and continue to be used to provide care to elderly people, with specific reference to the studied areas. Our findings indicate that most communities still believe that families and communities have the responsibility of caring for their elderly. However, owing to various changes, including urbanisation and intercultural diversities, less care is provided by families and communities to elderly people. For instance, experiences from the Chagga community show that, although care is vested in families, the youngest son plays a key role. He is required to stay within the confines of the family land and is given the biggest share of that land so as to ensure that he has the means of production and is able to meet the basic needs of his family and the parents. He is the overseer of the properties, parents, and his sisters when they return home to visit the parents.

Apart from families, communities also have mechanisms for helping the elderly in the event of the family's failure to provide. In both Kilimanjaro and Mara, it was learnt that community support is provided through community members either working together to help the family with a specific task, such as housing construction, or giving direct contributions like food, based on the capacity of individual community members. The support is provided through schemes such as *msaragambo* in Kilimanjaro and peer support groups, commonly known as *nzagu*, in Mara. These models have long histories in the communities. For instance, being predominantly farmers, pastoralists, and fishermen, Mara community members revered the elderly in the following manners, as echoed by a study informant:

> The valuable part of the slaughtered goat, like the fillet and abdomen, was usually reserved for the elderly people in the community, and some of the fishermen were setting aside some fish for elderly care. This was a norm. It made older people feel respected and assured them that they were correctly taken care of by the community members.

Arrangements like these help to ensure that no older person is left without help in case of difficulty. However, participants observed that this valuable indigenous form of support is in decline due to selfishness, moral decay, and feelings that the government and other institutions can help. Community members no longer feel obliged to provide for the elderly, nor are there strong mechanisms to ensure that this form of support is revitalised and maintained. These findings confirm those by Spitzer and Mabeyo (2011) in a study that assessed the missing social protection in Tanzania. From this study it was evident that older people lacked adequate care and support from their families and communities, and so they have to continue to work in order to support themselves until they die. More than 60% of the 400 older people aged between 60 and 79 who were included in this study confirmed that they were still engaged in either agricultural or other economic activities to earn a living (Spitzer and Mabeyo, 2011, 95).

Based on this, social workers have a role to play in improving the situation by sensitising communities to the importance of maintaining indigenous practices of helping the needy, especially considering the fact that poverty rates in the country are high and government support to various vulnerable groups is inadequate. Failure to adopt and sustain such practices is likely to lead to the production of a generation that will be irresponsive to the needs of vulnerable groups.

Care for Children

The findings suggest that there are both indigenous and innovative approaches to the care of children. Historically, the care of children was viewed as a communal responsibility. Thus, every community was responsible for moulding children's behaviour, and parents accepted this collective responsibility. There were indigenous ways of passing on knowledge to children through storytelling and initiation ceremonies.

However, this pattern is now changing owing to the adoption of the 'modern lifestyle' where some parents do not like their children to be reprimanded by other community members when the children misbehave. A lack of fear of the community has led some children to become deviants and to be involved in criminal activity. Another change in care is associated with modernisation and the introduction of formal institutions of care for children, such as childcare centres. As a result, families surrender the burden of care to institutions instead of assuming their traditional roles.

The findings also suggest that there are various innovative approaches to the provision of care to children, particularly targeting those affected and infected with HIV/AIDS. According to a social worker from WAMATA Agency in Dar es Salaam (an NGO that works with people affected by HIV/AIDS), they have formed 'children clubs' which are run in schools by volunteers. These help children discuss issues that are of concern to them receive life skills education, and facilitate behaviour modification. Another innovative approach is the initiation of a Child Helpline. This is a free telephone hotline through which cases of abuse can be reported and are then directed to social workers for action.

Orphan Care

The findings show that communities have arrangements for taking care of orphans, which largely depend on the age of the child. These arrangements are rooted in traditional norms and practices. For instance, experience from the Chagga community is borne out by the following observations:

> When parents die and leave behind children of below 18 years without proper care, family members choose other people to take care of the orphans. If an orphan requires breast milk, one family member of child-bearing age is appointed and given a certain type of food (usually heavy soup) known as *mlaso*, made up of a mixture of beef, known as *kidomoyi*, and hot milk to stimulate the mammary glands for sufficient milk production. The approach ensures that babies continue to be breastfed and live together with their relatives. (Social welfare officer at the remand home, Hai, Kilimanjaro)

This practice was also applied to assist parentless children and those deprived of parenthood at a very young age for reasons other than death, such as sickness or imprisonment. When one of the children turned 18, he or she would then take over the responsibility of taking care of his or her siblings under the watchful eyes of the community, as illustrated in this quotation:

> In case one of the orphaned children had turned 18 and above at the time of the parents' death, he would be allowed to look after the other siblings and assigned a supervisor who would guide, direct, advise, listen, counsel, and provide them with emotional and material support. The chosen supervisor was required to possess a reasonable degree of maturity in terms of wisdom and good conduct in the eyes of his or her community. (Social welfare officer at the remand home, Hai, Kilimanjaro)

These arrangements should help children maintain family and community ties. However, they are undergoing drastic changes in the course of modernisation, urbanisation, and globalisation.

Widow Care

The findings confirmed that since time immemorial, communities had arrangements and systems of care for widows that varied over time and were based on cultural norms. A general and historical practice learnt from Kilimanjaro and Mara is that traditionally, widows were treated as 'a property for inheritance' (local leader, Mara). Hence, after the death of the husband (the breadwinner), an inheritor had to be chosen by the remaining family members. The selection of the inheritor was dependent on various factors, including: having good conduct and a good reputation; possessing reasonable resources to take care of the widow's and his own family; being married or having his own family.[7] The findings further suggest that in some instances, like in the Chagga community, the inheritor was allowed to have a sexual relationship with the widow, but the practice is now being discouraged to reduce the risks of HIV transmission. This approach is facing challenges today

---

[7]   A detailed explanation of this practice in Kilimanjaro is provided in the next chapter on *msaragambo* (Chapter 7).

owing to the increasing number of widows and orphaned children. The capacity of families is also constantly being exhausted. As a result, in urban settings, widows are taught entrepreneurship and income generation skills so that they can establish their own income generation activities that can help them to sustain their lives. Hence, organisations such as WAMATA formed self-help groups for women and other HIV/AIDS orphans' caretakers in order to help them generate income. This innovative approach is worth emulating.

There are also innovative approaches to helping women, including widows, particularly in relation to addressing the problem of violence, where a telephone helpline for reporting cases of violence against women was established by an organisation known as C-Sema.

Conflict Management Approaches through *Washenga* and *Wachili*

It was the intention of this study to explore and document the distinctive approaches that are used in conflict management, targeting both marital and other family conflicts. Although ethnic groups in Tanzania have different ways of handling conflicts, it was learnt from the Chagga group that they use the so-called *washenga* in resolving marital conflicts. The *washenga* are people who are commonly used in Tanzania as negotiators during the process of marriage. The *mshenga* (singular of *washenga*) is a representative of the groom and his family who is sent to the family of the bride to present a proposal for marriage and negotiate the pride price. He must ensure that he represents the family of the groom in the entire process of marriage until the wedding ceremony is completed. It was learnt that, in addition to this role, in the Chagga ethnic group, this person becomes an advocate and marital problem solver for the respective couple. It is only when the *mshenga* fails to find solutions to the conflicts that the matter is submitted to other authorities, such as courts, for further decision-making. Hence, the *washenga* are useful in addressing cases of domestic and gender-based violence as well. It was further pointed out that the *washenga* contribute a lot to stabilising families as they strive to ensure that marriages survive amidst potential challenges. Describing how the *washenga* are functional in resolving marital conflicts, a social worker in Kilimanjaro Region explained:

> In case there is a conflict in a marriage, the girl will not be accepted to return home and talk to her parents in the absence of the *mshenga*. In some families, if the girl returns to her parents, she will not sleep in her parents' house. Instead, the parents will find another place for their daughter to sleep, while waiting for the discussion with the *mshenga*. The discussion will be conducted along with a drink known as *mbege*. If the men feel that they are the ones to ask for forgiveness, they usually pluck a leaf from a tree known as *sare* and present it to either the girl or the family, asking to be forgiven.

If the discussion between the two families does not yield positive results, the parties are allowed to go to court for the arrangement of a separation or other possible solutions.

Apart from the use of washenga in marital conflict resolution, the Chagga also use local leaders, commonly known as wachili, who have the power to resolve conflicts and impose sanctions on those who break social norms. According to the views of a social worker in Kilimanjaro, the *wachili* are used to set boundaries and establish good farming practices in order to conserve the environment. However, they can also impose sanctions:

> For example, when a child reports to the clan chairperson that he or she is neglected or abandoned, the clan chairperson imposes sanctions on the perpetrator and if the deviant is an alcoholic, the clan chairperson orders social isolation against that person. Social isolation can be effected in clubs or pubs selling local brews, or the marketplace; and [he] will continue to make follow-up visits to see if that person has changed his behaviour or not. (Female social worker in Hai, Kilimanjaro)

Clan leaders are also used in Mara Region. They resolve conflicts and institute sanctions on those who violate set rules. They may impose a penalty known as *nzagu* in case a person has been accused of issues such as failure to fulfil his responsibilities to the family, wife, or children.

The use of such indigenous approaches has proven effective in solving problems because of the community's respect of cultural norms. However, some community members have pointed out that the application of these approaches is diminishing. Hence, it would be interesting to see if they could be revitalised and modified by ensuring that local leaders who are engaged in problem solving are educated in order to maintain professional ethics, such as respecting the confidentiality of clients' problems. An alignment of the traditional and conventional methods is, therefore, required in order to ensure synergy.

Indigenous Community Organising Approach through *Msaragambo* and *Saiga*

Our findings show that in Kilimanjaro and Mara Regions there have been long-established indigenous support and self-help schemes known as *msaragambo* and *saiga*, respectively. Through *msaragambo*, people work together and assist each other in the event of problems, such as the lack of food or shelter, and during crop cultivation, weeding, and harvesting. Similar self-help groups are called *saiga* in Mara. To get people to work, different mechanisms are used. For instance, in *msaragambo*, singing is done while working so as to stimulate and inspire people. Food and local beer known as *mbege* is prepared and people work in rotation. In *saiga*, peer support groups involving youth and the elderly are formed and they have a monthly schedule of activities to be achieved by the youth groups, while the elders' groups ensure the supervision of the planned activities. In both areas it was learnt that there are common meeting places for such groups, called *litongo* for the Kuria community in Mara Region and *mengeni* for the Chagga community in Kilimanjaro Region. There are also local councils, particularly in Mara, called *nzagu*, that have remained strong to date and are now recognised by the police force in matters of law enforcement. Through the two schemes, activities like building roads and the construction of houses are easily accomplished. In cases of failure to work together, community members make direct contributions to people in need, such as the elderly who lack support. These approaches can be adopted and replicated by social workers in helping different groups in need of support.

Innovative Approaches to Problem Solving: Village Community Banks

It has been found that there are innovative approaches, mostly in HIV/AIDS-related service provision, particularly targeting caretakers, women, and orphaned and the most vulnerable children. In order to combat poverty among caretakers of HIV/AIDS orphans, economic empowerment programmes, particularly through village and community banking (referred to as VICOBA), have been established in the sites where this study was conducted. Through VICOBA, community members are guided and facilitated by a trained officer to create informal and well-organised mechanisms for generating income and fighting poverty. They form groups and initiate a revolving fund, which is termed in Swahili as *upatu* or *mchezo*, from which members can save and borrow money to finance different projects. Through VICOBA, there is also a community service scheme known as *jamii* (meaning 'community'), where part of the profit is used to help the needy. It can finance education for poor students, provide services to the elderly, or provide capital to people with disabilities. The revolving fund helps members to start their own businesses. The operation of VICOBA is guided by norms, rules, and regulations directed towards goal achievement. There are also sanctions and punishments for potential defaulters. This model discourages the provision of cash support to people; instead, money is leant to earn returns and make a profit. Another advantage of this approach is that group members support each other on different occasions, including during weddings and in times of loss.

Based on the values of VICOBA explained above, social workers can adopt and replicate this system in combating poverty among their clients.

Strengths of the Indigenous Models

Based on the study findings, indigenous models are considered strong on the grounds that they are based on local discourse and knowledge. In this regard, they boast of being relevant to the local reality and, hence, banking on high local support. Echoing this, a social worker from Kilimanjaro said: 'The indigenous approaches are owned by people, they are sustainable, context-specific, and indeed helpful.'

Moreover, it has also been argued that indigenous models are very strong and helpful because they receive strong backup and sanctions from influential religious and local leaders. These models are also strong since they are available whenever necessary, people recognise and respect them, they can make very positive contributions to the development of the respective community, and they reduce the isolation of beneficiaries from their families and local communities; hence, people in need are helped while being able to stay within their communities. The approaches also ensure that common ways and values of life are maintained. For instance, supporting older people within their localities ensures the maintenance of cultural norms, interactions, relationships, and ways of life, something that would not be possible with institutional care.

While it was generally noted that the examined indigenous approaches have strengths, some of them need either to be abandoned or modified, especially when they contradict the principles of human rights or have negative effects on the parties involved. The inheritance of widows is among the practices that were recommended for discontinuation and condemnation.

Obstacles to Effective Adoption of the Models

The findings indicate that there are various impediments to the effective adoption of indigenous and innovative models. One big obstacle is that the indigenous models have not been documented. Another obstacle is that they are not backed up by laws and regulations and sometimes they might be in conflict with basic human rights, such as in the handling of cases like rape through indigenous approaches that fail to respect the human rights of the rape victim and to appropriately punish the perpetrator.

Another obstacle is the introduction of modern approaches and techniques, such as the use of advanced farming equipment like tractors, which simplifies agricultural work – one of the major activities done via the indigenous approach of *msaragambo*. However, it should not be taken for granted that the advancement in technology is a hindrance to the application of the indigenous models. Rather, technology can also be applied to improve and enhance these approaches. Moreover, political influence has been mentioned as a factor that may interfere with the adoption of indigenous methods. It was stated that commitments made by politicians, such as guaranteeing the provision of certain services, make community members believe that they do not have the obligation of helping each other in cases of need. Rather, they develop a dependency syndrome that 'the government will do'.

The findings suggest another factor hindering the effective implementation of the indigenous approaches, namely the introduction of formal systems of care for the elderly and children through institutions. It has been pointed out that some community members feel that these institutions have taken over their obligation to care for such categories of people. Hence, when they have an orphaned child or an elderly person who lacks support, they expect the government to fully step in. The introduction of a modern formal schooling system has also been found to be a factor that potentially affects the effective adoption of indigenous approaches. For instance, it was asserted that after the completion of their studies, the eldest sons are less likely to return home and stay with their parents, as it used to be in traditional societies. Instead, they send money or give the parents support from a distance and, in some cases, take them with them to more urbanised areas.

Modernisation through schooling has also been associated with alterations of some long-standing socio-cultural norms in African societies. As a result, children are taught 'modern' values that do not place adequate importance on intergenerational relations, for example.

Moreover, the introduction of formal governmental structures to deal with the provision of welfare has been seen as an impediment to the enforcement of indigenous models. It was learnt that, owing to the existence of social welfare departments, family members often report their problems to that department rather than to local leaders.

Another obstacle relates to social work training. It was learnt that training institutions do not adequately integrate these indigenous approaches into their curriculum. This was confirmed by both lecturers and students. A student from Kampala International University, Dar es Salaam branch, pointed out:

> There is no specific module on these approaches but lecturers just chip in aspects of indigenisation through modules like rural and urban sociology. However, in reality, students sometimes encounter problems in the field and must consult local leaders for support. They must be adequately prepared for this.

Regarding the adoption of innovative approaches, it was mentioned that the major obstacle is lack of resources to facilitate their formulation and implementation. Moreover, lack of literature and innovative skills among social work educators were also observed as an obstacle. A female educator from the Institute of Social Work in Dar es Salaam pointed that one obstacle is that educators 'do not think beyond the box – they hesitate to teach students how to think innovatively.'

Furthermore, the limited number of social work teaching staff constitutes a potential hindrance to the adequate consideration of indigenous approaches in teaching. A shortage of staff results in excessive workloads for existing teachers, leaving little time for innovation and preventing adequate engagement with and guidance of students to design and use innovative approaches.

Conclusion

The findings of this study confirm the existence of rich indigenous knowledge in the Tanzania context. Though the application of some of it may be diminishing, much still exists that can inform social work practice and training. To ensure the indigenisation of the profession, there is a need for a paradigm shift and transformation. In undertaking this paradigm shift and transformation, social work training institutions must review their curricula and ensure that indigenous, innovative and contextually relevant approaches are integrated into the teaching and research programmes and are adequately taught. Locally relevant theories, approaches, and principles for defining and addressing pertinent problems in the country must become part of the training. Social work trainers should strive to ensure that concepts and models related to African social work feature in the global literature of the discipline.

Students must also be practically oriented towards local realities. They should have more practical experience and do more fieldwork with communities. A female social work educator from the Institute of Social Work urged that both students and lecturers should not only work in their comfort zones but also deal with what they might be uncomfortable with. There should also be a change in students' research orientation. That means their topics should focus on what we really want to see changed. More research should be conducted and focused on rural areas. This will lead to the production of a research literature that can adequately inform practice and training. A change of attitude among social work practitioners is also required. They must be more flexible, innovative, and accommodative of new approaches that can help in providing examples of best practice. For instance, the overreliance on case methods in solving problems should be re-examined and should be geared more towards the local realities.

Communities also require sensitisation to the importance of maintaining, uplifting, and using culture-specific, indigenous approaches of helping and problem solving that are still useful. For instance, the *msaragambo* ideology and practice should be replicated in other communities to enhance collective action in problem solving. The youth should also be oriented to respect traditional customs and beliefs that used to guide problem-solving processes. They should learn that being modern is not synonymous with one's abandonment of good practices and values. While advocating the adoption of indigenous and innovative models, we caution that the process should not be construed as a replacement of the conventional Western social work methods. Rather, the indigenous and Western models should be used in a mutually complementary manner.

References

Kalinganire C and Rutikanga C (2014) *The Role of Social Work in Poverty Reduction and the Realisation of Millennium Development Goals in* Rwanda. Kampala: Fountain.

Kebede W (2014) Social Work Education in Ethiopia: Celebrating the Rebirth of the Profession. In: Spitzer H, Twikirize JM and Wairire GG (eds) *Professional Social Work in East Africa. Towards Social Development, Poverty Reduction and Gender Equality.* Kampala: Fountain, 161-172.

Kreitzer L (2012) *Social Work in Africa: Exploring Culturally Relevant Education and Practice in Ghana.* Calgary: University of Calgary Press.

Mabeyo ZM, Ndung'u ME and Riedl S (2014) *The Role of Social Work in Poverty Reduction and the Realisation of Millennium Development Goals in Tanzania.* Kampala: Fountain.

Mabeyo ZM and Mvungi A (2019) *Indigenous and Innovative Models of Social Work Practice in Tanzania.* Dar es Salaam: Mkuki na Nyota.

Rankopo MJ and Osei-Hwedie K (2011) Globalization and Culturally Relevant Social Work: African Perspectives on Indigenization. *International Social Work*, 54(1): 137-147.

Spitzer H (2014) Social Work in African Contexts: A Cross-Cultural Reflection on Theory and Practice. In: Spitzer H, Twikirize JM and Wairire GG (eds) *Professional Social Work in East Africa. Towards Social Development, Poverty Reduction and Gender Equality.* Kampala: Fountain, 15-28.

Spitzer H and Mabeyo ZM (2011) *In Search of Protection: Older People and their Fight for Survival in Tanzania.* Klagenfurt: Drava.

Twikirize JM (2014) Indigenisation of Social Work in Africa: Debates, Prospects and Challenges. In: Spitzer H, Twikirize JM and Wairire GG (eds) *Professional Social Work in East Africa. Towards Social Development, Poverty Reduction and Gender Equality.* Kampala: Fountain, 75-90.

Twikirize JM, Asingwire N, Omona J, Lubanga R and Kafuko A (2013) *The Role of Social Work in Poverty Reduction and the Realisation of Millennium Development Goals in Uganda.* Kampala: Fountain.

Wairire GG, Zani A, Machera M and Mutie PM (2014) *The Role of Social Work in Poverty Reduction and the Realisation of Millennium Development Goals in Kenya.* Nairobi: University of Nairobi Press.

Community Organising in Tanzania: Learning from the *Msaragambo* Model in Kilimanjaro Region

Zena M. Mabeyo, Abu Mvungi and William Manyama

Introduction

Available literature suggests that social work training and practice in Africa, in general, and Tanzania, in particular, suffer from a dearth of local experiences and realities (see for example, Osei-Hwedie, 1993; Rwomire and Raditlhokwa, 1996; Briggs, 2005; Gray, Coates and Yellow Bird, 2008; Osei-Hwedie and Rankopo, 2008; Chitereka, 2009; Mabeyo, 2014; Spitzer, 2014; Spitzer and Twikirize, 2014). This is despite the contention by Spitzer and Twikirize (2014) that locally relevant cultural practice, indigenous knowledge systems, and African ethical concepts constitute important elements for the success of any social work intervention. This should not be construed as shunning conventional approaches and social work theories, but rather to ensure that such approaches and social work theories are adequately informed by local realities that would allow them to develop appropriate and effective interventions.

This chapter draws on information from a recent empirical study on indigenous and innovative approaches of social work practice conducted in Tanzania. The study employed a cross-sectional research design with a qualitative research approach and gathered views from 62 informants, including social work educators, practitioners, students, community members and service users, local leaders, and eminent social workers/policy makers. This chapter describes and analyses *msaragambo* – one of the local approaches to problem solving in Tanzania. This is a specific form of community organising among the Chagga community of Kilimanjaro Region. The approach demonstrates how collective efforts and resources are organised and utilised to help poor individuals, settle disputes, correct behaviour, and care for the elderly, widows, and vulnerable children. The use of this approach is evidence

111

that indigenous problem-solving approaches are relevant and effective in specific cultural settings, notwithstanding the fact that they are not mainstreamed into social work practice and education.

The Historical Practice of the *Msaragambo* Model of Solving Problems

Msaragambo is a form of community organising practised by the Chagga ethnic group, which is a dominant grouping of the indigenous people of Kilimanjaro Region. The history of *msaragambo* dates from time immemorial. During in-depth interviews, the Chagga elders referred to it as a long-time community practice they learnt when they were growing up. The custodians of the *msaragambo* model were Chagga elders and other community leaders. Based on descriptions made by purposefully selected informants, *msaragambo* was a scheme where collective efforts of the community were used as a means to solve individual and community problems (see Fisher, 2012).

The *msaragambo* approach was more popular in the past, i.e. before the onset of colonial rule in Tanzania that ushered in the process of modernisation. It entailed people working together to accomplish community or individual (household) activities. Collective working teams moved from accomplishing one household activity to another. Through this approach, people were able to accomplish more in a day than when working individually. For example, they would prepare a farm or construct a house in a day. What was required of the hosting household (the household on whose property people were working) was to provide food and traditional beer (*mbege*) for the day. The working sessions were accompanied by songs which are said to stimulate the working spirit of those participating. In addition, the *msaragambo* practice enabled families and the community at large to institutionalise helping mechanisms for the needy, particularly orphans, widows, and the elderly.

Changing Patterns and Continuity of the *Msaragambo* Model

According to the Chagga informants, the *msaragambo* model has continued to take different forms in response to social changes in the community today. In the urban areas of Kilimanjaro Region and owing to social change, the form of the practice has changed but the spirit still remains. Chagga people in urban areas still embrace the spirit of contributing to community work, only that they now contribute money instead of providing labour support in community projects. This is explained by the fact that urbanisation and land shortage have forced them into towns where they are engaged in different activities and are not able to physically participate in community work. With the advancement of technology, the Chagga living in urban areas have taken *msaragambo* to another level, as they use media blogs to reach their members back home to make cash contributions.

Informants in our study pointed out that Chagga associations have been formed all over the country to respond to various needs and problems facing the Chagga people. These associations have their constitutions and members make contributions which are then used whenever a member is in need or when there is a developmental issue that needs to be implemented in their home areas. In Dar es Salaam, for example, there is one such association known as Legho Kilua Development Association (LEKIDEA). The association caters for the Chagga community's needs such as offering moral and material support to orphans, widows, and elderly people. Furthermore, the association enables the Chagga ethnic group to build and maintain vocational training centres, health facilities, primary and secondary schools, and roads in Kilimanjaro Region. The use of *msaragambo* to accomplish such community projects has been hailed as one of the reasons why the number of community-serving infrastructures such as health facilities, roads, and schools is higher in Kilimanjaro compared to other regions.

In-depth interviews revealed that the *msaragambo* practice among the Chagga went beyond issues of development. Informants indicated that the practice is also applied during festivities, such as Christmas and New Year celebrations. It is customary among the Chagga people to travel home during these festivities for more than just celebrating together with their parents. Our informants indicated that the main purpose of such yearly pilgrimages was primarily spiritual; that is to communicate with the forefathers (ancestors), offering sacrifices and performing other rituals believed to be an acknowledgment of the ancestors' important role in the success of the living and also in ensuring that they were free from bad omens. This also served as a way of enhancing family and community ties. According to the key informants, it is during such homecoming that family members with misunderstandings or conflicts are reconciled. This time is also used to take stock of progress of each member's activities in the urban areas, including discussing how to help each other as family and community members, sharing success stories of personal and community development, and accessing the opportunity to participate in family and community development projects. In addition, members share responsibilities in the family and community, including taking care of orphans, widows, elderly people, and poor people.

Notwithstanding its positive aspects, informants argued that the practice is gradually being weakened owing to technological advancement and the influence of foreign cultures. For example, with advanced technology, people are capable of performing tasks quicker without needing joint efforts. These include, among others, the use of tractors in agriculture as opposed to hand hoes. Similarly, some individuals can afford to hire labour to work on activities that previously would have needed the *msaragambo* practice to accomplish. The informants indicated that the *msaragambo* practice of helping is declining because the community fabric has been weakened and individualism is setting in. The norms and values that held the community together and engendered the helping practice have been eroded by politics, globalisation, and modernisation, which have bred a growing degree of selfishness in the community. The informants further pointed out that in the past, only adults participated in the *msaragambo* practices, and for one to be regarded as an adult, one had to undergo initiation rites known as *jando* (for boys) and *unyago* (for girls). Informants in both group discussions and personal interviews revealed that during this time, initiates were taught life skills and good manners, including showing respect for the elderly, during circumcision ceremonies or other social events. Boys were taught how to be good husbands and fathers while girls were taught how to be good wives and mothers, and, in all cases, how to be good members of the community. Through this practice, child behaviour was monitored and regulated. After these ceremonies, children were expected to comply with cultural norms and practices, one of which is togetherness and helping each other during times of need.

Underscoring that the initiation ceremony is an important part of socialisation in the community, informants and social work practitioners revealed that the decline of *jando* and *unyago* has created a vacuum in the practice of *msaragambo*. The decline of the social and cultural institutions has given way to other institutions biased towards Western culture to take over the role of shaping the next generation. At Marangu village in Moshi District, a male informant was of the strong opinion that reviving youth training (*jando* and *unyago*) at the community level was the only way of ensuring their success as adults and of upholding the continuity of community identity. The empirical data also shows that the outcry about moral decay in Tanzania today can be explained by the absence of locally based institutions that train children and youths in ethics, norms, and life skills (see also Masath, 2013).

The foregoing notwithstanding, informants, especially those from the rural areas, posited that the *msaragambo* model of solving problems has shown some resiliency. This explains the fact that it is a deep-rooted practice that is helpful to community members. It was emphasised both in the group discussions and in in-depth interviews that the *msaragambo* practice continues to help restore decent life and economic justice to the disadvantaged.

The Applicability of *Msaragambo* in Contemporary Social Work Practice

This section provides a linkage between the *msaragambo* activities and the contemporary field of social work practice to assess the extent to which the two relate to or differ from each other. Hence, in the following section we present how community organising through *msaragambo* works in helping different categories of the client population.

Elderly care

The informants revealed that the elderly were highly respected among the Chagga. This veneration of the elderly was based on the strong belief that they constituted the source of blessings in the community and that the elders were the fountain of wisdom and knowledge as they were expected to provide justice when there were misunderstandings.

Findings from the study showed that the community, through the *msaragambo* practice, assisted older people who had problems in obtaining food and sometimes shelter. This happened where the children and the families to whom the elderly belonged were not in a position to provide such support themselves, as pointed out by the following informant:

> We are helping the elderly when they have problems in our community. We sometimes assist them to build houses, giving them food through the *msaragambo* practice. This normally occurs when children have moved to the urban areas and abandoned their old parents in the rural areas. (A male social welfare officer, 34 years, Moshi Urban)

The informants further asserted that although the community was ready to offer services to the elderly people neglected by their children, the latter were punished for abdicating their responsibilities. The punishment could be in the form of a stern warning and at times via sanctioning and charging those children who failed to provide for their aging parents. One of the informants said:

> We usually convene meetings when needs arise… Children who fail to take care of their parents are warned and sometimes punished during the *msaragambo* meetings. The meetings are sometimes conducted when children come back for the end-of-year festivities. (A male informant, 58 years, Moshi Rural)

However, other informants remarked that changes are being currently observed in the Chagga community. Care for the elderly seems to be on a voluntary basis and not guided by customary laws and arrangements like before. This is attributed to modernity and urbanisation, which has busted the fabric that held the community together and, in its place, perpetuated selfishness among the Chagga community members. Some individuals today think of taking the elderly people to institutions even while they would be well capable of assisting in their care themselves. It is important to emphasise here that although the *msaragambo* practice is being eroded in the face of modernisation, it is still an important safety net for elderly support in the rural areas. In-depth interviews with the elderly showed a very high preference for the practice. In Hai District and Marangu village in Moshi District, for example, the elderly indicated that they were comfortable in the community and were not prepared to be moved into old people's homes. An elderly man at Marangu village pointed out:

> If my children and community fail to take care of me then what was the use of continuing to live? It is better to die honourably within my community.

It is important to point out here that, owing to the *msaragambo* practice, the elderly are not interested in institutional care. The emergence of such institutions, though not many in Kilimanjaro Region, is taken negatively by the Chagga community. This is because the elderly would much prefer continued social interaction with their family members and their community rather than being moved away to a life in institutions.

Childcare and correction of behaviour

Information from both FGDs and in-depth interviews clearly indicated that institutional care for children was unpopular in the Chagga community. The basis of that conviction was that community and family care was the best option for them. The following quotation from an informant at Marangu village in Moshi District is illustrative of the foregoing:

> Here in Marangu most of the problems are solved at the family and community levels through the *msaragambo* practice. We do not like institutions. One of the white men built a children's home but I am telling you the response has been very low. We do not have street children in our community due to strong family and community care. (A male informant aged 68, Marangu village)

This quotation emphasises the dominant local view that family and community care, through the *msaragambo* practice, is very meaningful because it keeps the family members close, facilitates the transmission of norms and values to the family members, and ensures the reproduction of the community. When probed on the issue of child abuse, the informants indicated that there were incidents of child abuse, but the culprits were severely punished by the family or community members in the same practice of *msaragambo*. This is very helpful and effective because community members were aware that the community would give a severe punishment, which, at times, amounted to being ostracised from the family and the community. For example, if a child reported to the clan chairperson that he or she was being neglected or had been abandoned, the clan chairperson would impose sanctions on the perpetrator, which might include ordering social isolation against that person. According to the informants, social isolation was very scary because one would be ostracised from social and community activities and services. This includes not being served in shops, kiosks, clubs, or pubs selling local brews, and in the marketplace. What is interesting here is that on imposing the punishment, the chairperson would make a close follow-up to see if that person had changed his or her behaviour or not and would look out for those who associated with the culprit.

In-depth interviews with social work practitioners in Moshi Municipality and Hai District showed that they were mostly supportive of and encouraged the family and clan members to take care of children, especially orphans, when their biological parents or guardians died. The practice was that children who had lost their parents and had no assistance were shared among aunts, uncles, or grandparents, through the *msaragambo* practice. The practitioners insisted that the care provided by institutions was not very much acknowledged locally. They emphasised that when parents died, the family members were responsible for taking care and even breastfeeding the babies (see also Spitzer, 2014). This is despite the fact that, as indicated above, the practice of *msaragambo* is now taking different forms in the urban areas of Kilimanjaro Region owing to the influence of modernisation. The urban communities are much more individualised and support institutional care instead of family care, as pointed out by a senior social welfare officer, who remarked:

> Despite the recognised benefits of family care, there are some family members and community members who still want to take their children to the institutions. We have people who bring their children to the social welfare office, which is not correct. We encourage family members and the community to continue assisting each other, since the care which is provided by the institution is not culturally sensitive. (A male social welfare officer aged 57, at remand home in Moshi Municipal Council)

While the *msaragambo* practice is still preferred by both the practitioners and the community, the former argued that there were some aspects of *msaragambo* that leave much to be desired, for example, solving problems related to child abuse. Here, the practice, in the name of togetherness, tends to avert justice for culprits accused of child abuse. Issues that need to be handled through the formal judicial system are withdrawn to be handled at the community level and, in the process, justice is denied. A case in point here is that serious and sensitive cases like the raping of children and women cannot simply be settled through the *msaragambo* practice. For example, it was reported that people would shy away from serving as witnesses in child abuse cases simply because they wanted to save the offending community member from severe punishment if their culpability was proven in a court of law. According to the social work practitioners, issues of child abuse go against the statutory laws. One of the social welfare officers reported:

> I had one case of a child who was raped by her father. We reported it to the police and the man was arrested. But when we were still collecting some evidence and witnesses, one of the family elders convened a family meeting in the practice of *msaragambo* and wanted the mother of the child who had been raped to withdraw the case because of the fear that the child's father would be jailed and, thus, they would not have any help. (A female social welfare officer aged 32, Hai District)

Drawing from the above, it is necessary to point out that although the *msaragambo* practice of correcting behaviour in the Chagga community seems to be very relevant, some aspects of the practice can contradict statutory laws and other human rights. Hence, social work practitioners advocated the revision of *msaragambo* in order to safeguard the best interests of the child.

On the correction of children's behaviour, the informants indicated that before the introduction of modern parenting education, children were considered a communal responsibility. Through the *msaragambo* practice, the whole community was responsible for the socialisation of the children, including observing their behaviour and even instituting punishment when correcting the child's behaviour. In short, everybody seemed to be the custodian of the children in the community in order to ensure good conduct in accordance with the social norms. This role is slowly diminishing today in the wake of modernisation and growing individualism. It is no wonder that today, some parents go as far as confronting teachers who reprimand and/or punish their children. The days when any older person could reprimand a child who was misbehaving are gone. The consequence of this for parenting is far-reaching in terms of upholding a certain morality. It is little wonder, therefore, that today there is a high incidence of deviant behaviour and child abuse (see also Gudadi, 2014).

Widow care

Through the *msaragambo* practice, families and communities had a number of local arrangements for ensuring the protection of widows, based on the idea of widow inheritance in order to meet the welfare needs of the widow and her children. An appointed supervisor had to ensure that the properties of the widows' family were secured and their physical and social needs met. This could be arranged during the end-of-year festivities or at any time when the needs arose. There were different modalities underlying such arrangements. For example, family members would appoint a brother-in-law to inherit the widow. Initially, the appointed family member could provide services and was allowed to have a sexual affair with the widow, but today this is no longer openly practised owing to the existence of sexually transmitted diseases like HIV/AIDS, religious teachings, and condemnation by human rights activists. In cases where there was no brother-in-law, another respected man in the community would be appointed for that purpose. The appointed man, with the approval of the elders, must fulfil certain requirements, such as having good conduct and a good reputation, having reasonable resources to take care of the widows' children, and being married or having his own family.

However, social work practitioners were sceptical about utilising this family model as a way of solving widows' problems. This is attributed to the contradictions underlying the practice, particularly regarding the potential misuse of such an arrangement by potential supervisors. Thus, owing to continued family tensions and violations of women rights, social work practitioners emphasised that widows' cases should be forwarded to courts of law.

From a social work perspective, not every aspect of the *msaragambo* practice is desirable or practical for our contemporary times. Hence, it has to be adopted selectively, depending on the nature of the problem being resolved. In this case, it could be averred that the practice contradicts a number of human rights and other legal provisions and could even be construed as promoting violence against women. It does perpetuate gender inequality since women are treated as either the property of the man's kin or as obviously not being in a position to meet their own needs.

Social justice and dispute settlement

The *msaragambo* practice has been very useful in providing justice and settling disputes among the Chagga ethnic group. It was revealed that when the Chagga people travel home at the end of the year, they discuss success and problems, including resolving potentially existing conflicts within their families and communities. At such occasions, punishment and sanctions are instituted against those who had misbehaved. Some of the issues which are brought to the attention of family and community meetings include, but are not limited to, matrimonial cases, maintenance cases, theft, and abuse. The punishments include the payment of fines, for example in terms of goats, bulls, sheep, or in other ways that may be deemed necessary by the family or community leaders.

In addition, the people of the Chagga ethnic group believe that people who tell lies when settling disputes are most likely to be cursed or would instantly die. This idea is related to belief in the magical powers of the leaves of a plant known as *masale*. So, people are not allowed and actually fear to give false explanations because they know they would mysteriously die. Thus, the *masale* leaf is perceived as a sacred object in the Chagga community and every member of the community has to respect its magical powers.

In this regard, *msaragambo* was employed to attain social justice and to settle disputes among family and community members. One of the informants said:

> There are community leaders called *wachili*. They set boundaries between farmers and maintain good farming practices in order to conserve the environment. So, we sometimes consult them in their areas as local leaders when holding meetings for matrimonial conflicts. In some other families, the tree leaves known as *masale* have been used to settle disputes between family and community members. Sometimes we use *masale* for solving matrimonial and affiliation cases. (A male social welfare officer, 34 years, Moshi Urban)

The empirical data showed that the *msaragambo* practice of solving problems in families is also used by social work practitioners in Kilimanjaro Region. In-depth interviews with practitioners showed how they used the family systems to resolve marital conflict. Below are the processes involved in settling matrimonial conflicts reflecting the *msaragambo* practice:

- Social workers first listen to the couples in conflict in order to assess the nature of the problem.

- If they think that the cases could best be resolved within the clan setting, they advise the couple to go back and meet their *washenga* (dowry negotiators). The belief is that the couple's families understand their case and their circumstances better than the social worker. If they fail to get assistance from the lower level, then the social welfare officer, whose intervention is governed by laws and regulations, would be involved. However, this could lead to a divorce, which could have been avoided if the traditional mechanism had been successfully utilised instead.

- The social work practitioners advise the couple to use family counsellors and local leaders. The counsellors are selected by either their own families or by members of their community. These people were/are responsible for providing material and moral support to family members. Today, few families have such family advisors or counsellors. In case the family fails to resolve the conflict, they advise them to consult their local leaders or religious and marriage advisers.

- There is also a marriage reconciliation council that operates hand in hand with religious and marriage advisors. The council operates at the ward level and could convene several meetings, depending on the nature of the problems, with its main objective being to rescue the marriage.

- In case the marriage council fails to reconcile the couple in conflict, even after the social work practitioners' advice, then the couple is provided with Police Form 3 to fill in and submit to a court of law to allow for divorce proceedings.

Moreover, the practitioners reported that they sometimes use the *msaragambo* practice when holding conflict negotiation meetings within families. They are usually asked to attend, especially when the family has matrimonial problems. In Hai District, social welfare officers reported that they are working together with family members. They normally hold a conference meeting at the family level with different parties involved in the conflict, whether it is matrimonial or anything that requires the presence of other people like the clan chairperson, religious leaders, etc. If they realise that the appointed clan chairperson is biased when making decisions on different cases, they replace him with another reputable person with integrity in the community, whom they expect to be free of bias. It was also reported that the sacred leaf of the *masale* plant was used to ensure that parties were telling the truth during the resolution of such conflicts.

Crisis intervention

The empirical data also indicated that the *msaragambo* practice has been used to address crises, especially hunger, in the Chagga community. Chagga community members were engaged in food production and used traditional granaries as food storage. By doing so, food security in the communities was ensured, including for times of disaster, such as famine, fire outbreaks, and floods. The community members participated in helping the victims of disasters to build houses, for example. In these cases, women usually collected grass and men went to the forest to find poles, while some also remained at home, making mud bricks.

The informants also pointed out that the *msaragambo* model had been employed by many non-governmental organisations (NGOs) that work with the rural Chagga community, carrying out the agenda of social and economic development. Below we provide an example of such an NGO that incorporates the *msaragambo* model into its practice.

Tanzania Women Research Foundation (TAWREF)

TAWREF is an NGO operating in Moshi Rural, Kilimanjaro Region. Activities performed by TAWREF include building houses, supporting orphans to get education, working in environmental conservation, and conducting research for evidence-based interventions. Social workers employed in this organisation viewed the Chagga community as being very cooperative and supportive through the utilisation of the *msaragambo* practice, even though it had undergone various changes over time. The social workers shared their best practices as having been demonstrated in assisting children, widows, and elderly groups through the *msaragambo* practice. According to them, their practices do not disturb the norms and values of the Chagga ethnic group. The informants pointed out that they do not impose interventions or models but rather use bottom-up approaches, as, for example, their model entitled 'standard of care' portrays. This is an innovative model in which the local community members are involved in identifying problems facing them and developing intervention programmes. In other words, this model starts with what the community considers to be the most burning issues and develop solutions based on their local experiences and realities. During interviews, the informants had the following to say:

> TAWREF is an exponent of the Mwalimu Nyerere ideology of *ujamaa* and self-reliance because it was very useful in terms of making people assist each other in their communities. So, we really capitalise on that ideology and we see that it

is working in our projects. We are currently running a house building project in partnership with the community members. The houses we are constructing are meant for the orphans, elderly, and disabled. (A female social worker, 57 years, TAWREF)

Further, the social work practitioners working with TAWREF remarked that they really supported the idea of traditional and modern social work working hand in hand, as the sentiments of this informant indicate:

People have to ask themselves how they lived before the coming of modern social work. Definitely, it was the families and communities which had some arrangement to cater for the needs of, let us say, orphans, the disabled, widows, and elderly people. So, TAWREF starts with what people have in the community and acts as a mere agent of change while not imposing interventions. (A female social worker, 45 years, TAWREF)

The above quote shows how indigenous models of social work practice can be integrated into social work interventions for solving problems from the family level to the community level. The informants believe that modern social work education should complement the indigenous knowledge systems if sustainable development is to be realised.

The analysis further shows that most of the governmental social work practitioners employ the *msaragambo* practice at the family level, especially in handing matrimonial and affiliation cases, while very little has been done in employing this model in solving problems that affect the whole community. Contrary to this, the informants who were working with NGOs reported that they employed the *msaragambo* practice for solving problems related to housing and poverty, and to provide assistance during crisis situations.

Conclusion

This chapter has attempted to describe and analyse the community organising practice of *msaragambo* in the Chagga community in order to show that it has been very useful in addressing individual and community problems. It has been noted that, despite its relevance, application, and importance, the *msaragambo* practice is faced with the challenges brought about by modernisation, which have a bearing on the way families and communities in Kilimanjaro Region respond to emerging social problems. It was particularly noted that the spirit of individualism is eroding the *msaragambo* practice. It was also revealed that not all aspects of the *msaragambo* practice are relevant, as some of them may run counter to the laws governing human rights and the best interests of the child. Given the current situation, we argue that cases related to violence against children, gender-based violence, and widows' welfare are beyond the *msaragambo* practices and need the attention of the modern courts of law. In addition, the *msaragambo* practice was applied differently by social work practitioners. While social workers employed by the government tended to employ it when dealing with matrimonial problems, those employed by NGOs found it useful when dealing with problems affecting the whole community.

The chapter has shown that some of the aspects of the *msaragambo* practice can offer alternative solutions to the problems faced by the Chagga community. The chapter has shown how social work practitioners can bring into the mainstream the eroded aspects of the *msaragambo* practice that are deemed positive for the development of the Chagga community. The practice can be revived and have an important impact on otherwise often resource-strapped social work interventions. Likewise, the concepts of *jando* and *unyago*, which used to be important youth training activities, can help in socialising youths to stay away from criminality and other problems and rather embrace work and a more responsible behaviour. This youth training is also significant because it would provide skills for a successful adulthood and for good parenting, both of which are currently found wanting. Social workers can also use the positive inclination towards community care to develop local centres based on the *msaragambo* practice to care for the elderly and for vulnerable children, without uprooting them from their cultural base. Since we see this model of community organisation to be very useful in addressing social problems and meeting various needs in the community, it should be integrated into social work training and practice.

References

Briggs J (2005) The Use of Indigenous Knowledge in Development: Problems and Challenges. *Progress in Development Studies*, 5(2): 99-114.

Chitereka C (2009) Social Work Practice in a Developing Continent: The Case of Africa. *Advances in Social Work*, 10(2): 144-156.

Fisher T (2012) *Chagga Elites and the Politics of Ethnicity in Kilimanjaro, Tanzania*. PhD Thesis Submitted to the University of Edinburgh, Scotland.

Gray M, Coates J and Yellow Bird M (eds) *Indigenous Social Work around the World. Towards Culturally Relevant Education and Practice*. Aldershot: Ashgate.

Gudadi LF (2014) *Dynamics of Juvenile Delinquency and Crimes in Arusha City*. Masters Dissertation Submitted to Sokoine University of Agriculture. Morogoro, Tanzania.

Mabeyo MZ, Ndung'u EM and Riedl S (2014) *The Role of Social Work in Poverty Reduction and the Realization of Millennium Development Goals in Tanzania*. Kampala: Fountain.

Masath B F (2013) Moral Deterioration: The Reflection on Emerging Street Youth Gangs in Musoma, Tanzania. *Social Sciences and Humanities*, 4(1): 101-111.

Osei-Hwedie K (1993) The Challenge of Social Work in Africa: Starting the Indigenization Process. *Journal of Social Development* in *Africa*, 8(1): 19-30.

Osei-Hwedie K and Rankopo M (2008) Developing Culturally Relevant Social Work Education in Africa: The Case of Botswana. In: Gray M Coates J and Yellow Bird Y (eds) *Indigenous Social Work around the World*. Aldershot: Ashgate, 203-219.

Rwomire A and Raditlhokwa L (1996) Social Work in Africa: Issues and Challenges. *Journal of Social Development in Africa*, II (2): 5-19.

Spitzer H (2014) Social Work in African Contexts: A Cross-Cultural Reflection on Theory and Practice. In: Spitzer H, Twikirize JM and Wairire GG (2014) *Professional Social Work in East Africa. Towards Social Development, Poverty Reduction and Gender Equality*. Kampala: Fountain, 15-28.

Spitzer H and Twikirize JM (2014) A Vision for Social Work in East Africa. In: Spitzer H, Twikirize JM and Wairire GG (2014). *Professional Social Work in East Africa. Towards Social Development, Poverty Reduction and Gender Equality*. Kampala: Fountain, 371-384.

Twikirize MJ (2014) Indigenization of Social Work in Africa: Debates, Prospects and Challenges. In: Spitzer H, Twikirize JM and Wairire GG (2014). *Professional Social Work in East Africa. Towards Social Development, Poverty Reduction and Gender Equality*. Kampala: Fountain, 75-90.

Culturally Responsive Social Work Practice in Uganda: A Review of Selected Innovative and Indigenous Models

Ronald Luwangula, Janestic M. Twikirize, Justus Twesigye and Stanley Kitimbo

Introduction and Background

Culturally responsive practice is often influenced by the extent to which social work practitioners apply indigenous and innovative philosophies, methods, approaches, and models. There is consensus among social work scholars regarding the need for the social work profession to develop and adopt models and approaches that promote culturally relevant social work practice. Conventional Western-oriented practice models have been challenged by a number of scholars as being largely irrelevant to local contexts, hence, presenting applicability challenges associated with contexts that are significantly dissimilar to those in which they were developed (Midgley, 1981; Osei-Hwedie, 1993 and 1995). Scholars such as Ife (2000), Gray and Allegritti (2002), Gray, Kreitzer and Mupedziswa (2014), Spitzer (2014), and Twikirize (2014) share similar concerns. Haug (2001 and 2005), Nagpaul (1993), and Nimmagadda and Cowger (1999) contend that social work models based on the British or American cultures are not universally relevant. Recent conferences in Africa with themes such as *Rethinking Social Work in Africa: Decoloniality and Indigenous Knowledge in Education and Practice* that took place in South Africa in October 2017 illustrate a continuing discomfort with the Western-oriented, mainstream theories and models of social work and the demand for culturally responsive social work practice and education. And yet to date, these models still dominate social work curricula in Africa, including in Uganda. During such conferences, panels, and meetings, social workers often criticise the Western social work models. Yet, they hardly invest in efforts to research, analyse, and document alternative models. Twikirize (2014), for example, questioned whether the practice models framed as part of indigenisation were documented.

Generally, indigenisation literature is skewed towards offering a framework for theorising and conceptualising indigenisation (see Midgley, 1981 and Gray et al., 2007), placing emphasis on the importance of culture and context in social work training and practice (Weaver, 1999; Spitzer and Twikirize, 2014). This in part explains the rather enduring phenomenon where the Western social work models are identified with inherent gaps in the African contexts, on the one hand, and their continued dominance on the continent, on the other. As a result, social work graduates less exposed to home-grown literature on indigenous and innovative models of social work practice struggle to make themselves relevant at service delivery and policy engagement levels. Under the PROSOWO project (*Professional Social Work in East Africa*), one of the important themes addressed was the indigenisation of social work in East Africa. Twikirize (2014, 75), reflecting on the experiences of international social work students on internship in Uganda, illuminates the reality of the indigenisation discourse in Uganda. She reports that students from universities in Europe characterised social work practices in agencies where they were placed as 'not social work' because it did not fit in their theoretical orientation.

In this chapter, we show how the social work profession in Uganda is repositioning itself to become culturally responsive and relevant in practice. We share examples of home-grown indigenous and innovative models of helping that can positively influence social work education and practice. We attempt to reawaken the indigenous voices which Gray, Coates and Hetherington (2007, 56) describe as silenced through the imported 'western thinking from Britain and the United States'. We argue that mere acknowledgement of the social work profession's ethnocentric foundation (Weaver, 1999) is not enough. According to Munroe et al. (2013), the indigenisation process involves a shift from Western, Eurocentric approaches to teaching a curriculum where the indigenous people are more visible. The documentation of these local models thus sets in motion the conditions necessary to achieve the indigenisation of the social work curriculum, that is, social workers having a clear understanding of the local values and appropriate models of intervention for effective service delivery to the community. The indigenous models presented fit very well within the call by Gray and Allegritti (2002) upon social workers to clearly define and describe indigenous models of social work helping.

Methodology

This chapter draws from data collected in a broader study conducted in Uganda under the PROSOWO project. The study was purely qualitative and aimed to analyse and document indigenous and innovative models of social work practice in Uganda. The study sites were the Northern Region (Gulu District), the Central Region (Rakai District) and the Western Region (Rukungiri and Mbarara Districts). These sites were purposively selected to represent the distinct cultural and ethnic groups in Uganda.

Gulu is the largest metropolitan district in Northern Uganda and also lies at the centre of post-conflict recovery, rehabilitation, reconstruction, and development. The Northern Region where Gulu is located suffered from a two-decade civil war (1986-2006), which affected the social fabric and cultural heritage of the Acholi, a predominant ethnic group in this region. Northern Uganda is historically known to be deeply traditional, with a rich community-oriented culture and traditional institutional set-up. Rakai District is found in the Central Region and has one of the oldest cultural institutions and the largest ethnic group in the country, i.e. Baganda. It thus provided an ideal site for studying an array of approaches and practices from a historical and contemporary perspective and how these relate to social work. Rakai is one of the districts that were much affected by the HIV and AIDS epidemic, which resulted in a large number of child-headed households. It thus provided a good opportunity to examine local models of dealing with the orphan crisis and, more generally, with household poverty and deprivation. The Western Region where Rukungiri District is located is home to the ethnic groupings of Banyankore and Bakiga. The different study sites yielded diverse and yet interrelated models of helping and problem solving that we present in this chapter.

The study used participatory methods of data collection, including individual interviews, focus group discussions, and case narratives. Data was collected from social workers or community development workers in the public service realm at district level (six in total) as well as in the civil society sector (seven in total). Other study participants were community and traditional leaders (eight in-depth interviews), community members and service users (seven focus group discussions); and five case studies. Data was transcribed verbatim, followed by editing for structural and grammatical errors. Interviews and discussions held in local languages were blind back-translated into English. Data analysis entailed the identification of patterns and themes using thematic analysis.

Indigenous and Innovative Models of Helping

In the course of the study, a number of indigenous and innovative practices were discovered. Although they varied according to the specific regions where the data was collected, most of them shared characteristics of mutual helping and community-oriented rather than individual practice or orientation. According to Ouma (1995), mutual help and reciprocity formed one of the indispensable principles that for long bound people together in the indigenous systems in a spirit of sharing and caring. In this chapter, we present a number of selected models to illustrate the notion of culturally responsive practices. The models presented address social work concerns such as child protection, socio-economic empowerment and security, and responses to HIV and AIDS. It is worth noting that the models presented are not unique to the study sites, but that they are a common feature of communities in Uganda. The chapter illustrates examples of the applicability of such indigenous and innovative models in mainstream social work in Uganda.

Village savings and loan associations: An innovative model for socio-economic empowerment

The developmental approach to social work is emphatic on empowering clients (Midgley and Conley, 2010). Particularly in low-income settings, as social workers strive for relevance, efforts are increasingly being committed to interventions that empower their clients as well as improve their socio-economic status. In Uganda, village savings and loans associations (VSLAs) form a common feature in efforts to empower clients. In all study sites, VSLAs were a common feature, with a range of similarities. Development literature attributes VSLAs to the international development organisation CARE, which introduced the approach first in Niger in 1991 (CARE, 2016). Since then, VSLAs have increasingly gained popularity in many parts of Africa, including Uganda.

Most of the problems that clients present to social work agencies in Uganda are strongly linked to poverty (Twikirize et al., 2013). Owing to this, social workers working with grassroots communities and groups in Uganda have embraced VSLAs as one of the mechanisms for supporting their clients towards economic empowerment. Under the VSLA approach, community members, with or without external support, mobilise themselves into groups of about 15-30 people to form a savings and loans association. The group sets its rules and procedures, determines the group leadership structures, the minimum and maximum amount of money a member can save per sitting, and the regularity of meetings (e.g. weekly or bi-weekly) during which members save a portion of their income into a pool from which they can borrow at very low interest. The group also determines loaning terms, including the loan amount (often two or three times one's savings portfolio), the interest rate on loans (usually 10%), the repayment period (often three months), the length of the saving cycle (normally a year), and the amount of a social or emergency fund that every member contributes during every sitting. Depending on the socio-economic status of community members, the minimum saving per sitting (cost of a single share) may range between 500 Uganda shillings (UGX) (approx. 0.14 US$) and 2,000 UGX (approx. 0.57 US$) for most VSLAs in Uganda, but some may set the value beyond that. The setting of the share price is done by the group members themselves, often at the beginning of the saving cycle, and it is maintained until the end of the cycle (Luwangula, 2015, VSL Associates Ltd, n.d.). At each meeting, every member is required to buy a minimum of one share and a maximum of five shares.

Members' savings are kept in a simple metallic box, which serves as a local safe. The local safe might be provided by a facilitating social work agency or purchased from group contributions. The custody of the savings box, kept under lock and key, is often entrusted to the group treasurer. The group chairperson, secretary, and treasurer may each have a key to only one of the three locks at any one time. However, as some groups' savings increase, they can choose to open accounts in formal banking institutions. This reduces the risk of losing money through theft or misuse due to rudimentary means of keeping the money in group members' homes. Such groups fix their deposits for a period of one year, which corresponds to a saving cycle.

Other than the regular savings, group members at every sitting contribute towards a social or emergency fund, often set at a rate much lower than the share price. The social fund is a contingency fund from which members borrow at no interest to cater for pre-defined emergencies such as the loss of a loved one, or the sickness of a member or his or her child. The members' savings serve as collateral. At the end of the saving cycle, the members share their savings and dividends, which they use for individual productive activities. Those willing to roll into a new cycle do so. But in-between the old and the new cycle, members may review their constitutions to address issues such as increasing the share price, or the admission of new members to replace dropped members or members unwilling to continue. With respect to gender, VSLAs attract both men and women, although at times in unequal proportions, with most groups constituting more women than men. For instance, in VSLAs that bring together a particular category of people such as widows, or persons living with HIV, women tend to be dominant.

Qualitative interviews and discussions with study participants underscored the critical role that VSLAs are performing in empowering people living on the verge of poverty. The participants recounted various benefits that have accrued from their membership of such groups, ranging from the acquisition of household items, house construction, and raising capital for starting small-scale businesses to other alternative livelihoods. Other common benefits especially relate to supporting children's education. Most participants do, in fact, borrow short-term loans from the VSLAs to pay school fees for their children. Whilst this might not be directly seen as an immediate economic investment, the education of children is, in fact, one of the most recognised means of socio-economic empowerment. Children's education also has the potential to break the cycle of poverty at household level.

Besides the economic benefits, participants also referred to the power that emanates from belonging to a group. Through these groups, some have been able to advocate for better services from the government. Although the VSLAs do not offer substantial financial services, most participants prefer to borrow from such groups rather than from formal banking institutions. This is both due to uncomplicated collateral requirements and the fact that in case of default on a loan, the members do not anticipate harsh repercussions since they virtually know each other and relate at a more personal level.

VSLAs constitute a social group work approach where the staff of social work agencies serve as group facilitators. Commonly referred to as community-based facilitators, these staff facilitate the savings and loans groups through the group formation stages. They go on to provide counsel to the groups whenever the need arises. Once the groups attain maturity, they are gradually left on their own. Mature groups facilitate the formation of new groups, in which case the members of the former assume the role of facilitators for the latter.

VSLAs are relevant to the Ugandan context on many fronts. To begin with, many of the social work clients are either poor or their problems and challenges are strongly linked to poverty (Twikirize et al., 2013). This is true for issues such as the failure of men to provide for their families – often resulting in conflict, gender-based violence, child labour, early marriage, teenage pregnancy, and school dropout. Moreover, where such challenges would be ameliorated through access to credit, most social work clients lack the capacity to access formal financial services, which require significant collateral such as salaries or fixed assets, which many lack. VSLAs create opportunities for social work clients to save and access credit that they otherwise would not access owing to bureaucracy, illiteracy, lack of collateral, and the cost of formal financial services. Hence, they contribute towards improvement of the welfare of the vulnerable groups. Through this model, social workers reasonably address their clients' life challenges such as children's school fees, health costs, food, capital for productive ventures, and lack of access to meaningful social protection in the wake of commodified social relations. In many instances, VSLAs have been a basis for community members to access government programmes that target organised and functional groups, such as Operation Wealth Creation, Community Demand Driven Development, Northern Uganda Social Action Fund, Youth Livelihood Programme, and Uganda Women Entrepreneurial Programme. Moreover, as household incomes improve, household stability also tends to improve. Through efforts to mobilise their clients to join and benefit from VSLAs, social workers are contributing towards improved social welfare of their clients.

Community organising models

Community organising is one of the core methods of social work that is mainly focused on community mobilisation, capacity-building, and empowerment. Staples (2004, xvii) argues that 'organising is based on the notion that ordinary people *can* and *should* join together to gain more control over their life conditions'. Staples (2016) further argues that together, community members set their own goals and take collective action to help themselves and that, based on this notion, 'the act of organising is an article of faith in community members' collective power, lived expertise, wisdom, competence, and judgement to bring about progressive change' (xx). In the following sections, we present two innovative practice models that take the form of community organisation in Uganda's context. These are *akabondo* by World Vision and *nkwatiraako* implemented by Rakai Counsellors' Association (RACA) – an HIV and AIDS-focused organisation in Rakai District in Central Uganda.

Akabondo: The household cluster approach

Akabondo – an equivalent of a household cluster approach – is more of an innovative than indigenous approach to problem solving. It was introduced by World Vision, a non-governmental organisation that operates in many parts of Uganda responding to the plight of vulnerable children and communities. The model involves mobilising community members in a neighbourhood to form groups of 15-20 households, and through these groups, to reflect on their problems and challenges, the cost of inaction, whether and how they would like to address their challenges and foster their own community development.

Akabondo is a Luganda word meaning a shell or sac that contains the eggs of a jigger. Whilst the analogy is negative, the implied message is positive. Within this sac, all the eggs are of the same size, and when they grow, they all progress together. In other words, they mutually support each other. Analogous to the eggs of a jigger in *akabondo*, members of the community within the neighbourhood are seen as belonging to the same context, having more or less similar social development challenges, and thus ought to lift themselves together out of their challenging situations.

Under *akabondo*, the neighbours identify what they consider to be their priority problems and aim to address them by using locally available resources. The approach involves identifying Trainers of Trainers (ToTs) from the clusters themselves, who facilitate the growth of the neighbourhood group while keeping the group focused. The process of identifying ToTs is done by community members together with social workers from the agency. The social work agency (in this case World Vision) facilitates the groups through the forming, storming, norming, and performing stages of group development (see Tuckman, 1965). The members of *akabondo* meet regularly to undertake activities of a common purpose geared towards collective problem solving. Some of the activities include collective farming to ensure food security, provision of informal education to pre-school children, and provision of counselling and guidance to children and adolescent youths. Essentially, this approach is engineered by the local communities themselves and, thus, addresses the ownership and sustainability gaps integral to common interventions by NGOs whose conception and operation is largely from outside the community, a practice that compromises sustainability and community stability.

Under the *akabondo* approach, community members acquire a sense of belonging, with a collective responsibility of working together to improve members' welfare. The members hold themselves accountable for their community development or lack thereof. The mentality is that when one struggles, for instance, with famine, disease, ignorance, illiteracy or poverty, the effects spill over to the neighbours. Thus, progress is not measured at individual or household level but in terms of community progress. The members reinforce each other, tapping into each other's strengths, while working to address their weaknesses. The sense of collective accountability is illustrated in the sense that:

> ...no one just looks and ignores intervening in matters where the neighbour's child misses school, immunisation, or suffers malnutrition. If I know it is a day for antenatal care at the health facility, I have the responsibility to remind my neighbour and his wife about it and to ensure that they actually go to the health facility. (FGD with members of *akabondo*, Rakai District)

> It is everyone's responsibility to ensure that in your own and in your neighbour's home, the sanitation is good, they have a pit latrine, women do not default on antenatal care visits, and we all plant food crops during rainy season... (FGD with members of *akabondo*, Rakai District)

By the time World Vision initiated this model, the organisation had worked in Rakai for at least 15 years. During this period, the organisation supported various interventions across the health, water and sanitation, education, environment, and child protection sectors. However, the models of intervention used to fall short of guaranteeing lasting ownership and sustainability of interventions in the supported communities. This was partly due to individualistic tendencies and a lack of appreciation of collective efforts and collective responsibility. This led World Vision to innovate the *akabondo* model that is engineered by the local communities themselves.

> We were awakened by the reactions of the community members when we started informing them about the pending closure of our Rakai ADP [Area Development Programme]. To us, we believed we had done a lot during the 15 years of service to the community across the five sectors of intervention. But people started asking us: 'So how are you leaving us? How shall we continue with life without you?' This was a wake-up call that our approach all along had a gap. That is when we thought about *akabondo*, and it has proven that it works. (World Vision member of staff, Rakai District)

This model was identified with a set of strengths, including: challenging externally driven approaches by NGOs; addressing core issues that affect communities as identified by community members; promoting social cohesion; and promoting adult literacy. The model also laid the foundation for members to form and join a social enterprise model – the village savings and loans association (VSLA). Through *akabondo*, members acquired various domestic amenities, for example solar power panels (at a subsidised price, having bought them in bulk as a group). A common granary for all members was constructed in one member's home, while water tanks, sanitation facilities (lit pit latrines with hand-washing facilities and garbage pits) were constructed in the respective members' households. These domestic amenities were very critical for addressing drought, poor sanitation, and food insecurity. Solar power addressed the lack of access to the hydro-power grid by many residents in Rakai but also fire accidents associated with candles. The model further eased the work of some social service workforce such as village health teams, para-social workers, and community development officers responsible for promoting food security, mobilising for the immunisation of children, domestic sanitation and hygiene, child protection, early childhood development, and addressing domestic violence. In terms of gender, relations between husbands and wives were said to have improved. Men appreciated their role in childcare, provision, and protection. Husbands and their wives in every household (for those married) participated in the neighbourhood group activities, including the sale and management of farm products, although this reveals less about men's and women's respective control over proceeds from the sale of produce.

Some of the challenges associated with the model are: the members' livelihood activities are agrarian, hence, dependent on nature, which impacts their harvest; and fears that the mutual obligation of group members towards each other may fade once the social work agency (World Vision) stops providing some form of leadership. That notwithstanding, the model is largely effective. It represents a form of social work approach where clients are enabled to reflect upon their own agency and make use of their resources to transform their situations. Such social work practice makes sense especially at a time when social work in Uganda has come under scrutiny by the political regime that questions the contribution of the profession to development. Considering the household, neighbourhood, and community challenges addressed by the *akabondo* model, including drought, poor sanitation, food and economic insecurity, poor attitude towards health service seeking, adult illiteracy, and lack of access to pre-primary education particularly in the rural setting, this practice model impacts positively on the lives of cluster members.

Nkwatiraako practice model

Nkwatiraako, literally meaning 'give me a helping hand' in Luganda, is a self-help group approach. In the context of the study, the approach involved People Living with HIV and AIDS (hereafter referred to as PLHA) forming groups through which they could collectively address their health, psycho-social and socio-economic challenges. This model with features of community organising was being applied in the Byakabanda Sub-County in Rakai District. The members of *nkwatiraako* were receiving HIV treatment, care, and support from the Rakai Counsellors' Association (RACA). But beyond HIV and AIDS-related medical and psycho-social support received from RACA, they shared the common challenges of daily living such as school fees for their children, hunger, drought, poor housing, and poverty.

For purposes of context, it should be stated here that, in the early days of the HIV epidemic in the 1990s and early 2000s, various actors, including RACA, provided a holistic care package to PLHA, ranging from medical care and food aid to livelihood support, and sometimes education support to the children of PLHA. In some instances, modest houses were constructed for critically vulnerable PLHA households. However, partly due to cuts in donor support, the intervention package to PLHA steadily reduced to medical treatment and psycho-social counselling, resulting in a response vacuum. This gap in formal provision compelled the PLHA to consider a self-help approach to address their challenges. Many groups of this nature have been formed across the country and are a major feature of the response to HIV and AIDS in Uganda. In this case we describe the *nkwatiraako* group approach to illustrate how such approaches function.

The *nkwatiraako* group approach was spearheaded by the local organisation, RACA, through their HIV and AIDS counsellors in 2005. The group started with seven members – four women and three men. By 2016 (at the time of this study), the group membership had grown to 31, although two of the founding group members had died. As has been indicated in the previous sections, most of these groups have more females than males, partly due to the fact that most males hesitate to disclose their HIV status.

The group members, with or without the support of the social work agency, conduct community HIV sensitisation and mobilisation for HIV testing, and foster disclosure of HIV status as one way of challenging HIV/AIDS-related stigma. These activities fit well within Goal 1 of the Uganda National HIV and AIDS Priority Action Plan (2015-2018), that is, to reduce the number of new youth and adult infections by 70% and the number of new paediatric HIV infections by 95% by 2020 (Uganda AIDS Commission, 2015a). The group also engages in the promotion of household sanitation and collective economic production. For instance, they collectively hire land, cultivate, sell produce in bulk, and share the proceeds. They further support the construction of modest houses for their very needy members. Activities involving food production and security, household sanitation, and housing support, among others, are in line with the social support and protection goal for PLHA articulated in Uganda's National HIV and AIDS

Strategic Plan. It is also in line with Goal 3 of Uganda's National HIV and AIDS Priority Action Plan (2015-2018) on reducing vulnerability to HIV and AIDS and on the mitigation of its impact on PLHA and other vulnerable groups (Uganda AIDS Commission, 2015b).

The group also ventures into income-generating activities. They buy household utensils such as plates and saucepans which they hire out to non-members during social functions. Group members in need of these items for a social event or activity do not pay any money. In 2011, RACA added a VSLA component to the group activities. Members were encouraged to form a VSLA group and RACA's support to the group came in the form of a savings box, ledger books, a stamp and stamp pad, as well as training, but not finances. By 2016, group members were each saving a minimum of 2,000 UGX (approx. 0.57 US$) and a maximum of 10,000 UGX (approx. 2.86 US$) per week. Alongside savings, every member at every weekly sitting was contributing 500 UGX as a social emergency fund. The emergency fund is borrowed from at no interest by any member in order to address emergencies such as buying school materials for their children, food, and transport to health facilities to access antiretroviral treatment. Members are also eligible to borrow from the group savings at a 10% interest for purposes of individual socio-economic improvement projects.

From a gender perspective, *nkwatiraako* was found to be predominantly comprised of females. This phenomenon is common in self-help groups. For instance, whilst Flynn (2013) underscores the impact of self-help on poverty alleviation and development in Uganda, Bamutungire and Kiranda (2010, 1) describe the self-help group approach as a women's 'thing' and a 'hidden treasure for women'. Flynn (2013) further makes reference to 2,600 self-help groups supported by a German organisation called Kindernothilfe (children's emergency help) in 27 districts in Uganda that registered an impact on poverty alleviation and development but with approximately 99% members being women. Understanding such gender dynamics is very important as, otherwise, resources can be misappropriated in attempts to engage men in self-help models, and yet they increasingly show less motivation to participate in group activities, preferring individual ventures. In general, men appear to engage more easily in revolving fund ventures while women can perform and identify more easily with self-help groups (Luwangula, 2015).

The appropriateness and contextual relevance of *nkwatiraako* as a model for community organising and development cannot be overemphasised. The practice model adheres to the principles of collectivism, sharing, reciprocity, and community empowerment. These are fundamental principles of traditional social protection and support systems in Uganda and in Africa at large (Ouma, 1995). The VSLA component enables people living with HIV/AIDS to economically meet their day-to-day challenges. Otherwise, they would have overstretched their social capital and would, in turn, be labelled by their relatives, family, and friends as a burden. Social capital is not an inexhaustible resource. Once it gets overstretched, relations get complicated. Essentially, this practice model is welfare-enhancing both to its members and the community at large.

Culturally responsive child protection practices: Traditional reception and rehabilitation approaches by *Twesitule* Women's Group in Rakai District

Compared to contemporary times, the phenomenon of children and young people falling out of family care was less common in the past. In the African and Ugandan tradition, the family was a very strong childcare institution. Parents and other relatives assumed the childcare responsibilities, often without needing legal enforcement. In many communities and cultures, the notion of orphanhood was not as devastating as it appears today, especially in terms of the care that orphans received from their surviving relatives. Surviving relatives, including uncles and aunts, assumed the care for orphaned children. Therefore, with or without the biological parents, children had a social father or mother figure who took up the care responsibilities. This helped to deal with various circumstances that would otherwise victimise a child as an 'orphan', including saving them from dropping out of family care. This, though, is not to suggest that such children had their rights totally guaranteed. In some instances, the family care environment characterised what Save the Children Sweden (2011) and Ganga and Chinyoka (2010) refer to as platforms for abuse and meting out violence to children. Nonetheless, such families offered basic care that prevented most children from becoming destitute. However, factors such as HIV and AIDS, urbanisation, the commodification of life, and poverty have increasingly constrained the capacity and, in some cases, the willingness of the extended family to provide the needed care for orphans.

In Rakai District, at the peak of the HIV epidemic in the early 1990s when children orphaned by HIV had no guarantee to be taken in by equally HIV-affected kin relatives or community members, a group of women called *Twesitule* Women's Group took an initiative to offer help to children in the form of traditional reception and rehabilitation services. *Twesitule* is a Luganda word literally meaning 'let us uplift ourselves'.

Twesitule Women's Group in Kyotera, Rakai District was started in 1991 by a group of women as a response to the adverse effects of HIV and AIDS, including orphanhood and the sickness of parents. The impact of HIV and AIDS in Rakai inspired the practice of traditional reception and rehabilitation of affected children and youth, as noted by the group founder:

> Here in Rakai, old people were dying a lot, leaving very many young children behind
> with no help. So, that influenced us to identify those children so as to give them a
> future by training them to make craft bags, necklaces, mats, and many other things.
> (Founder of the group)

The group rented a residential facility in a nearby semi-urban centre where children
with diverse vulnerabilities, including orphans, lost and missing children, and children
with errant behaviour were admitted and taken care of. The group supported children
through mainstream primary and secondary education as well as skills development
through vocational training. Despite being a women's group, both male and female
children and youths in need were admitted. Common vocational skills imparted to
the children included making crafts, such as beads and mats, weaving baskets, and
making other items. The children and youth were additionally trained in playing
traditional musical instruments, performing traditional dances, playing football, and
catering. Such training gave the children the opportunity to make music, dance and
drama performances focusing on sensitisation and community awareness about HIV
and AIDS. NGOs in Rakai focusing on HIV prevention, managing discrimination
and stigma, and protection of people living with HIV and AIDS hired these children
and youth groups to support their sensitisation campaigns. In some instances, it
was during such performances that exceptionally talented children were identified
and sponsored in school by other more established social work organisations.
Some schools also identified children talented in football and music and offered
them scholarships. Children in mainstream formal education were engaged in craft
making after school and during holidays, while those who were not attending formal
education spent their days at the centre.

Twesitule Women's Group helped children and youths to appreciate the essence
of hard work. Proceeds from the sale of products made in the process of training
the children were shared between the children and the women's group. The idea was
twofold: to enable the sustenance of the group since they had no external support;
and to motivate children through direct benefits from their participation. In the
former case, the proceeds were used to pay rent for the residential facilities, buy
children food and clothing, and partly to pay school fees for those in mainstream
education. From a child protection perspective, the practices of the group to some
degree present a form of child labour. However, close scrutiny of the model showed
that the group took care to allocate age-appropriate tasks to the children. Through
the age-appropriate and culturally acceptable tasks, the approach was seen as a way
of strengthening the ability of children to develop skills for self-reliance under the
supervision of caring adults.

The traditional reception and rehabilitation model by the *Twesitule* Women's
Group is arguably instrumental in contributing to problem solving at the individual,

family, group, and community levels. For instance, group activities turned out to be an important mechanism for children that would otherwise not attend school to access school, and to meet their basic survival needs such as food and clothing that their HIV-stricken households could not offer. It is possible to imagine the difficult, risky, and vulnerable state these children would be exposed to without this group's intervention, amidst no meaningful social protection to vulnerable households in Uganda. Thus, this group's model protected these children and youths from a myriad of life challenges, including exposure to street life, the worst forms of child labour, child trafficking, and falling into institutional care. The contribution by these women fits well into the increasingly consensual view that, particularly in African contexts, women are more sensitive to, and appreciate the childcare roles more than men (Luwangula, 2015).

The practice also fits well within the developmental approach to social work. Developmental social work calls upon practitioners to prioritise interventions that empower their clients (Midgley and Conley, 2010). Skills training is one of such interventions as it prepares children and youths for the successful transition to productive adult life (Luwangula, 2017). Moreover, considering the unique vulnerabilities that children and youths affected by HIV and AIDS are faced with, interventions geared towards according them the skills for independent living later in life are desirable. Such skills development interventions have been found largely effective in the Ugandan context among uniquely vulnerable categories of children, such as older street children (Luwangula, 2017). Skills development for HIV-affected children and other vulnerable children assures them of relative economic independence. From a social protection perspective, this contributes to transformative social protection as well as child-sensitive social protection (Devereux and Sabates-Wheeler, 2004; Department for International Development et al., 2009). Equipping children and young people with hands-on skills is a well-accepted social work practice in contemporary Uganda.

Discussion and Conclusion

The indigenous and innovative models presented in this chapter directly relate to the main themes of the Global Agenda for Social Work and Social Development geared to promoting social and economic equalities, promoting the dignity and worth of peoples, working towards environmental and community sustainability, and strengthening the recognition of the importance of human relationships (see Jones and Truell, 2012). The *nkwatiraako* model as well as the *twesitule* group model are underscored by principles of respect for the dignity and worth of individuals in the community while promoting the importance of human relations. Village savings and loans associations (VSLAs) serve a similar purpose but centrally promote the social and economic functioning of the members and their households. The same can be said of the *akabondo* household cluster approach. At the centre of all these practice models lies the motivation to promote community and environmental sustainability. Thus, they are not only culturally responsive and contextually appropriate but also have the potential for being replicated in other parts of the country and most other African contexts since they are strongly rooted in the ethic of *ubuntu* and mutual support. These philosophical underpinnings characterise most communities in Africa.

Cognisant of the weaknesses integral to the imported and less contextualised modern social work models in the African and Ugandan contexts, the propagation of indigenous and innovative models makes sense. It is timely for the social work profession to boost its contribution to the socio-economic development of Uganda. The indigenous and innovative models presented in this chapter, however, are rarely documented as practices geared towards cultural responsiveness, yet they form part and parcel of the indigenised practice. No wonder, Twikirize (2014, 75), in her comment on the social work practice discourse in some parts of Africa, contends that such practice has been 'unconsciously or sub-consciously adapted to the prevailing conditions, needs and expectations of the target groups'. We see a scenario where social work practice in Uganda increasingly reflects an integration of the traditional, indigenous, and local ways of helping. This, according to Twikirize (2014), is an attribute of indigenisation. Indeed, these practice models affirm Spitzer's (2014) characterisation of social work in Africa as unique and the solutions it offers as specific. Spitzer (2014, 15) reported that social work practices in Africa endeavoured to 'provide meaningful responses to the needs of people living at the grassroots level'. Reflecting upon those remarks, the mainstreaming of economic strengthening elements through VSLAs into all these models serves as a case in point. It strengthens the responsiveness of social work to the identifiable needs of clients which are strongly linked to poverty. The economic strengthening interventions are more justified since addressing issues of poverty, vulnerability, and social exclusion is central to social work's relevance in Africa. In Uganda, this is being realised through such indigenous and innovative models. A number of the presented models reflect the principles of reciprocity, altruism, and social cohesion which for long guaranteed the local populace access to services with or without financial resources (Devereux and Sabates-Wheeler, 2004; Barya, 2011; Ouma; 1995). To this extent, social workers adopt practices that they themselves and their clients identify with and appreciate.

Our arguments by no means imply that the imported social work models no longer have a place in the African and Ugandan contexts. Instead, we re-echo the necessity of the social work profession to reposition itself for purposes of achieving cultural relevance where social work principles and values become of greater essence. Arguably, the models presented in this chapter are strongly linked to the developmental social work perspective which recognises that social work agencies use investment strategies infused with community-based, participatory and rights-based interventions (see Midgley and Conley, 2010). Such social investment approaches are relevant in contexts such as Uganda where problems presented by social work clients as illustrated are generally economic, social, political, and environmental. The approaches used to respond to these structural challenges fit well within the social development paradigm.

Finally, although the indigenous and innovative social work practice models identified and documented here are as well associated with some limitations, they remain culturally relevant. It is plausible that if integrated into social work curricula, trainees will identify more with the curriculum content. This is premised on the empirical evidence in East Africa (Kenya, Uganda, Tanzania, and Rwanda) where over 70% of students and 67% of social work educators from 25 higher education institutions expressed concern about the dominance of textbooks and materials authored in North America and Europe (Twikirize 2014, 83). Indeed, integrating local models of helping into the mainstream social work curricula has the potential to strengthen the match between theory taught in the classroom and skills demanded in the labour market.

References

Bamutungire J and Kiranda G (2010) *The Self Help Group Approach: Unleashing Human Potential.* Self Help Group Approach Uganda Program, 2010. Issue No. 2. Available at: http://self-help-approach.com/wp-content/uploads/2016/03/SHAG_Newsletters_Jan_2010_final.pdf (accessed 18 July 2017).

Barya J-J (2011) *Social Security and Social Protection in the East African Community.* Kampala: Fountain.

CARE (2016) CARE Village Savings and Loan Associations Surpass 4 Million Members. Available at: http://www.care.org/newsroom/press/press-releases/care-village-savings-and-loan-associations-surpass-4-million-members (accessed 20 May 2017).

Devereux S and Sabates-Wheeler R (2004) *Transformative Social Protection.* IDS Working Paper 232. Brighton: Institute of Development Studies. Available at: http://www.ids.ac.uk/files/Wp232.pdf (accessed 27 June 2012).

Department for International Development, HelpAge International, Hope and Homes for Children, Institute of Development Studies, ILO, Overseas Development Institute, Save the Children UK, UNDP, UNICEF and the World Bank (2009) *Joint Statement on Advancing Child-Sensitive Social Protection.* http://www.unicef.org/aids/files/CSSP_joint_statement_10.16.09.pdf (accessed 30 May 2014).

Flynn R (2013) A Case Study of Rural Finance Self-Help Groups in Uganda and their Impact on Poverty Alleviation and Development. *Independent Study Project (ISP) Collection.* Paper 1688. Available at: http://digitalcollections.sit.edu/isp_collection/1688 (accessed 25 June 2017).

Ganga E and Chinyoka K (2010) Exploring Psychological Disorders Caused by Poverty amongst Orphans and Vulnerable Children Living Within Child-Headed Households. *Journal of Sustainable Development in Africa*, 12(4): 186-198.

Gray M and Allegritti I (2002) Cross-Cultural Practice and the Indigenisation of African Social Work. *Social Work/Maatskaplike Werk*, 38(4): 324-336. Available at: http://www.academia.edu/867611/Cross-cultural_practice_and_the_indigenisation_of_African_social_work (accessed 08 June 2016).

Gray M, Coates J, and Hetherington T (2007) Hearing Indigenous Voices in Mainstream Social Work. *The Journal of Contemporary Social Services*, 88(1): 55-66. DOI: 10.1016/1044-3894.3592.

Gray M, Kreitzer L and Mupedziswa R (2014) The Enduring Relevance of Indigenisation in African Social Work: A Critical Reflection on ASWEA's Legacy. *Ethics and Social Welfare*, 8(2): 101-116.

Haug E (2001) *Writing in the Margins: Critical Reflection on the Emerging Discourse of International Social Work.* Unpublished Master's Thesis, University of Calgary, Calgary, Canada. Available at: https://scholar.google.com/scholar?hl=en&as_sdt=0%2C5&as_vis=1&q=Haug%2C+E.+%282001%29+Writing+in+the+margins%3A+Critical+reflection+on+the+emerging+discourse+of+international+social+work&btnG= (accessed 20 June 2016).

Haug E (2005) Critical Reflections on the Emerging Discourse of International Social Work. *International Social Work*, 48(2): 129-135.

Ife J (2000) Local and Global Practice: Relocating Social Work as a Human Rights Profession in the New Global Order. Eileen Younghusband Memorial Lecture IFSW/IASSW Biennial Conference, Montreal 31 July 2000. Available at: http://citeseerx.ist.psu.edu/viewdoc/download?doi=10.1.1.576.5015&rep=rep1&type=pdf (accessed 20 June 2016).

Jones DN and Truell R (2012) The Global Agenda for Social Work and Social Development: A Place to Link together and be Effective in a Globalized World. *International Social Work*, 55(4), 454-472.

Luwangula R (2015) *Towards Rewriting Children's Bondage in Poverty and Vulnerability: Underscoring the Fundamentals to Realizing Children's Social Protection Rights in Uganda.* PhD Dissertation, Alpen-Adria-University, Klagenfurt.

Luwangula R (2017) Preparing Older Street Children for Successful Transition to Productive Adult Life: The Need to Prioritize Tailor-Made Skills Training Program in Uganda. In: Mafigiri DK and Walakira EJ (eds) *Child Abuse and Neglect in Uganda.* Cham: Springer, 311-334.

Midgley J (1981) *Professional Imperialism: Social Work in the Third World.* London: Heinemann.

Midgley J and Conley A (2010) (eds) *Social Work and Social Development: Theories and Skills for Developmental Social Work.* New York: Oxford University Press.

Munroe EA, Borden LU, Orr AM, Toney D and Meader J (2013) Decolonizing Aboriginal Education in the 21st Century. *McGill Journal of Education,* 48(2): 317-338.

Nagpaul H (1993) Analysis of Social Work Teaching Materials in India: The Need for Indigenous Foundations. *International Social Work,* 36(3): 207-220.

Nimmagadda J and Cowger CD (1999) Cross-Cultural Practice: Social Worker Ingenuity in the Indigenization of Practice Knowledge. *International Social Work,* 42(3): 261-276.

Osei-Hwedie K (1993) The Challenge of Social Work in Africa: Starting the Indigenisation Process. *Journal of Social Development in Africa,* 8(1): 19-30.

Osei-Hwedie K (1995) *A Search for Legitimate Social Development Education and Practice Models for Africa.* Lewiston: Edwin Mullen.

Ouma AS (1995) The Role of Social Protection in the Socioeconomic Development of Uganda. *Journal of Social Development in Africa,* 10(2): 5-12.

Save the Children Sweden (2011) *A Focus on Child Protection within Social Protection Systems: Transforming Children's Lives.* Available at: http://resourcecentre.savethechildren.se/sites/default/files/documents/5908.pdf (accessed 21 December 2012).

Spitzer H (2014) Social Work in African Contexts: A Cross-Cultural Reflection on Theory and Practice. In: Spitzer H, Twikirize JM and Wairire GG (eds) *Professional Social Work in East Africa: Towards Social Development, Poverty Reduction and Gender Equality.* Kampala: Fountain, 15-28.

Spitzer H and Twikirize JM (2014) Ethical Challenges for Social Work in Post-Conflict Situations: The Case of Africa's Great Lakes Region. *Journal of Ethics and Social Welfare,* 8(2): 145-150.

Staples L (2016) *Roots to Power: A Manual for Grassroots Organizing.* 3rd edition. Santa Barbara: Praeger.

Staples L (2004) *Roots to Power: A Manual for Grassroots Organizing.* 2nd edition. Westport, Connecticut and London: Praeger.

Tuckman B (1965) Bruce Tuckman's Forming Storming Norming Performing Team Development Model. Available at: http://www.businessballs.com/tuckmanformingstormingnormingperforming.htm (accessed 14 March 2017).

Twikirize JM (2014) Indigenisation of Social Work in Africa: Debates, Prospects and Challenges. In: Spitzer H, Twikirize JM and Wairire GG (eds) *Professional Social Work in East Africa: Towards Social Development, Poverty Reduction and Gender Equality.* Kampala: Fountain, 75-90.

Twikirize JM, Asingwire N, Omona J, Lubanga R and Kafuko A (2013) *The Role of Social Work in Poverty Reduction and the Realisation of Millennium Development Goals in Uganda.* Kampala: Fountain.

Uganda AIDS Commission (2015a) National HIV and AIDS Priority Action Plan (2015/2016—2017/2018). Available at: http://www.ilo.org/wcmsp5/groups/public/---ed_protect/---protrav/---ilo_aids/documents/policy/wcms_455259.pdf (accessed 26 March 2017).

Uganda AIDS Commission (2015b) National HIV and AIDS Strategic Plan 2015/2016-2019/2020. Available at: http://hivhealthclearinghouse.unesco.org/sites/default/files/resources/22280.pdf (accessed 26 March 2017).

VSL Associates Ltd (n.d.) Available at: http://www.vsla.net/aboutus/vslmodel (accessed 23 February 2017).

Weaver HN (1999) Indigenous People and the Social Work Profession: Defining Culturally Competent Services. *Social Work*, 44(3): 217-225.

9

Building Resilience through Indigenous Mechanisms: The Case of *Bataka* Groups in Western Uganda

Justus Twesigye, Janestic M. Twikirize, Ronald Luwangula and Stanley Kitimbo

Introduction

There is increasing emphasis on strengths and resilience perspectives in social work literature at the global level (e.g. Saleebey, 1996). Yet, little attention has been paid to indigenous ways of coping with adversity. A critical analysis of indigenous ways of coping could offer significant insights into the resilience literature in contemporary social work in Africa. In this chapter, we argue that difficult life circumstances such as poverty, sickness, and death may not necessarily lead to adverse outcomes for the affected people. Certainly, some people's social functioning is diminished by the experience of adversity. However, other people recover and thrive, following the experience of an adverse event. In our exploratory case study in Rukungiri District, Western Uganda, we found that people, through their local organisations known as *bataka* groups (burial societies formed by community members), exhibited numerous strengths in responding effectively to bereavement. Although *bataka* groups were initially presented using deficit-focused descriptors, they are quickly adopting strengths-focused descriptors such as *bataka twimukye* ('local people rise up'). We draw implications for the strengths and resilience perspectives in social work practice based on these findings. In subsequent sections of this chapter, we provide an overview of poverty, structural violence, and death as examples of adverse conditions, we introduce the methods used in conducting this study, present and discuss our findings, and summarise the conclusions we draw from the presented research.

Poverty, Structural Violence, and Death

Adverse conditions such as poverty, insecurity and vulnerability to risks and disasters are highly prevalent in sub-Saharan Africa (Sewpaul, 2014). Farmer (2003) has argued that while suffering is widespread in the contexts of power inequality, it is disproportionately experienced by the poor and powerless members of society who, ironically, are also the majority. Suffering attributed to macro-level social, political, and economic forces that the poor and powerless members of society unduly experience has been described as structural violence (Farmer, 2003; Sewpaul, 2014). While it also occurs in high-income countries, structural violence is mostly common in contexts of low-income countries. In Uganda, Okuonzi (2004) reported that liberalisation and the adoption of market principles in the provision of health services have placed too much responsibility on patients and their families to meet the costs of care. Unfavourable environments experienced by poor people create undue suffering, debilitation, and death. Although the suffering experienced by poor people is often embodied, it also occurs in psychological idioms such as low self-esteem, loss of control, anger, and insecurity – conditions that, in turn, may undermine physical health (McLeod and Bywaters, 1999).

As is usually the case, adversity often makes people miserable long before they eventually die. Whereas death is an inevitable and sad reality for every human being, in the context of poverty, managing it can be very difficult for families, relatives, and community members (Narayan et al., 2000). For example, poor households may have to sell their livelihood assets, borrow at high interest rates, and drift into more poverty in order to decently bury their dead. Death and associated funerals thus can be very costly and significantly undermine the affected families' and households' financial, social, and spiritual wellbeing (Case et al., 2013). Researchers have reported on the spread of burial societies in different parts of Africa. For example, in their early research in Botswana, Brown (1982) and Grant (1987) reported that burial societies were common in different communities in that country. Participants in Brown's (1982, 80) study described the burial societies as the 'most important, most progressive, and best organised of all organisations in the Kgatleng village'. Recent studies on burial societies conducted in Ethiopia by Teshome et al. (2012) and in Uganda by Jones (2007) have reported that these societies were widespread and critical in serving as insurance schemes for members.

In this chapter, we show how local people in Rukungiri District cope with the cultural expectation of giving a decent burial to their dead and how they turn death, which is a tragic experience, into a manageable one through *bataka* groups (burial societies). *Bataka* is literally translated as 'community members' among the Bantu ethnic groups, who are predominant in Western Uganda. Rukungiri District is inhabited mainly by the Banyankore/Bahororo and Bakiga ethnic groups, who are a constituent of the Bantu (Nzita, Mbaga-Niwampa and Mukholi, 1993). The Banyankore/Bahororo were historically stratified into two groups, Bahima, who were cattle keepers and political leaders and Bairu, who were cultivators and servants of the Bahima. The Bakiga, in contrast to the Banyankore/Bahororo, were agriculturalists who generally grew crops, such as sorghum, peas, millet, and beans. They also lived and worked communally. With regard to the political set-up, the Bakiga were largely a segmentary society in which political authority was held by respective lineage leaders. All three ethnic groups believed in a common ancestry known as *Ruhanga* (the creator) who, according to legend, had sanctioned their unequal social and political relations. They also believed in witchcraft and attributed misfortunes such as death to human malevolence.

This chapter is influenced by the perspective of Gitterman and Shulman (2005), who claim that people who experience serious adversity may recover and acquire continued adaptive functioning. The basis of such recovery, according to Gitterman and Shulman (2005), include the affected person's temperament, family patterns, external support, and environmental resources. We show how community members in Rukungiri District, Western Uganda, utilise especially external support and environmental resources to cope with death and its associated costs.

Methods

This chapter is written from data that was collected in a large study on indigenous and innovative social work practice models in East Africa under the PROSOWO project (*Professional Social Work in East Africa*). Data for this chapter was collected from Rukungiri District in Western Uganda. We adopted a case study design involving a qualitative research approach to data collection, analysis, and reporting (Babbie, 2010). In particular, we conducted in-depth interviews with four key informants, four focus groups, and one case narrative interview (Babbie and Mouton, 2001). Qualitative data collected was captured using audio recorders, transcribed verbatim, blind back-translated from the Runyankore-Rukiga language (commonly spoken in Western Uganda) into English and analysed in Microsoft Word. Analysis was conducted based on the thematic analysis method and aimed at generating themes and patterns from the data (Braun and Clarke, 2006). We received institutional review and ethical clearance from MildMay, Uganda, which operates on behalf of the Uganda National Council of Science and Technology.

Findings and Discussion

Three themes regarding building resilience by *bataka* groups for bereaved families emerged from our data. These themes are (i) origins and labelling of *bataka* groups; (ii) the role of *bataka* groups; and (iii) the strengths of this model. The role and strengths of this indigenous approach are discussed with regard to potential links to social work.

Origins and labelling of bataka groups

Participants reported that *bataka* groups (burial societies) were initially known as *bataka kwezika* (self-burial by local people) and were later identified with progressive names such as *bataka twebiseho* (self-help for local people), *bataka twimukye* (local people rise up) and *bataka tukwatanise* (local people cooperate). Participants also reported that *bataka* groups were probably the most prevalent and dominant mechanism for mutual aid in communities of Rukungiri District in times of death. Participants generally agreed that *bataka* groups were ubiquitous in Rukungiri District, with their formation often based on primary relationships such as kinship and neighbourliness among community members.

> One vibrant mechanism for self-help that community members have devised is forming *bataka* groups. At least, every village in Bwambara Sub-County has a *bataka* group. (Community development officer in Bwambara Sub-County)

> There are some *bataka* groups with a membership of 30 to 60 people. Membership often comprises a couple in each household in the village. At times when a family is extended, members form their own *bataka* group and the rest of the community members mobilise themselves to form other *bataka* groups. (Chairperson of para-social workers[8] in Bwambara Sub-County)

A number of factors were reported to have influenced the formation of *bataka* groups in Rukungiri District. These factors include (i) difficulty by families in organising decent funerals, especially due to poverty; (ii) the role of the AIDS pandemic; and (iii) the adaptation of local technology. Pertaining to the experience of difficulty by families in organising decent funerals for members, a cultural and opinion leader in Kanyanga village stated:

> We started a *bataka* group in this village after seeing individual families suffer in making burial arrangements for their members. Bereaved families lacked the necessary resources to organise funerals. Now, members of *bataka* groups bring the necessary resources such as food, firewood, and water, which makes organising funerals easy.

Because of the widespread household poverty which undermined members' capacity to give a decent burial to their loved ones, death was extremely traumatising. On this matter, the community development officer of Bwambara Sub-County stated:

---

[8]   A para-social worker has been described as the supervised paraprofessional practitioner or volunteer – often community-based – who serves the needs of children and families, particularly where social welfare systems are underdeveloped or severely stretched. (Linsk et al., 2010)

As there were no coffins, dead bodies were buried in mats. I was young, but I remember some of these things. Actually, in those days people used to believe that death was stinky because whenever there was a dead person, the entire place would be smelly.

Forming *bataka* groups, therefore, facilitated families to cope with the traumatising experience of barely being able to bury their dead, a fact that contravened members' social and cultural obligations. Because of the increasing population and frequent droughts, food and wood, which are essential to organising funerals, were getting scarce in Rukungiri District. In particular, in the context of death, firewood is important in at least two ways. Firstly, firewood is used in preparing food for the mourners. Secondly, firewood is used in lighting a fire around which mourners would camp at night for a vigil. Moreover, following burials among the Banyankore/ Bahororo, there would be four days of mourning if the deceased was a man or three days if the deceased was a woman (Nzita, Mbaga-Niwampa and Mukholi, 1993). The concern that death was 'stinky' is attributed to the practice by Banyankore/ Bahororo of keeping dead bodies in the house for long while waiting for close relatives to convene for the funeral (Nzita, Mbaga-Niwampa and Mukholi, 1993). As they were not embalmed, decomposing bodies were likely to be smelly.

With regard to the role of HIV and AIDS in influencing the formation of *bataka* groups in Rukungiri District, members of a *bataka twimukye* group in a focus group discussion in Bwambara Sub-County stated:

> AIDS started in Rakai District and then it spread to Rwenshama landing site, which is near Bwambara village in Rukungiri District. Because we are far away from the road, we started a *bataka* group to transport patients to the hospital using *engozi* [a stretcher]. Because of too many deaths, we devised means of helping ourselves, including forming a *bataka* group.

In a related study, Mukiza-Gapere and Ntozi (1995) reported that *bataka kwezika* (burial societies) in Western Uganda emerged in response to the burden that bereaved families encountered because of AIDS-related deaths that necessitated frequent burials. The formation of burial societies helped bereaved families to effectively manage funerals, as these societies contributed funds, for example, to buy a coffin and food for mourners. Members of burial societies also provided manual labour to undertake funeral-related activities such as digging the grave. Owing to the many deaths attributed to HIV and AIDS, the use of coffins for burial and giving short speeches were, in addition to the formation of burial societies, adopted as pragmatic choices in the context of much need (Mukiza-Gapere and Ntozi, 1995). Moreover, because many parts of Rukungiri District are inaccessible by road transport as a result of the hilly terrain, community members devised the use of *engozi* (locally made stretchers or ambulances) as the appropriate means of transporting patients and dead bodies. Commenting on the importance of being buried at home, Whyte (2005) noted that in a patriarchal Ugandan society, men were expected to be buried on their fathers' land. In contrast, women were expected to be buried on their husbands' land. Because of the impact of HIV and AIDS, coupled with the expectation of being buried at the *correct* home, there was need for a collective effort by community members to transport the sick or dead to their parents' or husband's home to be nurtured or to be buried (Whyte, 2005).

Additionally, the adaptation of local technology previously used to transport bridegrooms and kings contributed to the formation of *bataka* groups in Rukungiri District. The development of *engozi* (stretchers) based on local technology necessitated cooperation among community members as carrying a dead body or patient required collective labour. Members of *bataka tweyambe* in a focus group discussion in Kanyanga village stated:

> When we were young children, when a girl was getting married, her family would weave a litter to transport her to the bridegroom's home. Later when people here got stuck with patients, they modified the litter and made *engozi* to transport them to hospitals.

> We copied the idea of *engozi* from community members living in hilly areas of Kabale District who had devised means of transporting patients to the hospital and collecting dead bodies because they lacked better means of transport; generally, that is where the idea originated.

These accounts suggest that participants viewed the use of *engozi* in transporting patients and dead bodies as appropriate because they had previously used a similar technology to offer dignified transport for bridegrooms and kings. The central influence of adaptable technology in transforming burials and related funerals has been previously reported in Africa. For example, Van der Geest (2006) reported that the introduction of mortuaries (locally referred to as 'fridges') significantly altered the burial and funeral practices in Ghana. In particular, Van der Geest (2006) reported that prior to the establishment of mortuaries in the 1960s in Ghana, families ensured that their loved ones died at their respective homes and were hastily buried.

Role of bataka groups

In order to explicate the role of *bataka* groups, we start with a case example:

> Sharon (not real name) is a 31-year old[9] widow with five children; two sons and three daughters. The oldest is 20 years old and the youngest is eight years old.

---

[9]   We could not verify Sharon's actual age because registration of birth in rural Uganda is not common. However, we did not dispute her age at marriage because we are aware of the high prevalence of child marriage in Uganda.

She is a resident of the hilly Kanyanga village in Rukungiri District. Sharon was understandably sad when stating that her husband, whom she had married when aged 11 years, died of AIDS in August 2015. He was 17 years old when he married Sharon and died aged 37 years. He died after 10 years of sickness during which he frequently sought medical treatment. Sharon's husband died in the evening when he was carrying a sack of charcoal on a bicycle to the market. She immediately sought support from her burial society known as *bataka twezikye* for her husband's burial and funeral. Sharon was grateful for the timely support provided by her *bataka* group that enabled her to organise a decent funeral for her husband. Because her husband collapsed and died away from home, she could not afford hiring a private car to bring the body home; besides, the hilly terrain rendered the use of a vehicle impractical. As she expected, members of her *bataka* group helped to collect the body in *engozi* (stretcher). When she informed members of her *bataka* group of her husband's demise, they rushed to the site where '…my husband lay dead, put him in *engozi* and brought him home. Members of our *bataka* group immediately brought food items including beans, posho [maize meal], bananas, fetched firewood, and water, and prepared for the funeral which took place on the following day.' Members of Sharon's *bataka* group undertook all funeral activities for free as was the norm. Many members also expressed their kindness in words and encouraged Sharon to cope with the loss of her husband. According to Sharon, a few friends and relatives who were not members of her *bataka twezikye* supported her during mourning. For example, she received 200,000 UGX (approx. 55 US$) from one of her friends as condolence and her relatives frequently visited and counselled her.

As the case above illustrates, *bataka* groups play a critical role in supporting poor community members such as Sharon in times of death. While such support offered by *bataka* groups may seem modest for wealthy people, it is nevertheless sufficient to assist poor community members to overcome the hardships associated with death. Below, we examine the specific roles of *bataka* groups in detail.

Bataka groups play various roles to enable members to cope with challenges, especially related to bereavement. Such roles include (i) the provision of resources for organising funerals; (ii) the provision of counselling to bereaved families; and (iii) the provision of support for developmental activities. The provision of essential resources, such as a coffin and food, to assist bereaved members to organise burials and funeral ceremonies was perhaps the most critical role of *bataka* groups.

The main function of *bataka* groups in this community is to support members materially, when they have a funeral. *Bataka* groups comprise men and women; men often supply the coffin, firewood, dig the grave, while women cook and serve food to mourners. (Community development officer, Bwambara Sub-County)

Participants viewed *bataka* groups as responsible for undertaking funeral-related activities on behalf of a bereaved member. Supporting bereaved families to organise a decent burial for their loved ones as the core business of burial societies has been reported elsewhere in Africa. For example, Brown (1982) reported that burial societies in Botswana effectively performed their critical *functional role*, which is to support the burial of the dead. Brown (1982) also reported that while burial societies in Botswana usually bought food at the local store to be prepared for the funeral feast, money for the coffin was often handed over to the family to do the purchase.

Another key role of *bataka* groups, according to this study, is the provision of counselling to bereaved families, as the senior probation and social welfare officer, Rukungiri District, stated:

> Members of *bataka* groups provide counselling and psychosocial support to bereaved families. If a member has lost a husband, it is common to see some women seated close to her throughout the funeral, giving emotional support.

Evidently, members of *bataka* groups were viewed as capable of meeting the emotional needs of bereaved members. Because members of *bataka* groups are usually neighbours, bereaved families were aptly placed to receive emotional care whenever it was needed. Women, because of their primary nurturing and caring role, were likely to offer emotional support to bereaved fellow women members while men could provide such support to fellow men, thus emphasising the gendered dynamics of *bataka* groups. Hall (1987) also stated that women were most involved in providing emotional support and cheering up bereaved families. Increased participation of women in the provision of emotional support may also be due to the fact that caring in Uganda is generally regarded as a woman's responsibility (Twikirize, 2014; Whyte, 2005). Researchers in the past have similarly reported that burial societies have the capacity to alleviate the emotional problems of bereaved families. For example, Baloyi (2014) reported that mourners in Africa usually stood with the bereaved in the same way clients are reassured that the counsellor is with them in times of trouble. Mourners also prioritised exhibiting solidarity with the bereaved families to undertaking their usual work. Baloyi (2014, 5) stated that in Limpopo Province of South Africa, local chiefs and headmen mobilised community members against organising any other celebrations, including church services and parties, whenever death had occurred to ensure that community members 'identified with the mourners'. Hall (1987) described the provision of counselling, along with practical support such as cleaning the house, as secondary benefits to organising the funerals of members of burial societies.

Bataka groups sometimes extended benefits to non-members. For example, the chairperson of para-social workers, Bwambara Sub-County, stated:

> Some *bataka* groups extend support to relatives of members, such as uncles, aunties, sisters and brothers of *bataka* group members. Support is sometimes extended to relatives of members who live in faraway villages. For example, members of *bataka* groups hire vehicles to transport mourners to faraway places to attend funerals.

Membership of a *bataka* group apparently engendered a multiplier effect for primary members and their kin. The wide coverage of benefits attributed to membership of burial societies has also been reported elsewhere. For example, Brown (1982) earlier reported that, apart from covering members of a nuclear family as primary beneficiaries, burial societies often registered three or four secondary beneficiaries, including their parents and friends. Such secondary beneficiaries were also likely to be residing in distant communities from those of primary beneficiaries. In a related study, Baloyi (2014) reported that long distances did not impede African people from participating in funerals.

Finally, *bataka* groups were reported to have recently started supporting developmental activities of members. The chairperson, Nyakagyeme Sub-County, stated:

> *Bataka* groups now are including other ways of helping, such as lending money to members to facilitate them to undertake developmental projects. Currently, many *bataka* groups own furniture, such as plastic chairs, which is a good thing. *Bataka* groups are also beginning to cover medical bills for members.

The inclusion of a developmental agenda suggests that *bataka* groups were progressive and aspired to offer holistic support to members. Covering the medical bills of members also showed that *bataka* groups were capable of preventing some untimely deaths. The changing role of burial societies from being primarily focused on funerals to supporting a developmental agenda has previously been reported in other contexts. For example, Bouman (1995) reported that while the most prevalent and pervasive form of mutual assistance in the context of low-income countries was associated with death, mutual assistance had extended from the social to the economic domains. Such a development was attributed to the influence of other cultures that inspired innovations and adjustments, perfection, and institutionalisation of mutual aid groups. In view of these developments, Bouman (1995) compared mutual assistance to members in low-income countries to the insurance industry in high-income countries. Additionally, members of mutual aid groups also undertook individual and collective economic investment, community development, and public works (Bouman, 1995). Supporting a developmental agenda involved, for example, pooling labour or money to improve public facilities such as roads, schools, and health facilities. Liard (2007) similarly reported that mutual aid groups served economic functions in Ghana where they were referred to as *susu*. In the context of Liard's (2008) study, *susu* were informal schemes for saving money among low-income earners that were not served by formal financial institutions. Because of their perceived effectiveness in transforming the lives of members, the department of community development in Ghana used *susu* as benchmarks for setting up and training new groups in income-generating activities (Liard, 2008). *Susu* can be equated to the village savings and loans associations (VLSAs) which, in Uganda, are an innovative approach to self-help commonly adopted by women facing financial insecurity and unable to access credit from formal financial institutions because of unfavourable eligibility criteria (Musinguzi, 2015).

The developmental agenda suggested by *bataka* groups is relevant to the social development approach to improve social welfare, especially in the Global South (Midgley, 1995). This approach is distinguished from social philanthropy and social work by its scope of intervention. For example, while social philanthropy and social work mainly focus on helping individuals, the social development approach focuses on helping the community and on intervening in the wider social processes and structures (Midgley, 1995). The social development approach is thus comprehensive and inclusive as it caters for the population as a whole. The most defining feature of the social development approach is its emphasis on linking social and economic development to the extent that both are viewed as integral facets of a dynamic process of development (Midgley, 1995). Similarly, members of *bataka* groups viewed having enhanced economic capacity as an effective strategy for meeting their social goals, including giving a decent burial to the dead.

The developmental agenda of *bataka* groups is also associated with the empowerment model in social work, which addresses weaknesses of Western-oriented social work (Anderson et al., 1994). Such weaknesses include often viewing an individual as the sole target for social work intervention. Appropriate social work intervention should address the immediate needs and concerns of individuals and contextual (environmental) factors to prevent future distress and ensure improved quality of life for all. The empowerment model proposed by Anderson et al. (1994) comprises five dimensions, namely, the individual, social, educational, economic, and political empowerment. Individual empowerment, for example, depicts the client's 'strengths and capacities to positively impact its position in life' (Anderson et al., 1994, 80). Additionally, economic empowerment is described as the 'ability of each able member in society to obtain sufficient income to live a life of dignity, and one in which the basic needs of shelter, food, and clothing can be adequately fulfilled' (Anderson et al., 1994, 82). These are legitimate aims which *bataka* groups pursue in addition to managing bereavement-related distress.

In keeping with the indigenisation debate in social work practice, Kabadaki (1995) suggested that social workers should apply adaptable models to facilitate meeting of the social development needs of rural people in Uganda. These are the ecological model (life model), structural model, and integrated practice model. According to Kabadaki (1995), the ecological or life model is useful in assessment and intervention owing to its focus on the individual, the environment, and the interaction of both. The model encourages the use of various methods, such as casework, group work, and social action in intervening in clients' situations. The model could be applied in helping rural people in Uganda facing problems such as the loss of a spouse or a severe illness (Kabadaki, 1995). The structural model emphasises the need by social workers to change clients' environments, to link clients with resources, and to impart skills among clients for self-help. The model utilises the principles of generalist practice (Kabadaki, 1995). The integrated practice model draws on concepts from relevant social work practice models and seeks to promote competency and empowerment among clients as well as the normalisation of their situations. Importantly, this model is flexible with regard to the level of intervention; it recognises that individuals have the capacity to learn and, thus, to solve their problems if they are adequately supported (Kabadaki, 1995).

The application of the above models and approaches while intervening in situations such as those experienced by *bataka* groups in Rukungiri District is consistent with the idea of pragmatism. Midgley (1995) has referred to pragmatism as the use of unconventional approaches to social work education and practice in non-Western contexts. Anderson et al. (1994) have outlined the following characteristics of a pragmatic approach to social work practice: (i) dealing with social problems in a direct manner without relying on conventional casework methods; (ii) emphasising practical skills over theoretical skills in social work education, e.g. teaching students how to set up rural cooperatives and raise livestock; (iii) directing social work interventions to the most pressing needs and social problems, e.g. poverty; and (iv) adapting the principal of indigenisation (that is, practising social work in a manner that is appropriate to the people and the country). This pragmatic social work practice suggests adapting social work roles such as broker, educator, enabler, and therapist to the cultural and contextual situations of beneficiaries of social work help (Midgley, 1995).

Strengths of bataka groups

Some of the strengths of *bataka* groups identified in this study include (i) the capacity to mitigate financial hardships of bereaved families; (ii) the capacity to effectively mobilise mourners; (iii) the capacity to promote social relations among community members; and (iv) adhering to strict operational guidelines.

Pertaining to the capacity of *bataka* groups to mitigate the financial hardships of the bereaved families, the chairperson of para-social workers, Bwambara Sub-County, stated:

> Members of *bataka* groups no longer suffer financially to organise funerals for relatives. You will hear at funerals announcements that *bataka* group X has contributed 200,000 Uganda shillings [approx. 55 US$] as condolence; *bataka* group Y has contributed 500,000 Uganda shillings as condolence; and another one

has contributed 300,000 Uganda shillings as condolence. People in this village no longer sell land to finance funerals as it had been the case in the past.

Besides cash payments to the bereaved families, burial societies catered for major burial expenses such as a coffin, transport for mourners to attend funerals, firewood, and food. Because funds provided by one burial society were unlikely to cover all the funeral expenses, families registered with various mutual aid groups from which they received support in the event of the death of a family member.

Another reported strength of *bataka* groups was the capacity to effectively mobilise mourners. For example, a cultural and opinion leader in Kyanyanga village stated:

> Organising funerals in this village has greatly improved since the proliferation of *bataka* groups. Long ago, you would find a handful of people at the funeral; today, when a member of the *bataka* group dies, the group makes radio announcements and also informs members of nearby *bataka* groups.

In the context of *bataka* groups, attendance by a large number of mourners implied some reasonable material and financial support for the bereaved family in the form of condolences. It also signified respect for the bereaved families. The use of mass media, including radio, ensured that burial societies mobilised mourners both in the near and distant communities. Mobilisation of mourners for funerals using the mass media is common in the African context. For example, Grant (1987) reported that whereas news concerning death usually spread fast within a closely-knit Botswana society, bereaved families found it necessary to inform relatives and friends resident in distant communities by modern mass media, including radio and telegram.

The capacity to promote social relations among community members was another reported strength of *bataka* groups. For example, the senior probation and social welfare officer, Rukungiri District, stated:

> *Bataka* groups have contributed to strengthening of friendships and enabled people to know each other. While at the funeral, groups of people hailing from different communities and districts are introduced to mourners. We now frequently meet mourners from Kanungu, Kabale, and Bushenyi Districts, some of whom are our relatives or clan mates but whom we previously had not known.

Bataka groups thus provided a platform for effective networking and socialisation by community members. Moreover, funerals often attracted a large number of mourners from both near and distant villages who would have otherwise lacked opportunities for interaction and networking. In a related study, Hall (1987) reported that, besides serving as insurance schemes, burial societies facilitated the creation of a 'home-boy' network involving migrant members from rural areas of Zimbabwe or neighbouring countries. Members organised entertainment and social events to ensure the continuity of local practices and values away from their respective home villages or countries.

Being organised and conducted on strict operational guidelines was also regarded as a form of strength of *bataka* groups. For example, the community development officer, Bwambara Sub-County, stated:

> Members of *bataka* groups know rules and regulations which regulate their conduct. If, for example, a member dies at 2 p.m., by 2.30 p.m., the entire *bataka* group will have reported to the deceased's home. Everyone will quickly know that a member has died as soon as someone lights a fire in the deceased's compound, and failure to observe time is seriously punished.

This account suggests that members of *bataka* groups were disciplined and adhered to strict rules of conduct. Furthermore, prompt responses to emergencies such as death could be due to the fact that members live in close proximity with each other. Researchers in the past have reported that strict sanctions ensured the success of burial societies. Brown (1982), for example, stated that burial societies in Botswana operated on explicit authoritative rules which, in many cases, were written down. Even when rules were unwritten, members of burial societies knew and strictly adhered to them. Brown (1982) also stated that the rules governing operations of burial societies concerned critical aspects such as the prescription of fees to be paid by members, categories of beneficiaries covered, and procedures for claiming benefits. In the case of Rukungiri District, the practice varies from one group to another, depending on the literacy levels of the majority of group members. While some groups keep a record of basic rules, others operate on unwritten and yet well-known rules and regulations.

The above features exhibited by *bataka* groups are consistent with the strengths perspective in social work practice. The strengths perspective is a 'way of working with clients that shifts social workers away from a focus on clients' problems, deficits and labels towards interactions and interventions that focus on clients' strengths, abilities, resources and accomplishments' (Kondrat, 2010, 38). The strengths perspective is regarded as a radical departure from 'psychosocial approaches based on individual, family and community pathology, deficits, problems, abnormality, victimization and disorder' (Saleebey, 1996, 296). It suggests viewing all people positively with regard to their capacities, talents, possibilities, visions, values, and hopes, even if these may be suppressed by their unfavourable experiences and conditions. At the core, the strengths perspective suggests that social workers should endeavour to use positive language characterised by words such as empowerment and membership, search for people's strengths, recognise people's resilience, identify critical factors (comprising risk and protective factors), and promote a sense of community (Saleebey, 1996). While all these elements of the strengths perspective are generally applicable to most people's situations, in the context of *bataka* groups grappling with death, their strengths and resilience need to be emphasised. Strengths implies that individuals have the capacity to adapt and cope with the stressors they experience, maintain reasonable levels of functioning even when experiencing significant problems, and recover from trauma often with the use of social support. Strengths can be personal or environmental and can be exhibited by individuals, families, and communities (Kondrat, 2010). Resilience, according to Saleebey (1996, 299) is the 'continuing articulation of capacities and knowledge derived through the interplay of risks, and protections in the world'. It depicts the tendency by some people to continue to survive against the odds. The odds stacked against many people may be in the form of illness, poverty, stigma, or abuse.

In the context of *bataka* groups, poor community members strived to provide a culturally acceptable and decent burial for their loved ones amidst debilitating poverty and deprivation. Coping with this cultural expectation by activating mutual aid is a typical manifestation of resilience as it is recognised in social work practice (Saleebey, 1996).

Conclusion

There is no doubt that death is tragic and can destabilise individuals' and families' wellbeing everywhere in the world. However, such destabilisation is often exacerbated in the context of poverty and deprivation, as individuals usually cannot afford the costs of organising funerals that meet their cultural and societal expectations. In the context of Western Uganda, *bataka* groups are significantly contributing towards a protective environment where community members are better able to cope with distress associated with death and dying. Ordinary community members acquire this enhanced capacity to effectively respond to the hitherto catastrophic death through pragmatic use of locally available resources. The exhibited strengths of *bataka* groups in Western Uganda as a mechanism for coping with traumatic experiences manifest the enduring resilience of humans to overcome hardships, including death. This has important implications for social work with communities building on indigenous approaches and models.

References

Anderson SC, Wilson M, Mwansa L-K and Osei-Hwedie K (1994) Empowerment in Social Work Education and Practice in Africa. *Journal of Social Development in Africa*, 9(2): 71-86.

Babbie E (2010) *The Practice of Social Research.* 12th ed. Belmont: Wadsworth, Cengage Learning.

Babbie E and Mouton J (2001) *The Practice of Social Research: A South African Version.* Cape Town: Oxford University Press.

Baloyi ME (2014) Distance No Impediment for Funerals: Death as a Uniting Ritual for African People – A Pastoral Study. *Verbum et Ecclesia*, 35(1), Art. #1248. http://dx.doi.org/10.4102/ve.v35i1.1248.

Bouman FJA (1995) ROSCA: On the Origin of the Species. *Savings and Development*, 19(2): 117-148.

Braun V and Clarke V (2006) Using Thematic Analysis in Psychology. *Qualitative Research in Psychology*, 3: 77-101.

Brown C (1982) Kgatleng Burial Societies. *Botswana Notes and Records*, 14: 80-83.

Case A, Garrib A, Menendez A and Olgiati A (2013) Paying the Piper: The High Cost of Funerals in South Africa. *Economic Development and Cultural Change*, 62: 1-20.

Farmer P (2003) *Pathologies of Power: Health, Human Rights and the New War on the Poor.* Berkeley: California University Press.

Gitterman A and Shulman L (2005) The Life Model, Oppression, Vulnerability, Resilience, Mutual Aid and the Mediating Function. In: Gitterman A and Shulman L (eds) *Mutual Aid Groups, Vulnerable & Resilient Populations, and the Life Cycle.* New York: Columbia University Press, 3-37.

Grant S (1987) Death and Burial in Mochudi: A Study of Changing Traditions. *Botswana Notes and Records*, 19: 137-149.

Hall NP (1987) Self-Reliance in Practice: A Study of Burial Societies in Harare, Zimbabwe. *Journal of Social Development in Africa*, 2: 49-71.

Jones B (2007) The Teso Insurgency Remembered: Churches, Burials and Propriety. *Africa*, 77(04): 500-516.

Kabadaki KK (1995) Exploration of Social Work Practice Models for Rural Development in Uganda. *Journal of Social Development in Africa*, 10(1): 77-88.

Kondrat DC (2010) The Strengths Perspective. In: Teater B (ed) *An Introduction to Applying Social Work Theories and Methods.* Berkshire: Open University Press, 38-53.

Liard SE (2008) Social Work Practice to Support Survival Strategies in Sub-Saharan Africa. *British Journal of Social Work*, 38: 135-151.

Linsk N, Mabeyo Z, Omari L, Petras D, Lubin B, Abate A, Steinitz L, Kaijage T and Mason S (2010) Para-Social Work to Address Most Vulnerable Children in Sub-Sahara Africa: A Case Example in Tanzania. *Children & Youth Services Review*, 32: 990-997.

McLeod E and Bywaters P (1999) *Social Work, Health and Equality.* London: Routledge.

Mukiza-Gapere J and Ntozi JPM (1995) Impact of AIDS on the Family and Mortality in Uganda. *Health Transition Review*, 5: 191-200.

Musinguzi LK (2015) The Role of Social Networks in Savings Groups. Insights from Village Savings and Loans Associations in Luwero, Uganda. *Community Development Journal*, 51(04): 499-516.

Narayan D, Chambers R, Shah MK and Petesch P (2000). *Voices of the Poor: Crying Out for Change*. Oxford: Oxford University Press.

Nzita R, Mbaga-Niwampa and Mukholi D (1993). *Peoples and Cultures of Uganda*. 4th ed. Kampala: Fountain.

Okuonzi SA (2004) Learning from Failed Health Reform in Uganda. *BMJ*, 329, 1173-1175.

Saleebey D (1996) The Strengths Perspective in Social Work Practice: Extensions, and Cautions. *Social Work*, 41(3): 296-305.

Sewpaul V (2014) Social Work and Poverty Reduction in Africa: The Indelible Reality. In: Spitzer H, Twikirize JM and Wairire GG (eds) *Professional Social Work in East Africa: Towards Social Development, Poverty Reduction and Gender Equality*. Kampala: Fountain, 29-42.

Teshome E, Zenebe M, Mataferia H and Biadgilign S (2012) The Role of Self-Help Voluntary Associations for Women Empowerment and Social Capital: The Experience of Women's *Iddirs* (Burial societies) in Ethiopia. *Journal of Community Health*, 37(3): 706-714.

Twikirize JM (2014) Gender Perspectives in Poverty Reduction and Social Development. In: Spitzer H, Twikirize JM and Wairire GG (eds) *Professional Social Work in East Africa: Towards Social Development, Poverty Reduction and Gender Equality*. Kampala: Fountain, 56-74.

Van der Geest S (2006) Between Death and Funeral: Mortuaries and the Exploitation of Liminality in Kwahu, Ghana. *Africa*, 76(4): 485-501.

Whyte SR (2005) Going Home? Belonging and Burial in the Era of AIDS. *Journal of the International African Institute*, 75(2): 154-172.

10

Traditional Fostering in a Post-Conflict Context: The Case of Laroo-Pece Women's Association in Northern Uganda

Ronald Luwangula, Janestic M. Twikirize and Justus Twesigye

Introduction

The prevention of family separation and, in particular, children dropping out of family care is a matter of global concern with local relevance. Paragraph 6 of the Preamble to the United Nations Convention on the Rights of the Child (UNCRC) underscores the need for children to be accorded the right to grow, develop, and receive primary protection within the family setting. The United Nations Guidelines for the Alternative Care of Children (UN Resolution 64/142, 2010) urge countries to 'support efforts to keep children in, or return them to, the care of their family' and where separation is inevitable, 'finding another appropriate and permanent solution, including adoption and *kafalah*[10] of Islamic law'. The Guidelines give primary focus to family care for children, either by their parents or guardians, or when appropriate, other close (non-) family members. Article 8 of the UNCRC entitles children to family relations as a way of preserving children's identity. Article 9 of the UNCRC underlines that only on grounds of necessity, in the best interests of the child, by the competent authorities, and in accordance with applicable law and procedures should a separation of children from their families prevail. The African Charter on the Rights and Welfare of the Child (African Union Commission, 2016) prohibits the unjustified separation of children from parents (Article 19); entitles separated children to maintaining regular contact with parents unless not in their best interest

---

[10] The Islamic *Kafalah* is a form of alternative care where a family takes in an abandoned child, a child whose natural parents or family are incapable of raising him or her, or who is otherwise deprived of a family environment, without the child being entitled to the family name or an automatic right of inheritance from the family. (Assim, 2009, 44)

(Article 19(2)); and urges member states to undertake measures that support and build the capacity of parents (Article 20).

At the national level, the Uganda Constitution recognises the family as the natural and basic unit of society that is entitled to protection by society and the State. It provides for the minimisation of all conditions that may cause separation and outlaws undue separation (Art. 31(2)); Art. 31(5)). Under Article 34(1), children's right to know and be cared for by their parents or legal guardians is enshrined. The Children Act (as amended) 2016 guarantees children the right to live with their parents or guardians (Section 4(1a)), while Sections 5 and 6 give preference to bringing up children in a family environment. Uganda's National Alternative Care Framework (Ministry of Gender, Labour and Social Development, 2012) gives primary priority to keeping the family together and to prevent separation.

Amid emphasis on family care for children and the prevention of family separation by a score of international, regional, and national laws, guidelines, and standards, there is a shared view that for some inevitable reasons, such as conflict, some children find themselves falling through the cracks of less protective families. Chimanikire (2004) highlights orphanhood and separation from their families among the significant impacts of conflict on children, with boys and girls being affected differently. Particularly boys are forced to commit violent acts while girls suffer sexual exploitation. Owing to conflict, the duration of children's separation from their families tends to be lengthy, during which they suffer traumatic experiences. Moreover, as children experience conflict, leading to blurred identities, they find it hard to imagine their role in the post-conflict society (ibid.).

This chapter presents a traditional fostering model adopted by a group of women in Northern Uganda, analysing its potential for building resilience and for contributing to social capital and social development within the broad context of post-conflict situations. The paper draws from data obtained from a broader study conducted in Uganda under the PROSOWO project (*Professional Social Work in East Africa*). The study examined the indigenous and innovative models of social work practice in Uganda. While the study was broadly conducted in three regions of Uganda, namely North (Gulu District), Central (Rakai District) and Western Region (Rukungiri and Mbarara Districts), this chapter focuses on one indigenous social work model, namely the traditional fostering of children by LAPEWA identified in Gulu District. The term LAPEWA refers to a women's association in the two communities, Laroo and Pece (see further below).

The study was qualitative, adopting a practice-based research approach. The methods used included interviews with two LAPEWA leaders, a focus group discussion with LAPEWA members, and three extended case studies with LAPEWA members who, at the time, had foster children in their care. In addition, one in-depth interview with a foster child aged 15 and key informant interviews with two probation officers were held. Audio-recorded data was transcribed verbatim to facilitate capturing the originality of the views shared by the participants of the study and post-coded, guided by emerging patterns and themes. The research objectives and other issues from the emerging data facilitated the generation of themes. Essentially, data was analysed using a thematic analysis method.

Family Separation, Armed Conflict, and the Quest for Alternative Care

Worldwide, millions of children are said to be deprived of family care (Dozier et al., 2012; Walakira et al., 2014; Better Care Network, 2014). These include, among other categories, the orphaned, abandoned, and maltreated children. Walakira et al. (2016) identify children in residential childcare institutions and children in street situations as more visible among children deprived of family care and a protective environment. Globally, childcare institutions accommodate as many as eight million children (Save the Children, 2009; Pinheiro, 2006). Moreover, the Better Care Network (2014) notes that this number might represent an underestimation attributed to gaps in global statistics and the many unregistered children's homes worldwide. Children in street situations, specifically children 'of' the street, constitute a population of children deprived of family care. UNESCO (2017) estimates the number of street children at 150 million globally. Most run to the streets owing to domestic violence, drug and alcohol abuse, the death of a parent, family breakdown, war, natural disaster, and socio-economic collapse. In Uganda, just as at the global level, the statistics on children in childcare institutions is not very exact, but estimates point to between 40,000 and 50,000 children (Riley, 2012; Walakira, Dumba-Nyanzi and Bukenya, 2015), while the number of street children is estimated at 10,000 (UNICEF, 2015; Walakira et al., 2016). The Consortium for Street Children (2016) points out that in Uganda, 44% of street children connect with the streets at the very young age of between five and 10 years. While these two categories of children are deprived of their right to grow up in a nurturing family environment, particularly children living in street situations go without the basic needs. These children justify the need for alternative care.

Children in armed conflict and/or living in contexts recovering from conflict contend with many realities, including eroded family capacities to care for them (Walakira et al., 2016). Some of these children completely drop out of broken families while others fail to trace their families, since they become separated from their parents in situations of war while too young. This was the situation in Northern Uganda during and following the two-decade (1986-2006) civil war.

Formal and Informal Foster Care

Within the alternative care literature, the concept of traditional or informal fostering is uncommon. Literature gives an impression that fostering originated in modern times (see Johnson, 2005). Thus, there is a skewed impression that fostering in its strictest sense is basically a formal alternative care practice. However, situations where community members organise themselves to informally provide family-based care for separated children with whom they share no blood relations, can clearly be identified as informal foster care. Traditionally, child fostering in sub-Saharan Africa was not uncommon (Grant and Yeatman, 2012; Alber, Martin and Notermans, 2013). Though less popular, some literature shows that in traditional times, informal child fostering was widespread before coming under pressure from civil wars in many parts of Africa (Gale, 2008), economic hardships, and changing work patterns. In other instances where informal fostering is referred to, kinship care (children being cared for by people related to them) is implied (Johnson, 2005; Gale, 2008). Gale, in reference to Sierra Leone, contends that for countries recovering from civil war and engulfed by poverty, malnutrition, and limited access to adequate medical care, the community is the best setting for caring for separated children. Gale particularly describes what he calls 'stranger care' – a phenomenon where a child informally finds him or herself in the care of adults or households unknown and strange to him or her. This form of care arrangement is said to be common and useful in post-war settings.

Gale (2008) notes that as families and communities weaken or even collapse due to conflict, the need for child fostering grows. War leaves many children either without primary caregivers or, as they scatter for safety, unable to return home. Their agony is heightened by the fact that some children separated from their parents due to conflict find themselves at a crossroads regarding whether to define themselves as orphans or non-orphans since they are unaware of whether or not their parents still live. This was the case in Northern Uganda. According to Levey et al. (2016), the availability of care from other sources for orphaned children or children separated from their parents serves to ameliorate the loss of a parent (borne by children) and the hardship that comes with it. This is said to have a strong impact on such children's development. Corbin (1997) echoes the need to focus on children and families affected by armed conflict in Africa and underscores the essence of practitioners to understand the effect of their war-affected experiences on social services, health facilities, and educational settings. But for children separated from their parents, access to social services is often only tenable through alternative care.

Whereas young children are often exposed to conditions that rob them of meeting their basic needs for health and development (McElroy et al., 2012), children in conflict and post-conflict situations score even worse. Uganda is among the countries with many children failing to reach their developmental potential (ibid.). The Ministry of Gender, Labour and Social Development (MGLSD), UNICEF and the Economic Policy Research Centre (2015) report that, in Uganda, among all children aged zero to four, 55% live in poverty, of whom 24% (or one in five) live in extreme poverty. Among all children aged six to 17, 38% live in poverty, of whom 18% are in extreme poverty; 15.2% of all school-aged children (aged six to 17 years) never attended school in 2011, 33% of under-five-year-old children are stunted (low height for age), 13.5% are underweight (low weight for age), while 5% are wasted (low weight for height). Although these figures are silent on the disaggregation between: a) children living with their parents or guardians and those separated; and b) children in conflict and post-conflict and those in stable settings, the MGLSD and UNICEF (2014) and UNICEF (2015) both attest to the fact that children in conflict and post-conflict situations as well as separated children contribute highly to these figures.

Essentially, various alternative care options are advanced in the event of family separation, including kinship care, fostering, domestic adoption, intercountry adoption and, as a last resort, institutional care. The UNCRC as well as Uganda's Children Act (as amended) 2016, and the National Alternative Care Framework prioritise kinship care over the various formal alternative care options. However, as society increasingly becomes individualistic and materialistic and as social relations become commodified (Kasente et al., 2002), kinship care is increasingly compromised. Northern Uganda has not been spared from such realities. The conflict that affected the entire region made it difficult for separated children to benefit from both kinship and formal fostering since, more or less, everyone was hard-hit. Moreover, the effects of conflict, including the collapse of nurturing environments, transcend the end of the conflict (McElroy et al., 2012; International Refugee Trust, 2014). Moreover, as Santa Barbara (2006) observes, children are affected by the impact of war in specific terms. Their attachments are frequently disrupted in times of war owing to the loss or emotional unavailability of parents or guardians. In some cases they face total loss of adult protection and become even more vulnerable as 'unaccompanied children', as they are often referred to in refugee situations.

Socio-cultural Context

Gulu District (where data for this chapter was collected) is occupied by the Acholi of Luo ethnicity, said to have migrated from Bahr el Ghazal in South Sudan (The Northern Trumpet, 2017). The Acholi are a socio-political entity composed of chiefdoms headed by the *Rwot* (ruler) and an overall king. Culturally, the chiefdoms are responsible for the social order and social wellbeing of the Acholi people. The chiefs, for instance, mediate between conflicting parties and preside over cultural ceremonies geared towards maintaining harmony and social order, such as *mato oput* – a traditional ceremony that aims at restoring relationships and promoting forgiveness between clans that would have been affected by either an intentional murder or accidental killing (Tom, 2006).

The family takes a central role when it comes to the care for and the protection of children. Traditionally, the concept of orphanhood had little space in Acholi culture. Representing what Lajul (2013) describes as the traditional African philosophy among the Acholi, at any one point in time, a child had a father and mother figure, regardless of whether the child had lost his or her biological parent(s). However, the armed conflict disrupted the social order of the Acholi to the extent that the phenomenon of children without parental care gradually emerged. The phenomenon of night commuters, where children left their families every night to seek safety on the streets, ultimately resulted in increased numbers of street children and their permanent separation from their families (Spitzer and Twikirize, 2014).

The Lord's Resistance Army (LRA) conflict, that spanned two decades, severely undermined the capacity of families to care for their members, and children were the primary victims. More than a decade since the war has 'officially' ended, the Northern Region still grapples with the effects of the conflict, including a very negative score in child vulnerability indicators (Spitzer and Twikirize, 2013; Walakira et al., 2016). According to the MGLSD and UNICEF (2014), child poverty was found to be highest in Northern Uganda among children aged zero to four and six to 17. In the region, younger children were nearly three times more likely to suffer from poverty than children in the Central Region, while older children were twice more likely than their peers in the Central Region to be extremely deprived. The same report noted that Northern Uganda had the highest share of underweight children; children in the region expressed more worry of violence, including household or domestic violence, than in any other region except Karamoja; and 20% of school-age children had never attended school, a higher percentage than in all other regions. UNICEF (2015) remarks that the population of the Northern Region is among the poorest 20% of the country's overall population, with less than one in 10 children of secondary school-age attending school. It is against such a backdrop that Walakira et al. (2016) characterise these children as multi-dimensionally deprived, including cases of family separation, with adverse impacts on children's physical and psychological wellbeing.

Traditional Fostering by Laroo-Pece Women's Association (LAPEWA)

Traditional fostering forms an indispensable indigenous social work model. In the context of Northern Uganda, a less common, yet critical, form of alternative care for children – traditional fostering – is evolving, giving some children the chance to live and develop. In this chapter, we focus on traditional fostering as offered by a group of widows under their umbrella association called Laroo-Pece Women's Association (LAPEWA). Laroo and Pece are two communities in Gulu District in Northern Uganda. Hence, LAPEWA is a grassroots women's organisation. In the aftermath of the armed conflict, these women began taking on unaccompanied children living on the streets. The presentation that follows captures the philosophy underpinning the LAPEWA traditional fostering model, the transitions that the model has undergone, the motivations of the actors involved, the model's gender dimensions, the strengths and challenges integral to the model, and lastly its discussion and conclusion.

Philosophy of the LAPEWA Traditional Fostering Model

LAPEWA started in 1997 as an association of widows in Gulu District. The initial membership was 100 women from Laroo and Pece communities in Gulu who came together with the aim to economically empower themselves through a 'cash round' scheme. In this scheme, members regularly pooled money and gave it to randomly selected members on a rotational basis until all group members had accessed the funds. Over time, LAPEWA members began noticing a number of social problems in their communities which they felt needed attention, yet appeared to be neglected. One of these was the phenomenon of young street children who were being used by older street children and adults to commit crimes, such as breaking into people's houses, shops, and kiosks to loot. Once caught, some of these children faced death perpetrated by their victims and angry mobs. During such times of heightened conflict, there was less social order, and violence was often resorted to as a form of justice against any wrongdoer or perceived criminal. Yet, these children neither had anybody to offer them protection against exposure to such risk nor did they have an opportunity to return to regular family settings. Tension due to conflict was high and families were in disarray.

In 2000, the LAPEWA women rethought their focus to include traditional fostering of children. At the time, many children were victims of orphanhood, family disintegration, destruction of the social fabric, higher HIV rates, gender-based violence, street violence, and lawlessness. According to UNICEF (2011), these factors strongly contribute to children dropping out of family care.

> We resolved to go to the district and explain to the authorities that as women, we are seeing this unfortunate thing happening, we already have an association, and we need to help these suffering children on the streets. (LAPEWA leader)

The process of getting children off the street started out as a crisis response. As children got beaten, LAPEWA women who conducted foot patrols on the streets of Gulu town intervened, rescued the children, and took them to their homes. That was how they started fostering children. The process later evolved from a crisis response to a preventive one. Rather than waiting to rescue and attracting victimised children to their homes, the women developed mechanisms to identify children at risk and to offer them alternative care. For example, they staged drama performances and concerts in the streets of Gulu town and other neighbouring towns, such as Koch-Goma, Anaka, and Nwoya, with the intent to expose the plight of children and encourage these children to leave the streets for family life. Some of the drama themes were HIV and AIDS, the causes and manifestations of domestic and gender-based violence, how children get wasted on the street, and how children get injured when stealing.

Transitions Undergone by the LAPEWA Traditional Fostering Model

Whilst LAPEWA women started fostering children very informally, before long, their contribution received recognition. The concerts staged by LAPEWA members received public exposure. The Gulu District leadership came to know about them and, in due course, recognised the association members' traditional foster care practices. The recognition manifested itself through the linking of the women to the court which, in consultation with local leaders, encouraged and presided over these women's taking an individual Oath of Court that qualified them as persons fit to care for and raise children. The requirements to qualify as a 'fit person' is provided for in Uganda's Principal Children Act (Government of Uganda, 2016). The process of selecting fit persons involves communities identifying fellow community members whom they consider morally upright and trusted to care for children. The LAPEWA women's previously demonstrated moral character and concern for children made it easy for them to be selected by their community members and forwarded to court as suitable candidates for the position of fit persons.

As fit persons, LAPEWA members received children in need of family care from the Child and Family Protection Unit (CFPU) of the police and the probation and social welfare officers, the two primary social work units in charge of child protection in Uganda. For instance, whenever CFPU had to deal with the case of a child offender, such as being involved in stealing, they would refer them to LAPEWA. The court also assigned care responsibilities. Often, though not always, during court sessions, LAPEWA had a roster that defined which of their members were expected to attend court, stand as sureties for the child(ren) and, thus, return with those children for counselling and guidance. Sometimes, by the time of the court sitting, the women had already had the children (having been handed to them by the CFPU or a probation officer), while in other cases, they only got to link up with the child in court. In either case, the women first talked to the children in question and comforted them in preparation for the court session. The court, in the presence of the probation and social welfare officers, then released the children to the fit persons, thus sparing the children from ending up in the remand home, a form of institutional care for children in conflict with the law. Moreover, it is not uncommon to perceive and treat children in remand homes as perpetrators of crime as opposed to victims of child protection failures.

Sources of Motivation

Initially, the motivating force behind the actions of LAPEWA's traditional fostering was implied, that is, it came from the wish to save young children from the undesirable experiences of living on the streets. In addition, taking an Oath of Court propelled the LAPEWA members to keep active and carry on the daunting challenge of traditionally fostering children amid difficult and challenging socio-economic circumstances. As of 2016, 22 LAPEWA members had taken the Oath of Court. The women felt very trusted, appreciated, and recognised, especially in a legal sense. The status, exposure, and nature of responsibility that the title of fit persons accorded them was very motivating. As fit persons, they stood as sureties for children in conflict with the law. Instead of such children being remanded, they were handed to the fit persons to take care of and guide them until the next appointment to appear in court (after 21 days). During that time, the fit person counselled the child, attempted to find out from him or her what exactly had happened, and to see if the child accepted his or her guilt and was remorseful, or whether he or she was actually innocent.

The other sources of motivation were the opportunity to be linked to external support. For instance, between 2007 and 2012, LAPEWA women were linked by the district to external support from Save the Children for the first time. Save the Children offered a cash grant of 105,000 UGX (approximately 29 US$) to the fit persons for the 21 days they took care of the children as they awaited reappearance in court. In case the court acquitted a child, the fit person would take him or her on. This was followed by conducting family tracing alongside an assessment of the child's readiness to be reunited with the family. This involved working with the probation and social welfare officers. The cash grant facilitated transportation during family tracing and resettlement where it happened. If tracing yielded success and both the child and parents were ready to reunite, the child would be resettled; but if tracing proved unsuccessful or the family was unprepared to take in their child, the fit person remained with the child indefinitely.

To better understand the motivating factors, it is necessary to reflect on the fact that until 2007, these women had shouldered the responsibility of childcare for vulnerable children without any financial support. And after being weaned off the support in 2012, LAPEWA members continued to foster children as before. They continued receiving children from the police, from probation and social welfare officers, or from court, and sustained the tracing of the children's families using their own meagre resources, sometimes utilising their VSLA.

Gender Dimensions of the LAPEWA Model

The LAPEWA model was implemented by women, all of whom were widows. These women demonstrated a strong spirit of sacrifice and voluntarism. This seems to have been less appealing to men. However, the association opened its doors to both male and female children. The role of men in the process of traditional fostering basically became important at times when the *mato oput* ritual that preceded the fostering of children who had committed serious offences had to be performed. With time, the LAPEWA members' VSLA group admitted a few men, some of whom occupied leadership positions and offered guidance. At the time of the study, they had not been directly involved in fostering. The gesture of the LAPEWA members fits well in the frame of reference that women perceive and appreciate the childcare roles much better than men (Luwangula, 2015).

Strengths of the LAPEWA Traditional Fostering Model

This model was identified with significant inherent strengths. First, the contributions of LAPEWA members helped to close the gap left by the absence of a reception centre in Gulu District, thus saving children from potential institutionalisation. The LAPEWA model further constitutes a structure for conflict resolution at the community level. The women are a reference point for matters involving children to local leaders and community members. The model illustrates a gesture of sacrifice in modern materialistic and individualistic times. Sacrifice was manifested through regularly committing time to attend court sessions, working without any pay, and offering space to accommodate the office of the association. The foster parents were very much intrinsically motivated. A case in point is that, despite the challenges that the women had been put through by some of the fostered children, taking such forms as stealing their hard-earned income, property, or clothing, the women did not rethink their consideration to offer help. Another key strength is that, unlike formal fostering, this process does not require extensive paperwork and documentation. In formal fostering, a prospective foster parent has to prove his or her suitability to foster a child, go through a rigorous process of assessment by an Alternative Care Panel, and procure a Care Order. Traditional fostering is based on the sanction of the community regarding the prospective foster parent as being fit to take on the child.

Challenges Integral to the Model

Traditional foster parents faced various challenges. Some of the children taken in were unscrupulous even when embraced as members of the family. More often than not, these children had a history of being in conflict with the law, and some did not completely reform. Yet, in practice, the probation officers rarely visited the traditionally fostered children to support the foster parents in reforming the children. Some of the children stole from the foster household and disappeared with their loot. In one case, a foster parent had a cash box in which she kept proceeds from the sale of tap water. A foster child (aged about 13) took off with the entire cash box just two months after she had been taken in. Another challenge was the concealment of identity commonly reported among relatively older children. This made family tracing rather difficult. Some foster parents also experienced false accusations from foster children's biological parents or guardians once they had been traced. After the foster parents had struggled to raise, rehabilitate, and support the children in acquiring vocational skills, their parents or relatives might appear and claim that the foster mothers had abducted their children. However, the formalisation of foster care practices meant that the foster care parents were protected against such false claims. The fact that all the children under their care were known to the authorities meant that the foster parents were at least protected. Therefore, when such claims were made, the foster parents could contact the probation and social welfare officers, who then mediated between the foster parent and the claimants of the fostered child. The claims also set in motion the preparatory process for the reunion of the foster child with his or her parents a) once the claimants had been proven to be the genuine parents or guardians of the child; b) once the child had shown a willingness to be reunited; and c) if the reunion was assessed to be in the child's best interest.

Difficulties related to the costs of daily living also presented another challenge. Since Pece and Laroo are urban suburbs of Gulu town, the cost of living was high, given caregivers' survival in a monetary economy. The women had to use their meagre resources to cater for the fostered children's feeding, medical care, clothing, and other basic necessities. Moreover, in the event of sickness involving hospitalisation, the traditional foster parents forfeited their work to attend to the foster children in the hospital until they were discharged. Difficulties in meeting the foster children's education costs were also a daunting challenge, especially where the foster parents struggled to educate their own biological children. Universal Primary Education (UPE) schools were relatively expensive for the foster care parents. Some of the UPE schools in Gulu charged up to 36,000 UGX (~10 US$) while others levied up to 60,000 UGX per child per school term. The following remark illustrates the challenge:

When your biological children are going to school and you don't have enough money to send the foster child to school, too, the latter painfully remains at home. And you see the foster child miserably looking at the counterpart going to school every morning. The child appears withdrawn. You also feel bad. (LAPEWA member)

As a way of dealing with this challenge, some LAPEWA members approached school administrators and appealed to them to offer educational support to the fostered children. In one of the cases, a member of LAPEWA who was fostering two children whose mother had a mental health problem approached a Religious Sister of Mother Theresa primary school in Gulu, and the children were accepted at that school at no cost.

Discussion and Conclusion

The LAPEWA model was identified to have saved many children from various risks associated with conflict, including the high risk of developing mental health problems, common among children and adolescents exposed to armed conflict (Betancourt et al., 2013). It further saved children from early relationships and marriage, characteristic of vulnerable youths in conflict and post-conflict settings, including in Northern Uganda (Schlecht, Rowley and Babirye, 2013). The LAPEWA model also saved several children from potential institutionalisation in a context where the majority of childcare institutions are profit-oriented to the extent that any welfare improvements are seen as an encroachment on the profit margin. Uganda has witnessed the proliferation of childcare institutions (Walakira, Ddumba-Nyanzi and Bukenya, 2015), on the one hand, as a response to the weakening option of kinship care and, on the other hand, largely motivated by the potential monetary benefits of running such institutions and aiding international adoptions, rather than organising a childcare system based on benevolence. The effects of institutional care are well documented. These include, among others: inappropriate care for children; children falling short of love and affection (Csáky, 2009); developmental damage (ibid., citing Browne, 2009); attachment defects (Ainsworth, 1967; Abela et al., 2012; Bakermans-Kranenburg, Dobrova-Krol and Ijzendoorn, 2011); effects on neurological development, social and behavioural development, and cognitive development of children (Abela et al., 2012). On this note, traditional fostering, argued to be necessary in conflict and post-conflict settings (Gale, 2008), was seen as worthwhile. The traditional foster parents under LAPEWA offered nurturing environments, which is critically important in shaping young children's future health and development.

From a theoretical stance, this traditional fostering model can be interpreted as contributing to the resilience of children as members of the family and community. The support given to the child by the foster family serves as a response to a myriad of stressors and risk factors such as poverty, violence, abuse, and illness that undermine the healthy social functioning of the affected children. As children's exposure to vulnerability is ameliorated through traditional foster care, resilience is built, which, in turn, salvages the children from disposition to behavioural disorder (Ingram and Luxton, 2005). Thus, we infer that when these children benefitting from traditional foster care are rated along the vulnerability-resilience continuum (Ingram and Luxton, 2005), they are more likely to incline towards resilience with minimal possibilities of vulnerability, stress, and psychopathology compared to if they had remained out of family care. The care, support, and protection extended to the foster children in the form of formal mainstream education and vocational training enable them to relatively withstand shock arising from poverty and other risks.

The LAPEWA model further subscribes to the social developmental approach in promoting the welfare of children, their caregivers, and their community. The model attempts to promote the wellbeing of a cross-section of community members while, at the same time, linking them to economic development. According to Midgley (1995), social development is distinctively concerned with linking social and economic development efforts. The LAPEWA model sets in motion a set of strategies linked to economic development that foster the welfare of children, women, and the community. For instance, vocational skills training for fostered children assures the children of both social and economic benefits that transcend the individual children and reach well into the community. In practice, the beneficiary children become economically relevant to themselves, their families, and their community in the long run. At the same time, their status changes from one of a social problem to that of a social and economic asset to the community. Interpreted from the developmental social work perspective, vocational training for fostered children represents a social investment capable of 'enhancing the children's capabilities to participate in community life and the productive economy' (Midgley and Conley, 2010, xiii). Similarly, the VSLA approach to economic wellbeing by LAPEWA members translates into social wellbeing for child caregivers, the children under their care, the neighbourhoods, and the larger community. VSLAs, for instance, foster an enterprise culture among involved members. Such a culture is associated with promoting social change (Midgley 1995, 104). The interventions of LAPEWA thus represent what Midgley (1995, 38) refers to as 'deliberate human action' towards a process of change. The LAPEWA model takes a community-based form of intervention that, as Midgley (1995) argues, is very compatible with social development. Community-based practice interventions are further prioritised under the developmental social work approach as critical in promoting independent living of community members (Midgley and Conley, 2010). Evidence from Uganda attests that children rescued from street situations and supported to acquire vocational and apprenticeship skills are more likely to secure their own independent living and incline towards reduced involvement in crime (Luwangula, 2017). Such interventions become very relevant to social work practice.

Arguing from a social capital theory, the LAPEWA fostering model demonstrates a 'sense of community' as implied by Putnam (2000, cited in Keeley, 2007). The model further represents common facets that underline social capital, such as the resources inherent in social relations which facilitate collective action (Garson, 2006); 'tangible assets [that] count for most in the daily lives of people: namely goodwill, fellowship, sympathy, and social intercourse among the individuals and families who make up a social unit' (Hanifan, 1916, cited in Keeley 2007, 102). Traditional fostering is duly underpinned by social relations among members, trust, norms, common purpose, collective action, goodwill, reciprocity, sympathy, and social intercourse, all of which constitute elements and dimensions of social capital.

It is imperative to note that the relevance of this model transcends the post-conflict settings. The fact that the phenomenon of children dropping out of family care is not only attributable to conflict but also to other factors, such as parental separation, violence against children, orphanhood, child trafficking, and child labour, means that such children in need of alternative care can equally benefit from traditional foster care beyond post-conflict settings in Uganda and Africa. However, some conditions must pertain. First, there ought to be willing community members ready to offer community-based care for children deprived of family-based care. Second, social workers should have lived up to their obligation to popularise community-based care for children in need of alternative care. Third, community caregivers that volunteer to traditionally foster children are appreciated in some way, such as prioritising them in the allocation of government programmes, such as the Youth Livelihood Programme (YLP), Uganda Women Entrepreneurship Programme (UWEP), Operation Wealth Creation, and Northern Uganda Social Action Fund (NUSAF).

As a concluding remark, traditional fostering as an indigenous model of child protection has a clear place in social work practice, particularly as alternative care for children. Literature that presents the fostering of children as formal alternative care implicitly dismisses informal community-based care beyond kinship care for children in need of family care. It is, thus, in order that traditional models, such as LAPEWA, that render a cultural script of fostering underpinned by social distribution of childcare among adults regardless of relations, are popularised. This is because they have the potential to insulate children without family care against suffering. The model is thus relevant on many fronts. First, in the way it helps to protect children deprived of family care; and second, because it connects to the indigenisation discourse of social work, whose emphasis on culturally relevant social work practice and education cannot be overemphasised (cf. Rankopo and Osei-Hwedie, 2010; Gray, Kreitzer and Mupedziswa, 2014).

References

Abela A, Abdilla N, Abela C, Camilleri J, Mercieca D and Mercieca G (2012) *Children in Out of-Home Care in Malta: Key Findings From a Series of Three Studies Commissioned by the Office of the Commissioner for Children.* Available at: http://www.tfal.org.mt/MediaCenter/PDFs/1_COOHC.pdf (accessed 17 June 2014).

African Union Commission (2016) *African Charter on the Rights and Welfare of the Child.* Available at: http://www.achpr.org/instruments/child/ (accessed 13 June 2017).

Ainsworth DSM (1967) *Infancy in Uganda.* Baltimore: Johns Hopkins Press.

Alber E, Martin J and Notermans C (2013) *Child Fostering in West Africa: New Perspectives on Theory and Practices.* Leiden: Brill.

Assim UM (2009) I*n the Best Interest of Children Deprived of a Family Environment: A Focus on Islamic Kafalah as an Alternative Care Option.* LLM Dissertation, University of Pretoria, South Africa. Available at: https://repository.up.ac.za/bitstream/handle/2263/12678/assim.pdf;sequence=1 (accessed 30 July 2018).

Bakermans-Kranenburg JM, Dobrova-Krol N and Ijzendoorn VM (2011) Impact of Institutional Care on Attachment Disorganization and Insecurity of Ukrainian Preschoolers: Protective Effect of the Long Variant of the Serotonin Transporter Gene (5HTT). *International Journal of Behavioral Development.* Doe: 10.1177/0165025411406858.

Betancourt TS, McBain R, Newnham EA and Brennan RT (2013) Trajectories of Internalizing Problems in War-Affected Sierra Leonean Youth: Examining Conflict and Post-Conflict Factors. National Institute of Health. *Child Development* 84(2): 455-470.

Better Care Network (2014) *Children in Institutions: The Global Picture.* Available at: http://bettercarenetwork.org/sites/default/files/1.Global%20Numbers_2_0.pdf (accessed 16 September 2017).

Chimanikire DP (2004) *Plight of Children in Conflict and Post-Conflict Societies: The Case of Africa.* Available at: http://ir.uz.ac.zw/bitstream/handle/10646/7/chimanikire_plight_of_children.pdf;jsessionid=30F7A239AA4F6A4770F0AD1D0663E61D? sequence=1 (accessed 25 June 2017).

Consortium for Street Children (2016) *Street Children. A Global Picture.* Available at: http://streetchildren.org/wp-content/uploads/2016/04/CFSC_Map-2016_FINAL-Low-res_v21.pdf (accessed 16 September 2017).

Corbin J (1997) *Children and Families Affected by Armed Conflicts in Africa: Implications and Strategies for Helping Professionals in the United States.* NASW Press. Available at: https://

www.naswpress.org/publications/children/inside/armed-conflicts-africa-intro.html (accessed 16 July 2017).

Csáky C (2009) *Keeping Children Out of Harmful Institutions. Why We Should Be Investing in Family-Based Care*. Save the Children, London. Available at: http://www.savethechildren. org.uk/sites/default/files/docs/Keeping_Children_Out_of_Harmful_Institutions_Final_20.11.09_1.pdf (accessed 10 April 2014).

Dozier M, Zeanah CH, Wallin AR and Shauffer C (2012) Institutional Care for Young Children: Review of Literature and Policy Implications. *Social Issues and Policy Review*. 6(1): 1-25.

Gale LA (2008) *Beyond men pikin: Improving Understanding of Post-Conflict Child Fostering in Sierra Leone*. Feinstein International Center Briefing Paper. Available at: http://fic. tufts.edu/assets/Gale-Beyond-men-pikin-improving-understanding-of-post-conflict-child-fostering-in-Sierra-Leone.pdf (accessed 12 June 2017).

Garson GD (2006) *Social Capital Theory*. Available at: https://www.hks.harvard.edu/ saguaro/web%20docs/GarsonSK06syllabus.htmhttps://www.hks.harvard.edu/ saguaro/web%20docs/GarsonSK06syllabus.htm (accessed 21 May 2017).

Grant MJ and Yeatman S (2012) The Relationship Between Orphanhood and Child Fostering in Sub-Saharan Africa, 1990s-2000s. National Institute of Health. *Population Studies* (Camb), 66(3): 279-295. doi:10.1080/00324728.2012.681682.

Gray M, Kreitzer L and Mupedziswa R (2014) The Enduring Relevance of Indigenisation in African Social Work: A Critical Reflection on ASWEA's Legacy. *Ethics and Social Welfare*, 8(2): 101-116.

Government of Uganda (2016) *Uganda Children Act* (as amended 2016). Kampala.

Ingram ER and Luxton DD (2005) Vulnerability-Stress Models. In: LH Benjamin and J Abela (eds) *Development of Psychopathology: A Vulnerability-Stress Perspective*. New York: Sage, 32-46.

International Refugee Trust (2014) Decades on, Uganda is Still Feeling the Effects of the LRA Conflict. Available at: https://www.irt.org.uk/2016/10/18/decades-uganda-still-feeling-effects-lra-conflict/ (accessed 21 July 2017).

Johnson H (2005) Literature Review on Foster Care. Mkombozi. Available at: https:// www.crin.org/en/docs/literature%20review%20of%20foster%20care.pdf (accessed 13 June 2017).

Kasente D, Asingwire N, Banugire F and Kyomuhendo S (2002) Social Security Systems in Uganda. *Journal of Social Development in Africa*, 17(2): 157-183.

Keeley B (2007) Human Capital: How What You Know Shapes Your Life. *OECD Insights*. Available at: https://www.oecd.org/insights/37966934.pdf (accessed 30 May 2017).

Lajul W (2013) *African Philosophy: Critical Dimensions*. Kampala: Fountain.

Levey EJ, Oppenheim CE, Lange BCL, Plasky NS, Harris BL, Lekpeh GG, Kekulah I, Henderson DC and Borba CPC (2016) A Qualitative Analysis of Parental Loss and Family Separation Among Youth in Post-Conflict Liberia. *Vulnerable Children and Youth Studies*, 12(1): 1-16.

Luwangula R (2017) Preparing Older Street Children for Successful Transition to Productive Adult Life: The Need to Prioritize Tailor-Made Skills Training Program in Uganda. In: Mafigiri DK and Walakira EJ (eds) *Child Abuse and Neglect in Uganda*. Cham: Springer, 311-334.

Luwangula R (2015) *Towards Rewriting Children's Bondage in Poverty and Vulnerability: Underscoring the Fundamentals to Realizing Children's Social Protection Rights in Uganda*. PhD Dissertation, Alpen-Adria-University, Klagenfurt.

McElroy TAM, Atim S, Larson CP and Armstrong RW (2012) Risks to Early Childhood Health and Development in the Post-conflict Transition of Northern Uganda. *International Journal of Pediatrics*. doi:10.1155/2012/820290.

Midgley J (1995) *Social Development: The Developmental Perspective in Social Welfare*. London: Sage.

Midgley J and Conley A (2010) (eds) *Social Work and Social Development: Theories and Skills for Developmental Social Work*. New York: Oxford University Press.

Ministry of Gender, Labour and Social Development (MGLSD) (2012) *Uganda's National Alternative Care Framework*. Available at: http://www.alternative-care-uganda.org/alternative-care-framework.html (accessed 20 October 2015).

Ministry of Gender, Labour and Social Development (MGLSD) and UNICEF (2014) *Situation Analysis of Child Poverty and Deprivation in Uganda*. Available at: https://www.unicef.org/uganda/CPR_Summary final.2014(1).pdf (accessed 25 June 2016).

Ministry of Gender, Labour and Social Development, UNICEF and Economic Policy Research Centre (2015). *Situation Analysis of Child Poverty and Deprivation in Uganda*. Available at: https://www.unicef.org/uganda/CPR_-_statistical_analysis(1).pdf (accessed 25 July 2016).

Pinheiro P (2006) *World Report on Violence Against Children. Secretary-General's Study on Violence against Children*. New York: United Nations. Available at: https://www.unicef.org/lac/full_tex(3).pdf (accessed 17 July 2017).

Rankopo M and Osei-Hwedie K (2010) Globalisation and Culturally Relevant Social Work: African Perspectives on Indigenization. *International Social Work*, 54(1): 137-141.

Riley M (2012) *The State of Institutional Care in Uganda: Baseline Study*. Ministry of Gender, Labour and Social Development. Available at: http://www.alternative-care-uganda.org/resources/moglsd-baseline-study-institutional-care-in-uganda-june-2012.pdf (accessed 23 April 2016).

Santa Barbara J (2006) Impact of War on Children and Imperative to End War. *Croatian Medical Journal*, 47: 891-4. Available at: https://www.ncbi.nlm.nih.gov/pmc/articles/ PMC2080482/pdf/CroatMedJ_47_0891.pdf (accessed 30 July 2018).

Save the Children (2009) *Keeping Children Out of Harmful Institutions: Why We Should Be Investing in Family-Based Care.* London: Save the Children. Available at: https://resourcecentre. savethechildren.net/node/1398/pdf/1398.pdf (accessed 25 January 2015).

Schlecht J, Rowley E and Babirye J (2013) Early Relationships and Marriage in Conflict and Post-Conflict Settings: Vulnerability of Youth in Uganda. *Reproductive Health Matters*, 2(41): 234-242.

Spitzer H and Twikirize JM (2013) War-affected Children in Northern Uganda. No Easy Path to Normality. *International Social Work*, 56(1): 67-79.

Spitzer H and Twikirize JM (2014) Armed Conflict and Political Violence in Africa's Great Lakes Region: Challenges for Social Work Education and Practice. In: Spitzer H, Twikirize JM and Wairire GG (eds) *Professional Social Work in East Africa: Towards Social Development, Poverty Reduction and Gender Equality.* Kampala: Fountain, 351-370.

The Northern Trumpet (2017) *HISTORY: Acholi People and Their Culture.* Available at: http://tnt.co.ug/2017/07/02/history-acholi-people-and-their-culture/ (accessed 07 November 2017).

Tom, P (2006) The Acholi Traditional Approach to Justice and the War in Northern Uganda. https://www.beyondintractability.org/casestudy/tom-acholi (accessed 30 July 2018).

UNESCO (2017) *Street Children.* Available at: http://www.unesco.org/new/en/social- and-human-sciences/themes/fight-against-discrimination/education-of-children-in- need/street-children/ (accessed 16 September 2017).

UNICEF (2010) *Developing Alternatives to Institutional Care in Montenegro.* Available at: http:// www.unicef.org/montenegro/media_14535.html (accessed 09 September 2014).

UNICEF (2011) *The State of the World's Children.* Available at: http://www.unicef.org/ adolescence/files/SOWC_2011_Main_Report_EN_02242011.pdf (accessed 23 August 2014).

UNICEF (2015) *Situational Analysis of Children in Uganda.* Available at: https://www.unicef. org/uganda/UNICEF_SitAn_7_2015_(Full_report).pdf (accessed 23 March 2017).

United Nations (1989) *Convention on the Rights of the Child.* United Nations.

United Nations (2010) Resolution 64/142. Guidelines for the Alternative Care of Children. Available at: http://www.cpcnetwork.org/wp-content/uploads/2014/04/ UN-Guidelines-for-Alternative-Care..pdf (accessed 28 November 2014).

Walakira EJ, Ochen EA, Bukuluki P and Allan S (2014) Residential Care for Abandoned Children and their Integration into a Family-Based Setting in Uganda: Lessons for Policy and Programming. *Infant Mental Health Journal*, 1-7. DOI: 10.1002/imhj.21432.

Walakira EJ, Dumba-Nyanzi I and Bukenya B (2015). *Child Care Institutions in Selected Districts in Uganda and the Situation of Children in Care: A Baseline Survey Report for the Strong Beginnings Project. Kampala: Terres des Hommes Netherlands.* Available at: http://www.alternative-care-uganda.org/resources/baseline-survey-report.pdf (accessed 22 September 2016).

Walakira EJ, Muhangi D, Munyuwiny S, Matovu F, Awich E, Ddumba Nyanzi I, Kayiwa J, Akellot J, Mubiri P, Majugo J, Mutebi A and Ruiz-Rodriguez M (2016) *The State of the Ugandan Child – An Analytical Overview.* Kampala/Washington DC: USAID/QED. Available at: http://pdf.usaid.gov/pdf_docs/PA00M978.pdf (accessed 02 May 2017).

Rural Older Women's Survival in Uganda: Implications for Social Work with Older People

Sharlotte Tusasiirwe

Introduction

Despite the demographic and socio-structural changes in East African countries (EACs), social work with older people still remains a neglected field in social work practice, training, and research. Voices of older women remain marginalised in discourses on ageing and in feminist literature. Utilising a qualitative approach, life story interviews were conducted with 10 older women in South-western Uganda, to explore their subjective ageing experiences. This chapter presents these older women's stories of their personal suffering and survival despite the cumulative disadvantages experienced owing to their age, gender, socio-economic status, and living in rural communities. As the interviews show, these older women were not passive victims, as they talked of how they devised collective initiatives to ensure their survival, like engaging in cultivation, and by forming older women's support groups. This chapter argues that social workers working with older people need to listen to their voices to challenge the intergenerational structural disadvantages older women are experiencing and to inform the development of strengths-based interventions. The chapter begins with a discussion of the demographic trends and the socio-economic situation of older people in EACs before presenting the empirical findings on rural older women's survival and the implications for social work practice.

Demographic Trends in East African Countries

Current demographic trends in EACs indicate a growing and ageing population (UNPD, 2017). Although the proportion of older people aged 60+ years in EACs is still low (average 4.2%) compared to the younger population (average 43.6%)

(UNPD, 2017), this proportion is projected to double to 8.3% in 2050, coupled with a growth in absolute numbers of older people from over seven million in 2015 to over 30 million in 2050 (UNPD, 2015). As for Rwanda, the proportion of older people is projected to grow fivefold from 4.5% to 12% of the 21.2 million total population in 2050 (Spitzer and Mabeyo, 2017). In Uganda, the recent Uganda Bureau of Statistics (UBOS) report indicates today's proportion of older people to be already 5% (1.7 million) of the total population, which has more than tripled the 559,000 number of older people in 1969 (UBOS, 2017). Although statistics must be treated with caution, such an unprecedented demographic projection of a growing number of older people presents a challenge for both policy and practice, particularly to stakeholders working with older people, including social workers.

The increase in the ageing population is said to be accompanied by increasing longevity, given the expected rise in life expectancy in EACs. Populations are projected to live longer, past 70 years by 2050, with the exception of Burundi whose life expectancy at birth will be 67.4 in 2050 (UNPD, 2017). The increase in the number and the longevity of older people will occur despite mortality due to HIV/ AIDS. While the longevity of the population is a celebration for social development, it is also a concern because of its implications for support systems, given that there are higher chances that the very old may be in need of support and care. This is even of greater concern when these demographic changes are analysed in the context of the current socio-economic challenges and opportunities.

The Socio-Economic Situation of Older People

The majority of older people in EACs grapple with deepening poverty and increasing vulnerability, poor health and limited access to health facilities (Spitzer, Rwegoshora and Mabeyo, 2009; HelpAge International [HAI], 2008). Most of the older people have not benefitted from economic growth and development (HAI, 2008). In Uganda, income poverty is increasing (UBOS, 2017) and so is multi-dimensional poverty measured in terms of the Human Development Index (0.493) (UNDP, 2016). Older people (60+) are among the poorest in the country. The majority of older people live in rural areas where poverty is rife and where there are fewer services (UBOS, 2017). They rely on subsistence agriculture (83.4% of older persons), where they face price fluctuations, unpredictable weather, and irregular income. Half of the older people have never been to school and these are predominantly older women (UBOS, 2017). Poverty among older people is a concern, given its intergenerational implications beyond the older people themselves. It is likely to be passed on to children and grandchildren in instances where there are no assets to inherit from older parents and where poverty prevents children from accessing critical services such as education (HAI, 2008).

Older people in EACs are ageing without adequate social protection, both formal and informal (Spitzer and Mabeyo, 2011). Formal state-regulated forms of social protection cover a very small section of older people (Barya, 2011), given the linkage between education, formal employment, and benefitting from formal social protection (Spitzer, Rwegoshora and Mabeyo, 2009). Informal support, the customary family support which most of the older people continue to rely on, is also currently under stress (Aboderin, 2004). For example, older people in Tanzania receive small, unreliable, and unbalanced material and financial support from their children and community members (Spitzer and Mabeyo, 2011). Factors that have impacted the ability of the family to sustain support for older people include poverty and material constraints, as well as modernisation (Aboderin, 2004). Also, HIV/AIDS has increased the number of orphaned children and doubled the care burden for older people, especially for grandmothers (HAI, 2004; Schatz and Seeley, 2015).

Adopting a gender perspective on ageing in EACs indicates the feminisation of not only ageing, but also old age poverty and care work. Older women live longer than men and are likely to experience poverty and discrimination in access to services (HAI, 2008). Older women are more vulnerable if they are widowed, childless, and in declining health (Beales, 2000). Inequalities also exist in roles and responsibilities, where older women continue to predominantly carry out unpaid and unrecognised care for the children and other sick people (Schatz and Seeley, 2015). Also, older women dominate subsistence farming.

Despite older people's agricultural productivity and their intergenerational familial roles, a negative paradigm towards older people predominates in society, where stereotypes overshadow older people's resourcefulness. There is a persistent belief in the 'old age dependency ratio' where older people are portrayed as overly dependent, frail, and weak, yet, contrary to this view, the majority of older people have made and continue to make major contributions and most remain economically active (Aboderin, 2012). Nevertheless, older people are 'invisible' and are often excluded from development programmes (HAI, 2008). The political commitments made by governments in terms of policies and programmes for older people remain largely on paper, as governments struggle to ensure their implementation (Spitzer and Mabeyo, 2011).

Policy Interventions

Most East African countries have illustrated their full commitment to advance the wellbeing of older people through being signatories to key pan-African frameworks on ageing such as the African Union's Policy Framework and the Plan of Action on Ageing (Spitzer and Mabeyo, 2011). In these frameworks, governments are urged to incorporate issues of ageing and the needs of older people into national policies and programmes. Consequently, most EACs have put in place policies concerning older people, with Tanzania pioneering with its National Ageing Policy that promotes health care, participation, and income security for older people (Spitzer and Mabeyo, 2011). In Uganda, the Social Assistance Grant for Empowerment (SAGE), which is a direct income support scheme for older people focused on the individual, is being implemented where 25,000 UGX (7.5 US$) per month is given to selected older people in a district (Ministry of Gender, Labour and Social Development [MGLSD], 2016). Despite the benefits to individual older people who have been able to use this money to access health care, support education for their grandchildren, and to start income-generating activities, the scheme is constrained by its non-universal nature as it targets only the first 100 oldest individuals in a sub-county, and it is yet to cover all the districts of Uganda. It is projected to cover 40 out of the 112 districts by 2020.

Older people in local communities are still a neglected group, with only limited targeted interventions to address their needs. Social work interventions for older people are meagre in EACs, with gerontological social work remaining a neglected field of practice (Mali, 2016; Twikirize et al., 2014).

Social Work with Older People in East Africa

Despite the commitment of social workers to work with vulnerable groups to identify and ultimately challenge the causes of their disadvantage, social work with older people in EACs remains a marginalised field in both social work education and practice. In their study, Twikirize et al. (2014) found that, on average, only 1% of social work interventions in EACs target older people. This inattention to social work practice with older people is reinforced by a lack of adequate training and education in the field. Although social work educators train generalist social workers (ibid.), current social work training, practice, and research mostly target the children or men and women of reproductive age. The majority of social work students graduate without the necessary knowledge and skills vital for working with older people (Spitzer and Mabeyo, 2017).

Research on issues of ageing in EACs is still in its infancy (Aboderin, 2012; HAI, 2008). The voices of older people themselves remain hidden and their stories unheard (Spitzer and Mabeyo, 2011). Particularly, the voices of older women have been persistently marginalised within discourses on ageing and feminist literature (Hooyman et al., 2002). There is urgent need to make older women's subjective experiences more visible, with a focus on multiple aspects of diversity beyond just age and gender, to broaden our understanding of ageing (Hooyman et al., 2002).

In Uganda, older women of 50+ years of age are specifically excluded, for example, from national studies like the Uganda Demographic and Health Survey, which includes only women of reproductive age (15-49). The experiences of older women regarding what it is like to age in Uganda are not sufficiently documented.

This is the research gap the current study intends to respond to through exploring the lived experiences of women ageing in Uganda and their implications for social work practice. The study is aimed at privileging the voices of rural older women and their stories.

Setting and Methods

The study explores the subjective experiences of older women ageing in a rural community in Uganda. Participants were 10 older women aged 50+. While by legal definition in Uganda, an older woman is one aged 60 years and above, I adopted the age of 50+ for this study to highlight the social contexts and to take into account rural definitions of what constitutes an 'older woman', since official and legal definitions of this term hardly capture the realities of everyday life.

These older women were residents of Nyakabungo B village in Bwambara Sub-County, Rukungiri District, Western Uganda. Bwambara is a hard-to-reach area because of its geographical location, which impacts on its accessibility. It is located approximately 404 km from Kampala city and situated in Queen Elizabeth National Park. My research aimed to give an opportunity to older women from such a hard-to-reach area to have their stories told.

I conducted life story interviews with 10 older women (Atkinson, 2002). A combination of purposive and snowball sampling was used in the recruitment of these women. The interviews were conducted by the author in the local language, Runyankore. Open-ended questions, such as 'Please tell me about your life…' were asked to allow for free expression by the older women. Interviews were audio-recorded after verbal consent. Each interview lasted between one and two hours. The interviews were later transcribed into English.

After transcription, I read through the women's stories and conducted a preliminary analysis and summary of the themes from the data. I presented these preliminary findings to the women in a focus group discussion (FGD). The intention was to give the women an opportunity to hear and discuss the themes from the preliminary analysis of their life stories. The FGD was productive as it yielded a more nuanced discussion on the themes, with the women sharing more of their ageing experiences as a group. In order to manage and analyse the data for emerging themes, the computer software NVIVO 10 was used.

The study was conducted as part of a PhD project at Western Sydney University (WSU), Australia. Ethical approval was attained from WSU (H11927), the Makerere University School of Social Sciences (03.17.028), and the Uganda National Council of Science and Technology (SS4316). In this chapter, I present a portion of the overall analysis from the life stories of these older women. I discuss two key themes: the women's cumulative disadvantages and their struggle for survival. These themes, unfolding from insights from the women's life stories, are discussed in the light of existing literature. To ensure confidentiality, pseudonyms are used for the participants' names.

Findings and Discussion

The key outcome of this study was that older women are not passive victims but have spent a lifetime braving adversities and struggling to survive. The 10 older women told poignant stories of their suffering as a result of cumulative disadvantages across their lifespan (cf. Dannefer, 2003). In order to counter these disadvantages, they developed survival strategies, such as persistently engaging in the cultivation of food crops and forming cooperative, community-based support groups to help each other. This section will elaborate on the cumulative disadvantages faced by these women and then discuss their struggles for survival. Subsequently, the implications for social work practice are discussed.

Cumulative Disadvantages Characterising Older Women's Experiences

The older women in this study told stories of suffering due to a variety of cumulative disadvantages they had experienced across their lifespan, as girls and now as older women living in a poor rural context. They talked of gender-based discrimination in terms of the denial of opportunity to attain formal education, the exposure to early marriage, and a lifetime of engagement in the invisible care work and crop cultivation for home consumption. As a result of poverty, the older women were then also unable to educate their children, and thus were forced to subject them, particularly their daughters, to an intergenerational cycle of early marriage and subsistence farming.

The women in this study were aged between 50 and 80 years. They had little or no education at all. Most got married at a young age. They had to grapple with many hardships in their lives, particularly with poverty. They spent their lives working hard to survive. Most had been widowed. Of the two women who were still married, one was caring for her sick, disabled husband. All the women had children and grandchildren living with them, except one woman who had lost all her 11 children to unknown illnesses. The most pressing disadvantages the women talked of are elaborated below.

Lack of formal education

The women were denied the opportunity to attain a formal education. None of the 10 women in this study had completed the primary level of formal education. Seven had never set foot in a school at all. The reasons why they did not go to school were mainly that their parents were unable to afford school fees and were not interested in educating their female children. Sixty-two-year-old Prisca spent her childhood caring for her family:

> I am the first born and, you know, how they would belittle us, the first-born children. I was told to grow food for the rest of the family, cook food for them so that, as they came from school for lunch, they would find the food ready. (Prisca, 62)

Praise (80), on the other hand, said:

> I did not go to school because, in those days, they would say that girls should not go to school, they would get pregnant.

These older women's stories of denial of education are not unique, given that rural older women comprise more than half of the population of older people who have never been to school (UBOS, 2017). Since there is a strong correlation between education, formal employment, and social security in old age (Spitzer and Mabeyo, 2011), the failure to attain education by these older women means exclusion from the pension system, which leads to old age poverty and deprivation.

Child marriage

In line with the evidence that shows that girls from the poorest households and with no education at all are highly vulnerable to early marriage and teenage pregnancies (Republic of Uganda, 2015), the women in this study talked of their marriages at a young age. Prisca was 14 at the point of marriage, three women were 15, one was 16, two were 18, and the others 20. Their stories are cases of child marriage, which also represent an overwhelming majority of women's experiences in rural Uganda (UBOS, 2011). These women's experiences demonstrate the role played by poverty and economic disadvantage as both a means and a consequence of the early marriages in contemporary Uganda.

Intergenerational impact

The women in this study expressed concerns regarding their failure to afford education for their own children and the impact this has had on them. None of these older women's children had completed their secondary education. Consequently, the children had to go through related experiences of early marriage, large families, and dependence on subsistence agriculture for survival.

Prisca gave birth to 13 children, of whom three have died. Nine of her children could not complete primary education because of the lack of funding for school fees. Prisca tried to educate her last-born son, who went on to secondary level but also dropped out. Eight of her sons and one daughter are all married now. Prisca has 27 grandchildren. Prisca's children, too, depend on crop cultivation for survival and are only able to provide limited support, as she observed:

> Long ago they used to say that 'when a rabbit grows old, it sucks the breasts of its children'; but now for us they say that if you grow old, you better die. Your child is looking after his family, he wants to pay school fees for his six children, he has to look after his wife. Then how will he start looking after you, old woman? (Prisca, 62)

All the older women talked of how they received only limited support from their children. They blamed this mainly on the poverty experienced by their children, exacerbated by the large family responsibilities:

> Those [children] who live in the community, who can give you food? Their family burdens are enough for them, they are also poor, depending on digging. You even find some coming to their mothers asking for something to feed their families. So those whom we live with, surely, are in the same pain like us.

> Surely, those [children] we live with cannot help us most of the time because they are also so poor. (Older women, FGD)

The older women's children are prioritising their immediate families. Their parents are supported last, and when resources allow. The older women talked of how they could not be certain about the support from their children. This is parallel to findings of a study in Tanzania which showed declining support to older people from their children because of the general poverty situation (Spitzer and Mabeyo, 2011).

A lifetime of care work for children and grandchildren

Although most of the older women's biological children have grown and formed their independent families, the older women still live with and care for some of their children and grandchildren:

> Currently, the ones I am caring for are seven children. One of them is my daughter who has had a misunderstanding in her marriage. She is here with me and she has one child, though I have been living with that child. And I also have one grandchild, a child of my son who married the first woman, and she eloped, and I remained with that child from the time it was nine months old. (Treasure, 55)

Eight of the 10 older women were caring for at least two grandchildren. Seven were still caring for at least one of their biological children. Caring in this case involves meeting all the daily needs of life, including paying for school fees and other school-related materials, like uniforms for children attending school, providing food, shelter, and health care. While some of the grandchildren cared for by the older women had been orphaned by HIV/AIDS, the majority were not. These non-orphaned children belonged to the older women's adult children, especially their daughters who had conceived out of wedlock. When their daughters officially got married, they could not go to their husbands with these children because it is culturally inappropriate for a newly married woman to come with illegitimate children. These children are left behind under the care of the grandmothers. While attention has been drawn to older women's caring role to orphaned children due to HIV/AIDS (HAI, 2004), their care for non-orphaned children born out of wedlock is also an issue that needs urgent attention, especially in rural areas which have higher rates of teenage pregnancies and child motherhood (UBOS, 2011).

All in all, although older women's care work is ongoing, it is 'work' that is devalued, unpaid, and thus remains invisible, to the disadvantage of these older women. Care work done by these older women, and by the majority of other women, is not 'counted' as productive work. Yet, when it is provided by a paid care worker in, for example, an orphanage or an institutional nursing home, it is valued as work (Waring, 1997). Because of their engagement in unpaid work, older women are not entitled to any pension to sustain them in old age. As a result, the older women continue to struggle to survive, mainly through subsistence crop cultivation.

Cultivation 'against all odds'

Older women depend on the cultivation of different food crops for their survival. They engage in cultivation with skills and knowledge they have accumulated over a lifetime:

> I did not go to school. I grew up using my inherited knowledge only, the knowledge from parents. You know if you have a parent they tell you do this, do that, so I grew up in a family where they were doing only cultivation. (Prisca, 62)

Given their lack of formal education, crop cultivation is the older women's major survival alternative:

> It is digging, and when I get where I can dig and get paid, I go there and dig. For me, I could not continue with school after my father had died. Two months after he had enrolled me in school, he died and that is where I stopped. My mother refused to take me back to school so I resorted to digging and growing crops. (Rhonah, age unknown)

Older women grow crops, like beans, cassava, rice, and millet, which are their source of food and money to cater for their basic needs. They sometimes sell some of these crops and buy animals, like goats. These animals are assets that are sold to raise money to meet an emergent need, such as in cases of unexpected illnesses. Some of the older women also dig for money in other people's gardens. A whole day of digging attracts a pay of 5,000 UGX (around 1.5 US$).

Older Women's Struggle to Survive

Despite these benefits from crop cultivation, the women are facing challenges that make their survival a constant struggle. For instance, given their location in the national park, the food they cultivate is sometimes destroyed by wild animals.

Although they reported to the Uganda Wildlife Authority, they have not been compensated for their crops. The women have had to devise ways of guarding their crops from the wild animals. Three of the women have abandoned their main houses to live in small makeshift dwellings that they constructed in the gardens where they spend the nights chasing away the wild animals:

> When they come at night, we flash torchlight into their eyes, we shout at them and they go away. (Prisca, 62)

Although they have managed the wild animals, at the time of this study, they had faced severe drought for two consecutive seasons, which had dried all their food crops. As a result, the risk of starvation was the older women's most pressing concern:

> The dry season has been long, and it has made us lack food. You stay without lunch and sleep hungry, and for us older women, we are almost dying. (Janice, age unknown)

The lack of food had made caring for the grandchildren very difficult for the older women:

> Surely, we couldn't be finding it [care] a challenge because when you have food inside your house, when a child comes and eats, say, the sweet potatoes, and in the evening, you prepare cassava for them, that makes the end of the day. (Older woman, FGD)

Also, the labour-intensive cultivation has had a negative impact on the women's health, as it has been a cause of illnesses some older women are grappling with.

> You see, at this age, if I did not have children to take care of I would not be digging. It disturbs me a lot. Two times I have been attacked by a strong illness, a very strong illness that I even reached the extent of being admitted to Nyakibale Hospital. It was a very strong illness, and my vessels were getting blocked, and when I went to [Doctor] Rutahigwa's [clinic] they said 'This old woman is very sick because she does work a lot.' (Prisca, 62)

Despite these challenges, older women have found limited pathways out of subsistence cultivation. Against all odds, such as the severe weather, wild animals, and their poor health, they have persisted in cultivating food crops. This finding is parallel to findings in Tanzania where older people, even beyond 80 years, were involved in some agricultural activities and crop cultivation to cope with their different hardships and to earn a living amidst missing social protection mechanisms (Spitzer, Rwegoshora and Mabeyo, 2009). This economic activity of older women contradicts the persistent concepts of old age dependency ratios and the exclusion of older people from programmes on the basis that they are of a certain age and, therefore, economically inactive (Aboderin, 2012; HAI, 2008). Older women have also devised collective means of surviving through support groups.

Support groups: Older women as community leaders and mobilisers

Amidst growing impoverishment and exclusion from existing formal social protection mechanisms, older women have formed multipurpose community-based support groups to help them in their struggle for survival. All the 10 older women of this study were at least in one or more support groups, formed by the women themselves. They come together to support each other materially and emotionally, motivated by the proverb that '*Agaari hamwe nigo gaata iguufa*', which literally means 'concerted efforts break a bone'. The groups are based on the principle of collective solidarity. When faced with a need or problem, the women mobilised and organised themselves into groups to find local solutions. Thus, they have formed rotational digging groups where they support each other in crop cultivation. They have savings and credit groups where members access credit that they use to cover different emergencies, for instance buying food in times of crop failure or even investing in animals, such as goats.

For example, Prisca leads a digging group of 11 older women who cultivate for each other, particularly in the evenings. This group has helped older women to have extensive gardens with less hard work.

> I have benefitted from it [group]. You see, where those beans are it is two and a half acres. With my little energy, would I weed that whole garden and finish it? It would not be possible! But when I invited them [the group], in just two days we had finished the weeding. (Prisca, 62)

This digging group is multipurpose as it also has a savings component where the older women save 2,000 UGX per month (less than one US$). They use this money to buy household items, such as plates or plastic chairs for each member, on a rotational basis. They also contribute to buying meat during festive seasons like Christmas and Easter.

Fifty-five-year-old Treasure has also mobilised 30 older women who are grandmothers. They have formed a *bamukaaka/bamukadde* (grandmothers') group where they save 1,000 UGX per month. This is a savings and credit group (*biika oguze*). The women borrow this money to meet their diverse needs, such as paying for school fees and medical care.

> The group has helped me in that I am able to borrow money and buy medicine, and when I get it, I take it back. (Hellen, 74)

Despite the survival benefits accrued from the support groups, they largely benefit older women who are strong and are able to reciprocate. Older women spoke of how they are struggling to raise the money to save and maintain those groups, given the fact that they are engaged in less paid work and have caring responsibilities. Thus, the groups suffer from having a small financial base. The money saved by members is too little to help them materialise their innovative ideas in order to run income-generating activities that would take them out of poverty.

> We [the group] had planned that when we save and the money accumulates we buy goats, but this lack of food has not allowed the money to accumulate. (Kengiga, 55)

The older women were determined to start an income-generating activity of keeping goats. They even sought external support from the government. However, a government official told them that their age disqualifies them from benefitting from the current initiative, the Uganda Women's Entrepreneurship Programme.

> We were told at the sub-county headquarters that as older women at the age of 60 or 70 years and above that we could not manage such a group. (Nyanjura, 70+)

Similar experiences of exclusion by older women have been documented by HAI (2008), where older people are excluded from poverty reduction programmes despite the fact that they are among the poorest and have innovative ideas for income-generating projects. These local collective initiatives by older women remain unrecognised and unsupported by the social and community workers who design policies and programmes. Such initiatives could be supported as indigenous community-based alternatives.

Implications for Social Work Practice

The findings from this study clearly show the cumulative disadvantages older women are experiencing across their lifespan. These older women were denied their right to education which would have guaranteed them formal employment. This disadvantage exposed them to early marriage and dependence on subsistence cultivation to survive. Consequently, the older women failed to afford formal education for their own children, given their lack of engagement in a paid activity. This has had an intergenerational effect on the children as they, too, are constrained by poverty. This means that children are unable to provide the much-needed support to these older women. As this study has shown, older women continue to engage persistently in the cultivation of food crops for home consumption as the main source of their survival. This is amidst the challenges of bad weather and poor health. Additionally, they have mobilised themselves to form support groups, which have also been instrumental in their survival. However, older women continue to be constrained by the economic disadvantage and also through age-based exclusion from government programmes based on stereotypes that the older women are too old to engage in projects.

These findings have implications for social work practice. The findings give insights into not only the adversities older women are experiencing but also their resilience and attempts to find local solutions for their survival. Older women's skills and knowledge, their persistence and determination to cultivate, their support groups, are resources that social workers working with older women can tap into to inform the development of strengths-based interventions.

Social workers need to adopt a critical perspective in their practice where the legitimate voices of older people are heard (Ife, 1997). Social workers should explore ways to bring from the margins and strengthen rural older women's local groups and initiatives that are helping them survive. Social workers can also work with these groups in political activism and advocacy to address the needs of older people and to challenge the stereotypes that the majority of older people are inactive dependants. The voices of older women regarding their desire to engage in income-generating activities should be listened to and supported. In this case, social workers need to ensure that older people are included in poverty eradication and development programmes. The older women's support groups are at the frontline of poverty alleviation in their communities. Therefore, any efforts towards fighting poverty should target and strengthen these neglected community groups. Social workers need to challenge structural and gender-based discrimination and exclusion that girls and older women are experiencing to address this cumulative disadvantage. In summary, this chapter calls for social work interventions at micro and macro levels.

Given the demographic and socio-structural changes, all social workers will most likely work with older people and their families in the future. Therefore, social work educators need to incorporate concepts relating to ageing into the existing social work courses so that every student is effectively prepared with skills and knowledge to work with older people. Some social work educators may not have the expertise to teach ageing issues, but they have access to communities and older people who are willing to share their stories. Thus, a collaboration with older people will facilitate training based on the authentic experiences of the older generation. Specialised gerontological social work courses can also be introduced at master's level to allow more advanced training of professionals who can work effectively at macro-policy and planning levels.

Conclusion

In this chapter, I have shared the stories of suffering and struggle for survival, characterising women's ageing experiences in a rural community in Uganda. These experiences of older women are a result of cumulative disadvantage due to age, gender, and socio-economic rural background. Nevertheless, the older women are not just passive victims but have devised means of ensuring their survival, although their efforts continue to be constrained by the economic disadvantage and age-based exclusion from programmes based on ungrounded stereotypes that the older women are too old to manage income-generating activities. Here, social workers are very relevant to learn from and build on the initiatives devised by these older women in their struggle for survival in order to challenge the intergenerational structural disadvantages brought to light in their stories. Older women's voices regarding their struggles and their resilience must inform social work practice and training to avoid reinforcing the stereotypical thinking about older people. Indeed,

> …no pedagogy which is truly liberating can remain distant from the oppressed by treating them as unfortunates and by presenting for their emulation models from among the oppressors. The oppressed must be their own example in the struggle for their redemption. (Freire, 2000, 54)

References

Aboderin I (2004) Decline in Material Family Support for Older People in Urban Ghana, Africa: Understanding Processes and Causes of Change. *Journal of Gerontology*, 59B (3): 128-137.

Aboderin I (2012) Global Poverty, Inequalities and Ageing in Sub-Saharan Africa: A Focus for Policy and Scholarship. *Population Ageing*, 5(2): 87-90.

Atkinson R (2002) The Life Story Interview. In: Gubrium JF and Holstein JA (eds) *Handbook of Interview Research: Context and Method*. Thousand Oaks: Sage, 121-140.

Barya J-J (2011) *Social Security and Social Protection in the East African Community*. Kampala: Fountain.

Beales S (2000) Why We Should Invest in Older Women and Men: The Experience of HelpAge International. *Journal of Gender and Development*, 2: 9-18.

Dannefer D (2003) Cumulative Advantage/Disadvantage and the Life Course: Cross-Fertilizing Age and Social Science Theory. *The Journals of Gerontology*, 58(6): 327-337.

Freire P (2000) *Pedagogy of the Oppressed*. New York: Continuum.

HelpAge International (HAI) (2004) *The Cost of Love: Older People in the Fight against AIDS in Tanzania*. Dar es Salaam: HAI.

HelpAge International (2008) Older People in Africa: A Forgotten Generation. Available at: http://eng.zivot90.cz/uploads/document/205.pdf (accessed 13 October 2017).

Hooyman N, Browne CV, Ray R and Richardson V (2002) Feminist Gerontology and the Life Course. *Gerontology and Geriatrics Education*, 22: 3-26.

Ife J (1997) *Rethinking Social Work: Towards Critical Practice*. South Melbourne: Longman.

Mali J (2016) Social Work with Older People: The Neglected Field of Social Work. Available at http://dialogueinpraxis.net/index.php?id=5&a=article&aid=26 (accessed 13 October 2017).

Ministry of Gender, Labour and Social Development (2016) How 'Small' Grants are Doing Big Things in the Countryside. Available at: www.socialprotection.go.ug (accessed 7 February 2018).

Republic of Uganda (2015) Strategy to End Child Marriage and Teenage Pregnancy 2014/2015-2019/2020. (Available at https://www.unicef.org/uganda/NATIONAL_ STRATEGY_ON_CHILD_MARRIAGE-PRINT_READY.pdf (accessed 23 October 2017).

Schatz E and Seeley J (2015) Gender, Ageing and Care Work in East and Southern Africa: A Review. *Global Public Health: An International Journal for Research, Policy and Practice,* 10(10): 1-16.

Spitzer H and Mabeyo ZM (2011) *In Search of Protection: Older People and their Fight for Survival in Tanzania.* Dar es Salaam: Drava/Mkuki na Nyota.

Spitzer H and Mabeyo ZM (2017) Social Work with Older People: Perspectives from East Africa. In: Gray M (ed) *The Handbook of Social Work and Social Development in Africa.* New York: Routledge, 133-144.

Spitzer H, Rwegoshora H and Mabeyo ZM (2009) *The (Missing) Social Protection for Older People in Tanzania: A Comparative Study in Rural and Urban Areas.* Feldkirchen/Dar es Saalam.

Twikirize JM, Spitzer H, Wairire GG, Mabeyo MZ, Rutikanga C (2014) Professional Social Work in East Africa: Empirical Evidence. In: Spitzer H, Twikirize JM and Wairire GG (eds) *Professional Social Work in East Africa. Towards Social Development, Poverty Reduction and Gender Equality.* Kampala: Fountain, 189-216.

Uganda Bureau of Statistics (UBOS) (2011) *Uganda National Household Survey 2011.* Kampala: UBOS.

Uganda Bureau of Statistics (2017) *Uganda National Household Survey 2016/2017.* Kampala: UBOS.

United Nations Development Programme (UNDP) (2016) *Human Development Report 2016: Uganda.* Available at: http://hdr.undp.org/sites/all/themes/hdr_theme/country-notes/UGA.pdf (accessed 11 October 2017).

United Nations Population Division (UNPD) (2015) *World Population Prospects: The 2015 Revision, Key Findings and Advance Tables.* New York: United Nations.

United Nations Population Division (2017) *World Population Prospects: The 2017 Revision, Key Findings and Advance Tables.* New York: United Nations.

Waring M (1997) The Invisibility of Women's Work. The Economics of Local and Global "Bullshit". *Canadian Woman Studies,* 17(2): 31-38.

12

Exploring the Efficacy of the *Bashingantahe* Institution as an Indigenous Model of Problem Solving in Burundi

Susan Muchiri, Jacqueline Murekasenge and Serges Claver Nzisabira

Introduction

Amid constant political instability and subsequent and cyclically recurring periods of violence that have characterised Burundi and that attracted the attention of different authors, the country has also cultivated traditional methods and strategies for peace settlement. These strategies, which have also been regularly undermined, especially in more recent times, include the institution of *bashingantahe*. The institution is well known to be one that trains people, mostly men, to be *abashingantahe* (wise men of integrity), whose primary role is to solve conflicts at different levels of Burundian society, particularly at the grassroots level. Traditionally, *bashingantahe* are believed to be guardians of society, and they are also called upon as advisors. Not everyone can be a *mushingantahe* (singular form), as someone who aspires to such a role must have specific qualities and virtues.

It is important for social work education and practice in post-conflict societies such as Burundi to be inspired and informed by such indigenous institutions' strengths for effective interventions at the micro, meso, and macro levels. In this chapter, the relevance of the *bashingantahe* institution for social work practice is expounded.

Methodology

Between 2016 and 2017, an empirical study on indigenous and innovative models of social work was conducted within the framework of the PROSOWO project.[11] The main objective of the study was to explore indigenous, culture-specific, and innovative methods and models of social work practice in Burundi. The qualitative study was conducted in Bujumbura, Gitega, Muramvya, and Rumonge Provinces. The study was conceptualised as practice research with participants involving a sample of six focus group discussions (FGDs), five interviews with local leaders (*abashingantahe*), six interviews with social workers, and one interview with a policy planner from the Ministry of Human Rights, Social Affairs and Gender (*Ministre des Droits de la Personne Humaine des Affaires Sociales et du Genre*).

Burundi: A Brief Historical Overview

Burundi has been an independent country since 1962. Before being colonised initially by Germany (1896-1918), then by Belgium (1918-1962), the country had been led by a monarchical dynasty for centuries. It is a small country, landlocked between Rwanda to the north, the Democratic Republic of Congo and Lake Tanganyika to the west, and Tanzania to the south and the east. It is also one of the most densely populated countries in Africa. The population is made up of four ethnic groups: the *Baganwa*, the *Bahutu*, the *Batutsi*, and the *Batwa*. These 'ethnic' groups speak the same language and share the same culture, history, and territory (Dexter and Ntahombaye, 2005). At present, three ethnic groups, the *Batutsi*, *Bahutu*, and the *Batwa,* are officially recognised. The *Baganwa* were the tribe from which the kings came.

Burundi has experienced turbulent times in its history. In 1965, Hutu army officers attempted a coup against the Tutsi-dominated government that had come to power at the end of Belgian colonial rule. In 1972, in retaliation for massacres of Tutsis, the government organised the murder of an estimated 150,000 Hutus, forcing hundreds of thousands of others into exile. In 1988, tensions in the Northern provinces erupted into violent conflict and caused new massacres of Hutu. In 1992, President Pierre Buyoya altered the constitution to permit multi-party elections, and the Hutu-dominated political party FRODEBU achieved electoral success in June 1993. When Tutsi soldiers assassinated the new civilian Hutu president Melchior Ndadaye in October 1993, armed Hutu groups retaliated against Tutsi civilians. In 1994, the newly appointed FRODEBU president, Cyprien Ntaryamira, along with

---

[11]   PROSOWO (*'Professional Social Work in East Africa'*) is a project to promote social work in the East African Community. It has been implemented in five countries (Burundi, Kenya, Rwanda, Tanzania, and Uganda) under the Austrian Partnership Programme in Higher Education and Research for Development (APPEAR) for the project period 2016-2018.

Rwandan president Habyarimana, was killed when their plane was shot down in Kigali – an event that triggered the 1994 genocide in Rwanda. In his place, Sylvestre Ntaryamira became president (University of Massachusetts, Political Economy Research Institute, 2006). In 2015, a political crisis marked by violent acts and large numbers of refugees and displaced people shattered the country again.

These changes in the political arena also heavily impacted on the society and its communities. Civil strife has left Burundi struggling with social problems that have affected families and communities. Rampant poverty and a high internal and external displacement crisis meant that communities in Burundi have had to find a way of coping with these social problems so that a relatively peaceful life could continue, both for individuals and families.

Overview of Local Helping Processes in Burundi

The horrific and repeated conflicts have affected Burundians economically, socially, and politically at the national, local, family, and individual levels. However, Burundi, like other African nations, has also had traditional strategies for resolving social problems, both at the community and the family levels. Unfortunately, these strategies seem to have been undermined, rather than strengthened, especially in more recent times.

The strategies were learnt and nurtured through the family, as the first and most important institution in society. According to Ntahobari and Ndayiziga (2003), the family is seen as the first institution to provide a frame of reference for each individual. It is also a child's first place of learning about life. It is where children first come to understand what society holds dear and what it condemns. It is where the basis of their identity is formed. Traditionally, the family also had the role of consolidating harmony and unity among its members and with the immediate community. It was likewise responsible for everyone's subsistence and their protection. Everyone was born into, and grew to achieve their full potential, within a family. Subsequently, since it played such a major part in the construction of one's personality, personal failures were attributable to the entire family and reflected badly on the whole community (Ntahobari and Ndayiziga, 2003).

According to Ntahobari and Ndayiziga (2003), traditionally, peaceful settlement of conflicts was the norm. A number of methods might be used, depending on the circumstances. Initially, an amicable settlement (*kwumvikana*) would be sought. Eventually, an emissary would be sent to try and obtain reparation (*kumutumako umushingantahe*). Acting through an emissary made it possible to avoid direct confrontation between the parties. If a settlement could still not be reached, recourse would then be made to the *bashingantahe*. In the rare cases where one of the parties did not accept the judgement handed down, an appeal would be made to a higher authority. It was, however, extremely rare for decisions to be referred to the royal court. This might happen in cases of serious conflict, such as those involving murder. It is important to note that, traditionally, there was a concern to bring together the parties to the conflict and achieve reconciliation, rather than just handing down judgement, as is the case today. The aim was, first and foremost, to reunite and reconcile, not to punish (Ntahobari and Ndayiziga, 2003).

Historical Overview of the *Bashingantahe* in Burundi

As Gahama (1999) explains, the history of the *bashingantahe* institution dates back to the time of the first monarchy in Burundi, and its first king (*mwami*) Ntare Rushatsi in the 17th century. He argues that during the 'investiture' ceremony, a stick was handed over to the newly 'invested' *mushingantahe* as a symbol of justice. Gahama adds that the king had been advised by *samandari* – the well-known comical figure – to establish the *bashingantahe* institution (Gahama, 1999).

According to Ntahombaye et al. (1999*), umushingantahe* is a term that combines two words: '*gushinga*' (to plant or to fix) and '*intahe*' (a ficus stick, symbolising justice and equity), literally meaning the one who plants the stick into the ground. Dexter (2005) adds that it is so named because of the court stick, *intahe*, that the *bashingantahe* strike on the ground rhythmically and in turn to insist on the importance of the words they use and the decisions they make while arbitrating conflicts. The institution has been transmitted from generation to generation. The word *ubushingantahe* means, on the other hand, the set of values underlying the *bashingantahe* institution (Dexter and Ntahombaye, 2005, 10). This term can also be used to refer to any other person, mostly men, who adhere to the values of *bashingantahe*. Nindorera (2003) adds that the *bashingantahe* institution, therefore, is a traditional institution consisting of the *abashingantahe* (more than one adult male who exemplifies *ubushingantahe*, 'wise men' or 'men of integrity').

Ntahombaye et al. (1999) describe the qualities and virtues required of a *mushingantahe*: he should have a mature personality, with a sense of truth, sharp intelligence, industriousness, self-reliance, and a sense of justice and responsibility. These attributes are said to ensure that the person had a well-balanced personality, implying that he had a high sense of honour, was a moderate, wise, and experienced person, who was self-controlled, able to compromise in social dealings, and was a man who could express himself in the right way as well as measure his words (Ntahombaye et al. 1999, 12).

Dexter and Ntahombaye (2005) add other essential qualities, such as experience and wisdom, a heightened sense of justice and equity, a concern for the common good, a sense of moderation and balance (in his words and acts), dedication, and the love of work. In addition to these qualities, they explain that a *mushingantahe* should have the moral and intellectual qualities of truthfulness, discretion, a sense of dignity, honour, and courage, as well as be self-sufficient (Dexter and Ntahombaye 2005, 11).

Women and members of the *Batwa* could not be invested as *bashingantahe*. Gahama (1999) explains that, in the olden days, women were used to try cases and settle disputes, but the king withdrew this privilege from them as they had apparently proved incapable of keeping secrets. He also argues that in Burundian customs, women were not invested as *bashingantahe* because, traditionally, it was believed that '*nta ntahe y'umugore*' – a Kirundi expression which means that a woman should not be a judge (Gahama, 1999). Dexter and Ntahombaye (2005) confirm that women were traditionally excluded from being invested as *bashingantahe* in their own right. The agreement was that they were invested together with their husbands as *bapfasoni* (persons of wisdom and integrity) but did not have the right to deliberate with the men nor render judgement. Clearly, from a human rights perspective, this constitutes social exclusion and gender-based discrimination, and it is aspects like these that social workers would have to be cautious about in dealing with traditional cultural institutions and practices.

Ntahombaye et al. (1999) state that the comical figure called *samandari* may have advised the king to set up the *bashingantahe* institution. Nindorera (2003) explains the idea of the king's interdependence (or collaboration) with his subordinates through the following story: One day *samandari* was cooking vegetables in the palace and asked the king to keep an eye on his pot for a short while. He went away and when he came back, he found that the volume of his vegetables had been greatly reduced. He then accused the king of having eaten his vegetables. Confused and ashamed, the king asked him to keep silent and promised him whatever he wanted. *Samandari* laughed and told the king he was trying to show that sometimes people could lie and accuse others in an unjustified way. *Samandari's* message was that the country needed an institution to avoid injustice and unfairness (Nindorera, 2003).

The *bashingantahe* were the legal guardians of society (*indingizi y'igihughu*). According to the Kirundi proverb '*umwami agirwa n'abagabo*', the king cannot rule without the support of the *bashingantahe*, or '*kananira abagabo ntiyimye*', meaning a prince that does not listen to the wise counsel of the *bashingantahe* cannot be crowned king (Ntahombaye, 1999). These proverbs show the crucial role played by the institution in society, to help the king in resolving conflicts and disputes in the country. In addition, the institution was expected to advise the king and make sure that the people were cohabitating in social harmony.

According to Niyonzima and Fendall (2001), the expression '*ganza sabwa*' (the king rules and reigns) suggests a tradition of remarkable stability and harmony. To some extent, the long-standing monarchy in Burundi did hold people together in harmony and unity. The phrase in Kirundi that best suggests the tradition of political stability is *'umwami aca amateka ntaca agasunikano'* (the king makes laws, he never makes troubles) (Niyonzima and Fendall, 2001, 16).

Qualifications of the *Bashingantahe* Institution

Traditionally, for adult men, the utmost ambition was to join the circle of the *bashingantahe* institution (Nindorera, 2003). Ntahobari and Ndayiziga (2003) add that the role of the family and society was to teach their children the values of humanism and social responsibility based on the virtues of justice, equity, truthfulness, and honesty, including being a role model for society.

Joining the *bashingantahe* institution was viewed as an honour for the family. As Nindorera (2003) confirms, parents tried their best to help their children earn this place in the social hierarchy and, thereby, receive that honour. A child who obeyed and helped one's parents, worked hard, respected and assisted others, did not lie, and respected the good of others, was more likely to earn consideration. Within a family, such a child might be appointed *samuragwa* (one who inherits the father's authority within the family and could inherit his father's seat in the institution). Normally, the *samuragwa* position would go to the elder son if he was considered a good son, according to his conformity to the education he received. Therefore, it was easy for a *samuragwa* whose father was a well-known wise man to become a *mushingantahe* (Nindorera, 2003). Most respondents in our study confirmed that it was not easy to be a *mushingantahe,* and that it was a long and arduous process to get the best and wisest people in each particular part of the country.

Ntahombaye et al. (1999) view the *bashingantahe* institution as a pillar and a foundation of society. They argue that the institution epitomised a code of social rules, which ensured social harmony and stability. Ntabona (1999) indicates that the role of *mushingantahe* was to ensure that there was harmony in his social environment as he was expected to contribute to the reconciliation and mutual consultations (within families and neighbourhood) and the protection of people and their properties. In summary, the role of the *mushingantahe* in case of conflict between people was and continues to be: give advice (*guhanura*), settle cases (*guca imanza*), and send the individuals to the court (*kumurega*) (Ntahombaye et al., 1999).

To become a *mushingantahe* was a process. As Dexter and Ntahombaye (2005) state, the community would discern the qualities and virtues of a *mushingantahe* over a period of years and his character would be tested. Often a young man would be chosen as a candidate based on his qualities. On the other hand, he would ask to be considered for investiture. He would then undergo gradual integration into the judicial functions with the help of a mentor *(umuhetsi)*: At first he would be an observer and take in the teachings of the *bashingantahe*, then he could become an auxiliary, associated with the investigations, and then, gradually, he would be allowed to attend the deliberations in the resolution of conflicts. However, he would not be able to participate in the judgements until his own investiture. Before the investiture, the candidate must have enough beer available to share with the entire community, according to the hierarchy of the *bashingantahe*. During the final ceremony, the candidate would be presented by his mentor and, subsequently, be invested (*kwatirwa*) by his peers, at which time he would take an oath of commitment (*indahiro*) and receive the *intahe* (Dexter and Ntahombaye, 2005, 12).

The *bashingantahe* institution was so highly regarded that there would be severe punishment for any *mushingantahe* who betrayed its honour. If the *mushingantahe* did not follow the laws of the institution, he would be stripped of the honour. Ntahombaye et al. (1999) note that disclosure of secrets about preliminary investigations, the violation of social taboos (like entering the house of his married daughter), or any other forbidden acts, were liable to sentences leading up to a *mushingantahe's* demotion. The sanctions often included social exclusion, such as forbidding him from sharing beer with others (*kumucira umukenke*) or forbidding him and his family from fetching water from the same source as the others (Ntabona, 1999, 78).

Current Roles, Efficacy, and Limitations of the *Bashingantahe* Institution

The *bashingantahe* institution continues to play a very important role in contemporary Burundian society. As Ntahombaye and Nduwayo (2007) point out, through a justice of proximity and a conciliation approach *(intahe yo ku mugina)*, the *bashingantahe* are still highly relevant in the resolution of familial and social conflicts, or in disputes over land (Ntahombaye and Nduwayo, 2005, 266).

Moreover, the *bashingantahe* hold strong moral, social, and political responsibilities. They also have a duty to set a good example with regard to promoting the virtues of *bashingantahe* within society. Socially, the *mushingantahe* is responsible for settling and resolving disputes and conflicts, thus contributing to peace and order in his social environment. It was from among the influential *bashingantahe* that the administrative authorities would choose their advisors (Gahama, 1999). As the indigenous legal and moral institution, the *bashingantahe* played and still play an important role in the resolution of conflicts over land (Ntahobari and Ndayiziga, 2003).

While a formal justice system was introduced after the removal of the monarchy, officials continue to see the importance of the *bashingantahe* in listening to the citizens and helping them to resolve social conflicts. The 'institution of notables', as the *bashingantahe* are also referred to, was charged with reconciling parties in disputes in any civil case falling under the jurisdiction of the communal tribunal at the *colline* level (the hill as the lowest level of administration). The law provided that the communal tribunal ask whether the parties had their dispute heard by the *bashingantahe* before bringing it to the court. It was also required that the *bashingantahe* provide a written transcript of the proceedings, including a summary of the evidence and the proposed settlement. However, the court would not be bound by the settlement proposed by the institution of notables (Dexter and Ntahombaye, 2005).

The PROSOWO study in Burundi shows that even today, the *bashingantahe* institution still plays a critical role in society by being the mediator between community members at the grassroots level. A male respondent from Bwiza put it like this:

> The *bashingantahe* institution collaborates with communities and across all levels of society in issues related to conflict resolution.

Leaders in the community are needed to solve social conflicts, which, if not addressed early, can cause larger social problems. From the study it was reiterated that the *bashingantahe* help in solving family conflicts, social problems, and conflicts between individuals, and are sought after for advice. Even today when people have conflicts among themselves and find no way of resolving them, they turn to the *bashingantahe*, because court cases usually take time. In contrast, the *bashingantahe* are able to help and resolve issues much more quickly.

It can be observed that the *bashingantahe* institution watches over society. They are relied upon for wisdom and arbitration, particularly in situations of misunderstanding and conflict. In good times, such as at a marriage, *bashingantahe* play the role of counsellors and will often be called upon to give 'words of wisdom' to the newly married couple (*ijambo*). There is no social issue too small or too big for the *bashingantahe*. It can also be observed that, because it is a group of people, it helps in handling the most complicated social issues as they bring their minds together to find a solution.

The peace-making role of the elders is one of the most important legacies of Burundi's culture (Niyonzima and Fendall, 2001). The *bashingantahe* today act as peacemakers in reconciling citizens during land disputes and family problems. They are also involved on peace and security boards which have been put in place at each *colline* by the government.

As leadership for the community, the *bashingantahe* institution remains crucial. Leadership is the process of guiding the development of a group and its members. The goal of effective leadership is twofold: to help the group and its members to achieve goals that are consistent with the value base of social work practice, and to meet the socio-emotional needs of the group's members. As can be observed in the institution, transformational leaders are those who display high levels of competency and trustworthiness, inspire and motivate members with their vision, stimulate independent and creative thinking among members, and individualise members by understanding their personal needs and goals (Toseland and Rivas,

2005). A leader has to be a person that can help the people he leads to move towards a certain objective. The *bashingantahe* are community leaders and they are known to lead their people in various social activities towards community cohesion and solidarity. Our study respondents strongly agreed that the *bashingantahe* were and still are people of respect, honour, and moral integrity, and if they did not abide by these virtues, then they would be stripped of that honour.

According to Toseland and Rivas (2005), transformational leadership models suggest that such a leader should be a charismatic role model with a vision, who helps members to align their own goals with those of the group and with larger organisational goals. Leaders need to be people that easily draw out others around them so that they can achieve community goals together. In this regard, the *bashingantahe* could qualify to be transformational leaders, since those vested with this status must display dynamic qualities. Even today, not everyone is chosen to be a *mushingantahe*, and there are certain traits and characteristics that are required for one to be chosen.

While the institution is a good model of leadership, several limitations can also be observed. According to Burundian customs, women were not invested as *bashingantahe*. There is a well-known saying that '*nta ntahe y'umugore*' (a woman cannot act as a judge). For social work, this is a concern, especially in contemporary society where gender equality is crucial in the development of communities. Spitzer and Twikirize (2014) point at the challenging link between ethical social work practice, the male-dominated *bashingantahe* system, and widespread gender inequality and sexual violence in Burundi. With *bashingantahe*, there are clear limitations concerning the role and place of women in solving social problems. The respondents revealed that women occasionally helped when it came to marital cases. The women would work with the married woman while the *bashingantahe* would work with the man. Currently women are not found in the *bashingantahe*, which puts them at a disadvantage because they do not have a voice in addressing social issues which may concern them. But it was also revealed through the study that they do play a secondary role and can be advisors to their husbands. Those that have such qualities as required for and exhibited by the *bashingantahe* then become known as *umupfasoni* (a wise woman).

The ethnic group of the *Batwa* were also excluded from that institution because they were largely considered to lack common sense (Ntahombaye, 1999). This group was and still is a minority in Burundi, and when they are excluded from the community it remains difficult for them to progress. This can be observed today as the *Batwa* still lag behind in education and other social development aspects.

The *bashingantahe* are chosen with regard to certain criteria. However, in contemporary society there is a need to be knowledgeable about the law. Owing to their ignorance of the written law, the *bashingantahe* may make their decisions without taking that law into consideration, thus depriving someone of their lawful rights (Dexter and Ntahombaye, 2005). Today, this may limit their effectiveness.

Linkages and Lessons for Contemporary Social Work Practice in Burundi

The *bashingantahe* as an indigenous moral and legal institution has a variety of traits that can inform social work. Culture-specific, community-based social work is well advised to align its interventions with locally relevant networks, structures, and belief systems (Spitzer, Murekasenge and Muchiri, 2014). According to a widely acknowledged international definition (IFSW, 2015), social work is a practice-based profession and an academic discipline that promotes social change and development, social cohesion, and the empowerment and liberation of people. In addition, social work insists on the principles of social justice, human rights, collective responsibility, and respect for diversity. Social work engages people and structures to address life challenges and to enhance wellbeing. Thus, integrating principles of the *bashingantahe* institution in practice and theory can bring needed change in Burundian society.

Within Burundian traditional pedagogy, young people are initiated and trained to become mature and socially responsible people. Likewise, social work education may enhance the preparation of future social workers to become socially responsible and to integrate the values of *bashingantahe*, such as to develop a mature personality, or to nurture a sense of truth, justice, humanism, and a good sense of judgement. Most of the respondents in our study confirmed that a *mushingantahe* cannot be installed if he does not show certain qualities, because these are the qualities that will make him efficient in helping the community. These are the qualities that have helped the *bashingantahe* institution thrive all these years. Thus, social workers can teach the values of the *bashingantahe* institution in individual and family counselling, as well as in community interventions, so that the community can develop these values as a way of preventing conflicts. As stated earlier, leadership is crucial in working with communities, families, and individuals. National agencies seek to change local communities through the introduction of new ideas, but the power structures of these national agencies of change may be different from the power structures of local communities. Therefore, local power structures need to be considered and understood in order to avoid potential failures of initiatives and projects in the community (Chitere, 1994).

The social work profession integrates individual, family, group, and community work to contribute to sustainable development. This implies that social work helps clients resolve their problems. Our research indicates that family issues were often resolved by the *bashingantahe*, and the families in conflict would take beer to the *bashingantahe* institution and share the beer as a sign of reconciliation. However, the reconciliatory influence of the *bashingantahe* is not only limited to family issues but sometimes extended to larger societal issues. The government of Burundi recognises the importance of the institution. Dexter and Ntahombaye (2005) point out that from January 1987 until April 2005, Burundian law provided a role for the *bashingantahe* within the judicial system. This is important for social work because it highlights the need to work hand in hand with the *bashingantahe*. Therefore, the practice of social work with communities may need to strengthen its collaboration with local leaders, including the *bashingantahe*. According to Dexter (2005), communal law directs the administrative institution at the *colline* level to work with the *bashingantahe* of their area for the conciliation, mediation, and arbitration of neighbourhood conflicts. Thus, social work in Burundi can borrow a leaf and integrate the *bashingantahe* into their course curricula for areas such as conflict resolution, working with individuals and families, and other social work courses.

Additionally, social work theory can integrate *bashingantahe* conflict management techniques. Active listening is one of the techniques that is used by both *bashingantahe* and social workers. In Burundi, after listening to the problems, there is usually a time of evaluation called *umwiherero*. Thereafter, advice or judgement can be passed. According to the traditional process, which is also adhered to nowadays, prior to any decision-making, the *bashingantahe* attempt reconciliation through an informal process. They provide advice (*guhanura*) through patient and careful use of language. After listening to the parties, they would repeat the facts, showing that they have been listening, and inspiring the parties also to listen to each other and to have an open mind. They use commonsense terms in characterising the case and in explaining their reasoning to the members of the public who are attending. If these techniques fail, the second and last stage is arbitration. In this case, the *bashingantahe* become judges and render a decision. There is also the possibility of lodging a complaint before a higher court in case one is not satisfied with the rendered decision (Dexter and Ntahombaye, 2005). Social work is also concerned with communities', families', and individuals' challenges related to stable socio-economic development. Thus, social workers may utilise similar skills in dealing with communities in the Burundian context.

Professional social work is also concerned with conflict resolution and with maintaining a stable and sustainable society. Thus, the *bashingantahe* institution can be a good model for social work to employ in bringing about sustainable development in Burundi. The prevention and peaceful resolution of conflicts are closely linked to education in a culture of peace and human rights. Among these institutions, the family, structures of social relations, and institutions of social harmony and conflict resolution should be mentioned, including the *bashingantahe* (Ntahombaye and Nduwayo, 2007).

There are three mechanisms for the functioning of the *bashingantahe* system, especially with regard to peaceful conflict resolution: mediation, conciliation, and arbitration in case conciliation fails. The following principles have to be respected since they come from commitments made during the appointment (*ukwatirwa*): adhering to undertakings (*kugumya ibanga*); neutrality; dialogue and conciliation (*kuja inama*); consensus and joint decision-making; a sense of the common interests and responsibility; insistence on the truth, discretion, and impartiality (*kugumya ibanga*); acceptance of the procedure (free oral expression in public) and the authority of the institution of elders; voluntary participation (*agatuku k'abagabo*); and the sense of compromise and tolerance that makes consensus possible (Ntahombaye and Nduwayo, 2007). These are similar to the basic principles and ethical practice in social work. Since social workers work with communities, families, and individuals, there is bound to be conflict – over resources, ideas, ideology, etc. Thus, the practice of culture-specific conflict resolution is a skill social workers need to cultivate.

The *bashingantahe* institution entails three kinds of commitments and obligations:

Moral obligations: The *mushingantahe* has the duty to set a good example with regard to promoting within society the virtues of justice, honesty, and truth. He is expected to be a 'granary full of peace'. According to the code of ethics of social work, a social worker has a moral obligation to society (the client, their colleagues, and the profession). Thus, in integrating aspects of *bashingantahe* in social work theory and practice, the social worker becomes a granary full of peace and will thus be accepted by the community.

Social obligations: The *mushingantahe* is not only a person officially invested and entrusted with the settling of disputes and contributing to peace and order in his environment but he also holds a duty to protect the weak. A core principle in social work is advocacy, where the social worker fights for the rights of the minority. As a result of advocacy, social workers have brought changes to communities where people had never dreamt of a better chance in life. Similarly, the *bashingantahe* institution was and is still efficient, because they fight and advocate for those that are being unfairly treated in their society. This is the reason why many respondents still agree that even today, when individuals have a problem, one of the first places they seek help from is the *bashingantahe* institution. This advocacy can be integrated into community interventions in social work practice.

Political obligations: It was from among the most influential *bashingantahe* institution members that the king and other administrators chose their advisers to better run the country (Gahama, 1999). As a result of this close relationship with political leaders, it can be observed that through the history of the *bashingantahe* institution, they have played the critical role of advisors to those in power. This tradition also proved successful in the democratic system of government. Today, the *bashingantahe* institution still plays its role of advising those in power from the grassroots level to the higher administrative levels. In social work practice, social workers are also often consulted in order to shape policies. Therefore, social workers can work with the *bashingantahe* and the government in positively influencing social policies.

According to the social workers we interviewed, the *bashingantahe* often help with conflict resolution in society and in achieving social justice as well as resolving social problems. The main objective in social work is to bring change to communities. Social workers can work with the *bashingantahe* to develop and improve effective and innovative models for problem solving in Burundi's communities.

Most of the respondents in our study agree that the *bashingantahe* are still relevant and effective today because it is easy to access them as they usually reside within the same area as others. They are the leaders at the grassroots level and are able to understand the people. Their advice is also free, and one does not need to pay anything. However, the parties that need reconciling need to bring beer to be shared after the reconciliation.

Today, the courts still rely on the *bashingantahe* to help them out. According to our study, most people with conflicts opt to first pass through the *bashingantahe* institution before going to the court system. If the *bashingantahe* are unable to resolve the problem, then the warring parties can decide to go to court. At the court, the *bashingantahe* can be called as witnesses to testify on what has been going on and the judges seek information from the *bashingantahe*. In social work within the community, the *bashingantahe* can be incorporated, both for family therapy and in community work, as they are the eyes at the grassroots level and thus are knowledgeable about issues that can be crucial in therapy.

Though the *bashingantahe* institution had been weakened by the time of the 1993 crisis, many people have realised that, wherever the *bashingantahe* functioned well, it was possible to limit damage from the crisis, and even to prevent it. They tried to discourage people from fleeing and to remain united on their *collines*. For those who did flee, the *bashingantahe* would seek them out later to encourage them to return. Following the crimes committed during the crisis, they succeeded in gathering people who were too fearful or resentful to associate and initiated a movement of dialogue and reconciliation among them, sometimes in collaboration with the local authorities (Dexter and Ntahombaye, 2005). This shows that the institution is still very effective in Burundian society. Even during the crisis that the country has undergone, the *bashingantahe* have tried to remain neutral so as not to let society disintegrate. After the crisis, the *bashingantahe* have been seen to try and bring conflicting people together so as to bring back harmony in the community.

To sum up, working with communities calls for social workers to collaborate with the local administration and leadership of the given context. Through collaboration with the *bashingantahe* institution, which is still highly influential in contemporary Burundi, social workers can strengthen social relationships through the enhancement of social harmony and mutual understanding at all levels of society, thus also contributing to the overall social development of the country.

Conclusion

This chapter has examined the indigenous institution of the *bashingantahe* in Burundi and its efficacy in solving social problems. Historically, the *bashingantahe* were practitioners of traditional law. Their responsibilities were to settle conflicts, to investigate and to try cases based on the philosophy of arbitration and reconciliation rather than repression (Ntahombaye et al., 1999). Our research has found that some of the *bashingantahe* practices and values are still relevant, even though the institution itself is no longer as effective as it used to be. *Bashingantahe* were involved in handling social problems ranging from individual issues, family conflicts and marital problems, to land issues and political strife, as well as other conflicts common to society.

Although years of war have affected the *bashingantahe* institution, it has endured civil conflict and political instability and is still much at work at the community level. Social workers can work hand in hand with them to revive and promote the application of the positive aspects of this institution in peace building and community development. As has been noted, the *bashingantahe* often urge citizens to solve their problems through negotiations. Social workers today are required to use the same approach and to cooperate with the *bashingantahe* to develop the basis of peace and harmony in the community that is needed to empower people to focus on development. In addition, in order to be chosen as a *mushingantahe*, potential candidates were required to adhere to principles such as transparency, truth, justice, and wisdom. Similarly and ideally, social workers today should share a conviction for these same principles in order to make their work of helping communities to avoid conflicts more productive and efficient so that a focus on future social and economic development is made possible.

Moreover, by showing good moral behaviour as well as being a loving and faithful steward of truth and justice, a *mushingantahe* was and continues to be an example in society. Equally, social workers must strive for these qualities in their promotion of sustainable development and their defence of and advocacy for minorities in society, because without such attributes it is difficult to fulfil the role of mediator and reconciliatory agent. It must also be remembered that penalties were given to any *mushingantahe* who violated the work ethics of the *bashingantahe* institution, so it is important for social workers in the field to also observe their work ethics and, in cases of misconduct, legal measures should be applied.

Since the 2015 unrest, Burundi has again been experiencing a difficult time, and the contribution of social workers is as urgent as ever in order to help in community integration so that peace and security can flourish and so that the community can finally make a step forward in sustainable development. From the results of our study, we are convinced that social workers, together with traditional institutions such as the *bashingantahe*, are crucial in helping to solve social problems and to promote sustainable development in Burundi.

References

Chitere CP (1994) *Community Development: Its Conceptions and Practice with Emphasis on Africa.* Nairobi: Gideon S. Were Press.

Dexter T and Ntahombaye P (2005) *The Role of Informal Justice Systems in Fostering the Rule of Law in Post-Conflict Situations. The Case of Burundi.* Research Report. Geneva: Henry Dunant Centre for Humanitarian Dialogue. Available at: https://www.files.ethz.ch/isn/26971/CaseofBurundi.pdf (accessed 21 August 2017).

International Federation of Social Workers (IFSW) *IFSW's Policies 2015.* Berne: IFSW.

Gahama J (1999) The Origin and Evolution of Bashingantahe. In: Ntahombaye P, Ntabona A, Gahama J and Kagabo L (eds) *The Bashingantahe Institution in Burundi. A Pluridisciplinary Study.* Bujumbura: Presses Lavigerie, 7-35.

Nindorera A (2003) *Ubushingantahe as a Base for Political Transformation in Burundi.* Available at: http://genderandsecurity.org/sites/default/files/ubushingantahe_as_a_base_for_political transformation_in_burundi_2.pdf (accessed 11 Aug 2017).

Niyonzima D and Fendall L (2001) *Unlocking Horns: Forgiveness and Reconciliation in Burundi.* Newberg: Barclay Press.

Ntabona A (1999) *The Bashingantahe Institution: From Tradition to Modernity.* In: Ntahombaye P, Ntabona A, Gahama J and Kagabo L (eds) *The Bashingantahe Institution in Burundi. A Pluridisciplinary Study.* Bujumbura: Presses Lavigerie, 12-78.

Ntahobari J and Ndayiziga B (2003) The Role of Burundian Women in the Peaceful Settlement of Conflicts. In: UNESCO: *Women and Peace in Africa: Case Studies on Traditional Conflict Resolution Practices.* Paris: UNESCO, 11-26.

Ntahombaye P and Nduwayo G (2007) Identity and Cultural Diversity in Conflict Resolution and Democratisation for the African Renaissance: The Case of Burundi. *African Journal on Conflict Resolution,* 7(2): 239-274.

Ntahombaye F et al. (eds) (1999) *Ibanga ry'Abashingatahe mu Burundi.* Bujumbura: Presses Lavigerie.

Spitzer H and Twikirize JM (2014) Ethical Challenges for Social Work in Post-Conflict Situations. The Case of Africa's Great Lakes Region. *Ethics and Social Welfare,* 8(2): 135-150.

Spitzer H, Murekasenge J and Muchiri S (2014) Social Work in Burundi's Post-Conflict Society. In: Spitzer H, Twikirize JM and Wairire GG (eds) *Professional Social Work in East Africa. Towards Social Development, Poverty Reduction and Gender Equality.* Kampala: Fountain, 149-160.

Toseland RW and Rivas RF (2005) *An Introduction to Group Work Practice.* Boston: Pearson Education.

University of Massachusetts, Political Economy Research Institute (2006) *Modern Conflicts: Conflict Profile. Burundi (1993-2006).* University of Massachusetts Amherst. Available at: www.peri.umass.edu/fileadmin/pdf/dpe/modern_conflicts/burundi.pdf (accessed 25 October 2017).

13

Ikibiri in Burundian Society: An Indigenous Model of Solidarity and Collaboration

Susan Muchiri, Jacqueline Murekasenge and Serges Claver Nzisabira

Introduction

Burundi is a small country (27,830 km²), landlocked between Rwanda to the north, the Democratic Republic of the Congo and Lake Tanganyika to the west, and Tanzania to the south and the east. It is also one of the most densely populated countries in Africa (approximately 11.2 million people and 470 inhabitants/km²). With 90% of a growing population depending on agriculture, arable land becoming scarce, and close to 65% of its population living below the poverty line, Burundi has serious problems of development (Dexter and Ntahombaye, 2005).

Burundi achieved its independence in 1962. However, its history as an independent country has been afflicted by political instability and cyclical and persistent violence. The country was led by a monarchical dynasty for centuries, before being colonised initially by Germany (1896-1918), then by Belgium (1918-1962). According to Timpson, Ndura and Bangayimbaga (2015), precolonial Burundian society was characterised by kinship that tied the Hutu, Tutsi, and Twa together in a web of collaboration and interdependence. Belgian rule did not leave Burundi well placed to create an ethnically harmonious nation. Timpson, Ndura and Bangayimbaga (2015) explain that Burundi's post-colonial context has been vastly marked by persistent ethnic inequalities in education and in the social, political, and economic sectors.

Like other African societies, Burundian traditional culture is collective. As Ibrahima and Mattaini (2017) describe, this collectivism as a cultural pattern and as a value system emphasises the extended family, community, caste, tribes, and related groups. Thus, members of these societies carry a sense of obligation to their collective community. *Ikibiri* is one of Burundi's cultural patterns, which the present chapter views as a model of solidarity and collaboration that inspires the social development of contemporary Burundi in its post-conflict era.

The President of Burundi, Pierre Nkurunziza, in his speech to the nation in 2014 defined *ikibiri* as teamwork aiming at the accomplishment of a given task in a short period of time (Présidence de la République du Burundi, 2014). The *ikibiri* system in Burundi was and still is a practice of unity through which the elders bring together their community's strength in order to help each other. Working together is the main objective of the *ikibiri* system (Ministry of Education, Higher Education and Research, 1987). In contemporary Burundi, the term *ibikorwa rusangi* is also used as a synonym of *ikibiri,* especially when referring to activities organised at the community level for matters of public interest, such as the building of schools and roads or the cleaning of public places.

Timpson, Ndura and Bangayimbaga (2015) argue that despite the dividers that complicate intergroup conflicts in Burundi, there are some socio-cultural connectors (*ikibiri* is one of them) that could provide the foundation for conflict mitigation and violence prevention, and, hence, give hope to the quest for sustainable peace and development. Timpson and colleagues add that these socio-cultural connectors include valuing one's family, especially one's children, customs that are grounded in the ethic of *ubuntu* (humanity to others), characterised by the values of humanism, goodness, compassion, forgiveness, wisdom, empathy, generosity, hospitality, and kindness (Timpson, Ndura and Bangayimbaga, 2015).

Regarding the political violence that has plagued East African countries and the implications of that violence, Spitzer and Twikirize (2014) argue that each country's context (the post-conflict situation in Burundi and Uganda, or the post-genocide era in the case of Rwanda) requires individual responses in terms of reconstruction and development efforts, peace building and reconciliation, psycho-social work and trauma healing, and social work interventions. Based on research done in Kenya, Rwanda, and Uganda, Spitzer (2017) adds that there is empirical proof that the community is at the centre of social work practice. The case of Burundi is not entirely different, even though no research has yet been done on this matter. In this context, the qualitative research done in 2016 has identified *ikibiri* as an indigenous model that can help in the processes of problem solving in post-conflict Burundian society, a society that is suffering from the consequences of political instability and violence as well as from extreme poverty. This is important for social work education and practice because, as Sewpaul (2014) argues, in the wide range of absolute and relative manifestations of poverty, interventions to alleviate this poverty remain the *sine qua non* of social work practice.

In traditional Burundi, there were institutions, socio-cultural values, practices, and rites that guaranteed social harmony and peaceful conflict resolution. These are part of the cultural heritage that need to be protected but also adapted for current circumstances (Ntahombaye and Nduwayo, 2007). These institutions include the institution of *bashingantahe* (the council of elders, see the previous chapter) as well as *ikibiri* as a way of unity, solidarity, and collaboration. In contemporary Burundi, these institutions and practices are used to maintain social cohesion among the different communities at the grassroots level.

Methodology

From September 2016 to October 2017, an empirical study under the PROSOWO (*Professional Social Work in East Africa*) project was conducted with the main objective to explore indigenous, culture-specific, and innovative methods and models of social work practice in Uganda, Kenya, Tanzania, Rwanda, and Burundi. The study was conceptualised as practice research with participants involving social work and social development practitioners, community members, local cultural and opinion leaders, and policy makers. In Burundi, the qualitative study was conducted in Bujumbura, Gitega, Muramvya, and Rumonge Provinces. The study involved a sample of four focus group discussions (FGDs), five interviews with local leaders, six interviews with social work practitioners, and one interview with a policy planner from the Ministry of Human Rights, Social Affairs, and Gender (*Ministre des Droits de la Personne Humaine des Affaires Sociales et du Genre*).

Conceptual Framework: Mutual Aid and Social Work

Communities in Africa and in Burundi have used mutual aid from time immemorial but it is only in the 20th century that mutual aid has become a formal term. Social work emphasises engaging people and structures to solve their problems; hence, the profession is well-advised to identify mutual aid structures and groups at the grassroots level in order to have a meaning and tangible impact of its interventions. It is clarified in the international definition of social work by the International Federation of Social Workers (IFSW) and the International Association of Schools of Social Work (IASSW) that social work is a practice-based profession and an academic discipline that promotes social change and development, social cohesion, and the empowerment and liberation of people. Principles of social justice, human rights, collective responsibility, and respect for diversity are central to the social sciences, humanities, and indigenous knowledge, and social work engages people and structures to address life challenges and to enhance wellbeing (IFSW, 2015). In line with this definition, working closely with communities, in general, and with mutual aid groups, in particular, can turn out to be an effective and sustainable route for social work practice in African contexts to fulfil the profession's mandate.

Mutual aid can be found within self-help groups that are often successful in helping individuals with certain social or personal problems. Self-help groups are voluntary, small group structures for mutual aid and for the accomplishment of a specific goal. They are usually formed by peers who have come together for mutual assistance in satisfying a common need, overcoming a common handicap or life-disrupting problem, and bringing about desired social and/or personal change (Zastrow, 2004).

Mutual aid and/or self-help groups are made up of people who have personal experience of the same problem or life situation, either directly or through their relatives or friends. On the one hand, a good number of studies explain that mutual aid and/or self-help groups have an important role in addressing health-related issues. In combination with professional assistance, mutual aid and/or self-help initiatives may promote physical and mental health, improve and enrich members' lives spiritually, socially, and politically (Munn and McVicar, 2006). Banks (1997) adds that members of mutual self-help groups come together because of the desire to produce collective goods within the group and to enjoy these products together. In this case, people want to be helped, but they also want to return that help to someone else in the group for the added benefit of the helper's wellbeing (Banks, 1997). On the other hand, self-help/mutual aid groups use giving circles, which involve individuals pooling their resources and deciding on the ways they shall be used, aiming at serving group members in their material betterment or for other philanthropist activities, and for providing resources to the community (Eikenberry, 2006). In the case of Kenya, *vyama*, also known as 'merry-go-rounds', aim at improving members' personal welfare or creating collective investment via *harambee*, referring to self-sufficiency (Wairire and Muiruri, 2017). According to Banks (1997), mutual groups are also known for their success in reconciling individuals with opposing political views and in educating its members in order to become more concerned and active citizens (Banks, 1997).

Similarly, in *ikibiri*, community members come together to accomplish tasks that cannot be achieved individually or would, if attempted to be done individually, demand a lot of time. This can be done to meet the needs of the community in general or for an individual member of that community. Moreover, the social work profession insists on using the participatory approach in addressing social problems at different levels of their activities.

Zastrow (2004) argues that self-help groups emphasise face-to-face social interactions, the assumption of personal responsibility by their members, as well as emotional support. They are frequently 'cause'-oriented and promulgate an ideology or values through which members may attain an enhanced sense of personal identity. Self-help groups are successful because members have an internal understanding of the problem, which helps them to help others (Zastrow, 2004).

Mutual aid does not cost anything, as people come together for social or psychological help and contribute what they can for the development of the individual or the community. Zastrow (2004) adds that any person with a personal problem can use self-help groups in the same way as others use social agencies. An additional advantage of self-help groups is that they are generally able to operate with a minimal budget (Zastrow, 2004). Mutual aid as a central facet of community development can historically be traced to the progressive era, which placed an emphasis on citizen participation. Efforts were focused on community-level intervention intended to integrate residents into the larger society. In both urban and rural areas, the interest was in helping residents develop their own organisations to more adequately serve their needs (Green and Haines, 2002). Even today, people come together through various mutual aid systems to help one another.

Falola and Jennings (2003) explain that in West and Central Africa, societies that focused on charitable, recreational, political, and economic functions for members who often shared the same language and ethnicity, can be traced back to the 18th century. The collective and community organising principles translated into mutual aid societies. The Yoruba in West Africa, for example, utilised mutual aid societies as early as the 18th century through the *ajo* and *esusu* saving institutions. Each member paid dues into a collective fund that would then be made available for individual loans (Falola and Jennings, 2003). In the same way, for as long as Burundians can recall, the system of *ikibiri* has existed, as people kept seeking ways to help each other.

The *Ikibiri* System: An Indigenous Model of Solidarity and Collaboration

The word *ikibiri* means 'working together' and reflects a highly valued tradition of cooperation in Burundian culture (Bridgeway Group, 2017). Participants in this study highlighted social solidarity, collaboration, and cohesion as foundations of the *ikibiri* system. As mentioned previously, within East Africa there is a very strong culture of giving to social causes that has evolved over time and is still thriving. This is a culture based on the traditional African communal values of reciprocity and mutual aid and on the principle of *ubuntuism*. In Kenya, this was manifested in the spirit of *harambee* (Mutua, 2009).

The *ikibiri* system in Burundi was a practice of unity through which the elders brought together the community strength in order to help each other. Working together was the main objective of the *ikibiri* system (Ministry of Education, Higher Education and Research, 1987). People would come together to accomplish a task that they could not perform by themselves and thus needed others to help them with. This is how one of our study respondents referred to it: 'When people are together,

God is with them' (male social policy planner, Bujumbura). Most participants in our study noted that when people get together, they are able to do much more than when one person does something alone, and they feel happy about the collective benefits produced by the teamwork.

Ikibiri is mainly practised in agriculture and construction. There is a saying in Burundi that the neighbour is like a relative, and the concept of *ikibiri* exemplifies this. In a similar fashion, the discipline of social work looks at developing communities by bringing people together and helping them to organise themselves to fulfil their social responsibilities towards community development. According to Zastrow (2004), initiators and members of mutual aid groups perceive that their needs are not or cannot be met through existing social institutions. They, therefore, decide to look for other ways to fulfil their needs, one of these ways being the use of mutual aid groups to be able to develop themselves. There is a Kirundi proverb that goes, 'If you work alone, you will not cultivate a good season' (*Mushingantahe,* one of the wise men of the council of elders). To produce better results, the community deems it necessary to assist one another through the *ikibiri* system of solidarity and collaboration in various social activities, such as weddings, funerals, and crises. Social work similarly relies on communities to foster social cohesion through solidarity and collaboration for optimal community development.

Ikibiri was also linked to the notion of barter trade. As narrated by a *mushingantahe* respondent in our study, historically, barter trade was a good way of helping each other between people from different regions. If one region was well known for something and another region lacked it, then the communities would help each other through trading their goods, leading to the development of both communities. Social work insists on group work as well as on community intervention, intending to help people help themselves. Today, community groups can be assisted by social workers using *ikibiri* as a strategy to come together in small groups to meet the social or material needs of the community or of individual members of the community.

In addition, *ikibiri* as a concept of mutual help within communities has been adopted by some organisations, such as the Red Cross, as an indigenous system to enhance their work with communities. IFRC (2015), for example, reports that the Burundi Red Cross anchors its humanitarian work in local understandings. In dealing with disasters, the Red Cross employs the *ikibiri* system, showing how important it is as a model for solidarity and collaboration. Similarly, social workers can use the *ikibiri* system to enhance their work in communities as *ikibiri* brings people together for mutual benefit. In the Burundian context, there seems to be no better method than *ikibiri* to enhance community wellbeing, social cohesion, and social responsibility.

Roles of the *Ikibiri* System

In the following section, we provide an overview of the key roles of the *ikibiri* system.

A strategy for economic development

In mutual aid, people come together to achieve greater results than they could achieve by themselves. According to our study, the *ikibiri* system helps people not only to understand that they need to help each other because one never knows when one might also need help (Rumonge respondent), but it is also a way to teach people that helping each other is the responsibility of every member of the community and a way of showing humanity within the community.

If a person does not help others, then he or she will be excluded and when he or she has a problem, no one would step in to help them (*mushingantahe* respondent). This shows that it is important for people to be there for each other to promote solidarity among themselves. When one does not help or get involved in social activities, it means the person is excluding himself or herself from society. Thus, in turn, when such an individual has a problem, it will be difficult for them to turn to the very society they rejected earlier.

According to a study respondent in Bwiza, *ikibiri* helps to speed up work and to strengthen unity and social cohesion. It was and continues to be used in various tasks such as cultivation, transporting an ill person to hospital, during a tragedy or bereavement, and for the construction of houses for vulnerable people. During *ikibiri*, people would dig, labour, harvest, and make granaries, and because there were many people working together, the work would be finished faster and more efficiently, and the harvest would be larger (*mushingantahe* respondent).

Burundi's president Pierre Nkurunziza had this to say on *ikibiri*:

> The Kirundi proverb going that one man can only steal one cow did no invite our ancestors to organize mass attacks to loot more. Instead, this proverb means that getting together increases productivity, as could be noticed in team work called 'Ikibiri'. On this occasion, a huge property was ploughed in one day or two at most. [...] As recommended by the Constitution of the Republic of Burundi in Article 74, every citizen has a duty to contribute by his work in the construction and prosperity of the country. I welcome the fact that many Burundians are now at work, and especially how they are involved in community work. This has allowed community development to accelerate in a short time as compared to the situation before. As I said before, and it is even obvious, since we launched the community development work program, we have achieved a lot by our own hands, and progress is very notable in all Communes. (Présidence de la République du Burundi, 2014)

Through the *ikibiri* system, productivity is increased because people can dig a very big field quickly. An area that would take over a month to finish can be finished in one day. *Ikibiri* strengthens unity and love in the community (*mushingantahe* respondent).

Social work has a role to play in enhancing bonds between individuals through different activities in which each member of the community finds interest. Twikirize et al. (2013) point out that the social work profession is not only a problem-solving profession but functions as an agent of change that aims to empower individuals and groups and to promote harmonious relationships. Likewise, contemporary social work aims to bring individuals, families, and communities together so that they can face their socio-economic challenges. People use *ikibiri* to help each other develop. People can call neighbours to help cultivate their land and this would be done for free, with the person that has called upon their neighbours providing food and beer for those who have come to help. This would help the people develop themselves.

A strategy for unity and solidarity

Our study shows that *ikibiri* is still being used as a system of solidarity and collaboration. People still help each other to till the land, during weddings or funerals, and even in reconstructing houses, schools, or hospitals that had been demolished because of civil wars or natural disasters. According to Ntahombaye and Nduwayo (2007), to this day, the *colline* or hill continues to be the first basic structure of political and social organisation of the state, a real pillar of Burundian society with a strong interrelatedness of the various components – the *Bahutu*, the *Batutsi*, the *Batwa*, and the *Baganwa*. Its organisation of daily life is stamped with unity and solidarity in its daily social and economic activities, such as deeds of mutual help (*ikibiri*), particularly in difficult moments when, for example, a family member dies, or in celebrations of the various stages in life (birth, marriage, appointment of a noble, ending of funeral rites) (Ntahombaye and Nduwayo, 2007). In line with this observation, our study found that *ikibiri* continues to serve as a means of strengthening solidarity, where people meet and work together and, in the process, strengthen community cohesion. According to Burundian culture, beer, as an essential part of the celebration of *ikibiri*, is crucial in social life because it shows that people are together. This strengthens social bonds cemented by trust and reciprocity, as it is culturally not easy to share beer with someone that you are in conflict with.

Ikibiri, the traditional system of solidarity and collective action, is being taken up again by many groups. This is happening in spite of bad experiences with the cooperative movement that had been promoted in the region in the past (Oltheten, 1999). It is a cultural concept that the community can easily relate to and, therefore, will be willing to work with. As a result, it can be observed that different organisations are using *ikibiri* to help the community develop themselves.

According to Cournoyer (2005), social work is not a solitary endeavour. It is a social profession, grounded in a perspective on a person and a situation, and is motivated by a mission to serve individuals and society as a whole. Social workers are deeply involved with others. Therefore, in using *ikibiri*, social workers have an opportunity to get involved with the community.

A strategy for helping vulnerable groups

Our study confirms that through the *ikibiri* system, vulnerable groups in the community, such as the elderly, are taken care of by family members with the help of society (Gitega resident). Accordingly, the neighbour (*umuzimyamuriro*) is viewed as a relative or a member of the family. When a person encountered a social problem, therefore, others would come to assist, and people would even ask for help from the neighbouring hills (Muramvya resident).

When people are vulnerable, it is not easy for them to be effective. Hence, in developing the community, people help one another. If a house collapsed, for example, the community would come together to help. Neighbours would also help each other with seeds for cultivating, farm animals, or food (Bwiza resident). Building a house is no easy task, meaning it would require a large group of people to come together to help the person that had been left vulnerable. Today, people still come together in *ikibiri* to help one another in crises, for example during floods, which are common in certain areas of Burundi.

According to our study, people would not hesitate to help someone in need and that is why there is no payment for any work or help given to one in need. Most respondents agreed that help was done out of love, concern for others, and concern for the good of the community.

According to our study, people can easily tell when a person has a problem and, therefore, they will work together to help that person. During weddings, if the girl's father was found to be poor, the community would come together (*ikibiri*) to help the family in preparing the wedding (Gitega resident). When there was a death in the community, people would come to join the family in mourning. The community would bring wood to the place of mourning for two weeks if the deceased was an adult, and for one week if it was a child. On the last day of the funeral ritual, the community would fetch water so that those in mourning could wash their hands (as a sign of cleansing from death) as recommended by Burundian culture (*mushingantahe* respondent).

These kinds of interventions might sound simple, but they have a significant impact on the social lives of community members since they are expressions of love, solidarity, and sympathy, and strengthen social relationships among community members. Similar to these ideas, Cournoyer (2005) argues that the nature of social work requires regular collaboration with others, in line with *ikibiri*, and a great deal of social support. He continues to rightly assert that social support includes formal and informal activities and relations that provide for the needs of humans in their efforts to live in society.

A strategy of community encouragement

According to Cournoyer (2005), among the needs of human beings is the need for other individuals and groups who can offer encouragement, access, empathy, role models, and concepts of social identity. This clearly identifies with *ikibiri* as a strategy for community encouragement, and if social workers use *ikibiri*, they can enhance their impact on the community. Mutual aid demands constant personal reflection even when it takes place via the interpersonal and is inherently psychological and social in concept and in action (Steinberg, 2010). When people get together, there is an energy that encourages and motivates them to move from one level to another and, thus, *ikibiri* as a system of mutual aid accomplishes the role of psycho-social support. In *ikibiri*, for example, women organise themselves in many activities such as farming, mourning, weddings, or sewing traditional baskets. The traditional baskets are used during weddings. People help the new couple prepare for their wedding, the women go to clean the groom's house and add decorations to make it look good (*mushingantahe* respondent). These activities are an encouragement and an assurance to the couple that they are not alone and that others are going to be there with them through their life.

Ceremonies are another way of bringing people together in *ikibiri*. Our study found no social activity where the *ikibiri* system could not be used. As long as more than two people are together and in unity, the *ikibiri* system can be relied upon. It has been a highly effective model of getting things done in Burundi. For example, when a new *mushingantahe* is being introduced, there is a ritual called *kwatigwa* (investiture of a *mushingantahe*). During this time, the community comes together to help with the preparation of the ceremony and beer is prepared for the ceremony.

It can be observed that because of this model of solidarity and collaboration, people do not tire easily because they are together with others who encourage them. This is the reason why during *ikibiri*, the community sing songs. According to a *mushingantahe* respondent, one such song goes like this:

Rima ntibagutange rima (Dig so that others cannot finish before us)

Turime hemwe (Let us dig)

Rima ntibagutange rima (Dig so that others cannot finish before us)

Rima mwa bakobwa mwe (Dig you girls)

Rima ntibagutange rima (Dig so that others cannot finish before us)

Rima! Rima! Rima! (Dig, dig, dig!)

From this song, it can be observed that *ikibiri* is a time of solidarity and collaboration. Being with others in the community is a source of encouragement for each other and a source of self-esteem and pride in being a member of the community.

Ikibiri also sustains unity and through this, people are able to do things they would not be able to do alone. There is positive energy for community members which fosters a sense of wellbeing and belonging in that particular community. Collaboration between community members makes them know that if anyone should encounter a social issue or a problem, there would always be people ready to help.

Ikibiri in Contemporary Society: Efficacy, Challenges, and Implications for Social Work Practice

Today, *ikibiri* may not be practised on the same large scale as before, especially because of developmental tendencies in society that have led people to be suspicious of others around them. Thus, people may be inclined only to help those they are close to, rather than helping the community at large, as was the case in the past. As a result of the changing times, *ikibiri* has now been adopted by associations and other organisations and, thus, has undergone a process of formalisation as opposed to the past where it had been an informal indigenous model. However, in these associations it is primarily used for economic development and, therefore, its other roles are being forgotten, mostly from the mere necessity to survive. This is a challenge because the concept behind *ikibiri* was to promote solidarity, cohesion, and collaboration in society.

As Midgley and Conley (2010) argue, developmental social work must emphasise not only clients' strengths and the importance of empowerment, but also requires that social workers' clients are provided with tangible investments that enhance their capacities and facilitate their participation not only in the productive economy but also in community life. They argue that a key feature of developmental social work and social development is the use of investment strategies (Midgley and Conley, 2010). In this regard, the *ikibiri* system can be used in social work practice as another kind of investment strategy or model to help clients meet their needs at the community level.

According to Zastrow (1995), it has long been asserted that similar needs exist in all cultures, but the moulding and shaping of those needs is culturally relative. Social workers must be cognisant of the ways in which cultural and other background factors affect perceptions, feelings, and expressions of these qualities (Zastrow, 1995). The Charter for the Renaissance of African Culture (2006) states that all human communities are basically governed by rules and regulations based on culture (Ntahombaye and Nduwayo, 2007). It is thus important for the social worker to be able to understand the culture of use of the *ikibiri* system in trying to help the community.

Today, *ikibiri* is still practised with some modifications, mainly due to the development of social and economic services, such as banks, civil society organisations, and cooperative groups. Therefore, social work can use this approach to integrate people from different stages so that they can cooperate to boost their development and to resolve disputes. Zastrow (1995) states that once a sufficient knowledge base has been acquired, social workers must incorporate this into practice to increase the effectiveness of their interventive activities. This implies that social workers have a duty to integrate the knowledge acquired about *ikibiri* into their social work practice.

Contemporary social work can borrow a leaf from the *ikibiri* model, for example during times of crisis, such as natural disasters, or family conflicts. During disasters, people lose their property, homes, food, and their own lives or those of their loved ones. It is difficult to individually assist the victims of a disaster but through the use of the *ikibiri* model, by mobilising the community, the victims can be assisted. Social work practice involves stepping in in times of disaster. Thus, social workers can use *ikibiri* to assist the victims of natural and man-made disasters people might be faced with today.

Ikibiri is and was not only used in times of disasters but for any issues related to the community that needed people to get together for the good. The aim of working together is to maintain unity and to promote solidarity as well as to strengthen relationships, which is a key component of the definition of social work.

Ikibiri and social work both focus on the social nature of societies and on how to resolve social issues. It is imperative, therefore, for social workers to understand how important *ikibiri* is as an indigenous method of solidarity and collaboration, and to use it in line with other professional methods. There are many social issues today that would be easily solved if communities came together. For example, Burundi has periods of famine. If the communities came together to plant, they could have a large harvest and store it for potential periods of famine in the future. Today, because of changes in the environment, there have been numerous incidents of flooding, and on these occasions the spirit of *ikibiri* can be fully harnessed as communities come together to help each other. When social workers are aware of these indigenous systems they can know how to integrate them in the sustainable development of communities.

From our study we found that *ikibiri* has many benefits for society. Many respondents agreed that when people work together, they encourage each other and are, thus, able to achieve more. Social work can use this, especially when people are engaged in work community development projects where they can be brought together to better develop themselves. It is worth noting that when people use *ikibiri*, production increases, compared to when people work alone. It is also a good way of saving time as there are many working together. Social work can adapt the *ikibiri* system, especially where crises occur in communities and people need to come together to find a solution as quickly as possible.

Ikibiri was used out of love for each other. For example, if a girl got married far away from where she had lived before, community members would go where she was now in order to help her. This was to show her new family that she had a family and friends who still cared. At the wedding, they would sing, '*Reka tumurerure nab'iwabo*' (Let us carry her, she has family) (*Mushingantahe* respondent). In integrating *ikibiri* into their practice, social workers can help community members to genuinely care for each other without vested interests, hence, promoting the spirit of *ubuntu*.

Social work today employs the use of associations to help the youth, women, men, or children. This can be a good avenue for integrating *ikibiri*. The association already brings community members together and hence, *ikibiri* can help in promoting solidarity, because they could also use *ikibiri* for activities that are not necessarily related to the association.

Conclusion

This chapter has looked at the *ikibiri* system as an indigenous model of solidarity and collaboration in Burundi and how it is used to help the community advance economically and socially. *Ikibiri* is the spirit of coming together for the good of the individual and the community. Our study indicates that it is an effective model of solidarity and collaboration among the Burundian people. From the study, many social issues where help was required were dealt with using the *ikibiri* system. Such issues were, for example, if one person had a farming issue (lack of a farm animal, needed help tilling the land, harvesting), in cases of death, for weddings or dowry ceremonies, the investiture of a *mushingantahe*, in cases of illness and other crises (civil wars that have destabilised Burundi in recent years, or natural calamities). As a result of everyone lending a hand, communities are able to achieve much. Today this model can be integrated with theories of social work so as to better develop communities and make them self-sustainable.

Ikibiri is an indigenous model of unity and solidarity in society through which the elders (*abashingantahe*) are able to help each other using the little they have and combine their strengths and their time to overcome societal challenges. As a Kirundi proverb says, '*Imitwe ikora ikoranye*' (Heads function well when they are together). The elders understand the importance of working together and how it can help to find answers to various social problems that people might face and that cannot be easily resolved by the individual alone. Therefore, the *ikibiri* system is needed to strengthen cooperation and unity in society and within communities, which, in turn, will help to overcome many of the existing challenges.

Burundian society, like other countries around the world, is affected by socio-economic problems rooted in long-standing conflicts and civil wars. There are many reasons why people might differ from each other in their opinions, ideologies, and affiliation to political parties, regional or ethnic loyalties. It is the role of social workers to connect society and to help people come together to discuss their differences and then use the system of *ikibiri* to organise them for their community development. As our study has indicated, during *ikibiri*, ethnicity, tribe, religion, culture, or region does not matter, as the people work together as one. According to a French proverb *'Union fait la force'* (unity is strength), today, communities need more unity than ever so they can achieve sustainable development. Therefore, social work can and should integrate *ikibiri* as one important socio-economic problem-solving tool in the contemporary Burundian context.

References

Banks E (1997) The Social Capital of Self Mutual Aid Groups. *Social Policy*, 26(1): 30-45.

Bridgeway Group (2017) Available at: www.bridgewaygroup.org/index/partners (accessed 4 September 2017).

Cournoyer B (2005) *The Social Work Skills Workbook*. 4th ed. Belmont: Thomson Learning.

Dexter T and Ntahombaye P (2005) *The Role of Informal Justice Systems in Fostering the Rule of Law in Post-Conflict Situations: The Case of Burundi*. Available at: https://www.files.ethz.ch/isn/26971/CaseofBurundi.pdf (accessed 21 August 2017).

Eikenberry A (2006) Giving Circles: Growing Grassroots Philanthropy. *Nonprofit and Voluntary Sector Quarterly*, 35(3): 517-532. DOI: 10.1177/0899764006287482.

Falola T and Jennings C (2003) *Sources and Methods in African History: Spoken, Written, Unearthed*. University of Rochester Press. Available at: https://books.google.bi/books?isbn=1580461409 (accessed 6 November 2017).

Green G P and Haines A (2002) *Asset Building and Community Development*. Thousand Oaks: Sage.

Ibrahima AB and Mattaini MA (2017) Social Work in Africa: Decolonizing Methodologies and Approaches. *International Social Work*. https://doi.org/10.1177/0020872817742702.

International Federation of Red Cross and Red Crescent Societies (IFRC) (2015) *World Disasters Report: Focus on Local Actors, the Key to Humanitarian Effectiveness*. Available at: https://ifrc-media.org/interactive/wp-content/uploads/2015/09/1293600-World-Disasters-Report-2015_en.pdf (accessed on 29 August 2017).

International Federation of Social Workers (IFSW) *IFSW's Policies 2015*. Berne: IFSW.

Midgley J and Conley A (2010) Introduction. In: Midgley J and Conley A (eds) *Social Work and Social Development: Theories and Skills for Developmental Social Work*. New York: Oxford University Press, xiii-xx.

Ministry of Education, Higher Education and Research (1987) *Dusome 6, Igitabo c'Umwaka wa Gatandatu*. Bujumbura.

Munn G and McVicar A (2006) Self Help Groups as Mutual Support: What Do Carers Value? *Health and Social Care in Community*, 15(1): 26-34.

Mutua M (2009) *Human Rights NGOs in East Africa: Political and Normative Tensions*. Available at: https://books.google.bi/books?isbn=0812241126 (accessed on 8 November 2017).

Ntahombaye P and Nduwayo G (2007) Identity and Cultural Diversity in Conflict Resolution and Democratisation for the African Renaissance: The Case of Burundi. *African Journal on Conflict Resolution*, 7(2): 239-274.

Oltheten T (1999) Participatory Approaches to Planning for Community Forestry: Results and Lessons from Case Studies Conducted in Africa, Asia and Latin America. Available at http://www.fao.org/docrep/006/x2103e/X2103E00.HTM#TopOfPage (Accessed 28 August 2017).

Ong'ayo O and Fransen S (2010) *Migration in Burundi: History, Current Trends and Future Prospects*. Available at mgsog. merit.unu.edu/ISacademie/docs/CR_burundi.pd (accessed 4 September 2017).

Presidence de la Republique du Burundi (2014) *Message to the Nation by H.E. Pierre Nkurunziza on the Occasion of the National Communal Day*. Available at: http://www.presidence.gov.bi/archives/spip.php?article5884 (accessed 4 September 2017).

Sewpaul V (2014) Social Work and Poverty Reduction in Africa: The Indelible Reality. In: Spitzer H, Twikirize JM and Wairire GG (eds) *Professional Social Work in East Africa: Towards Social Development, Poverty Reduction and Gender Equality*. Kampala: Fountain, 29-42.

Spitzer H (2017) Social Work in East Africa: A *Mzungu* Perspective. *International Social Work*, 1-14. doi.org/10.1177/0020872817742696.

Spitzer H and Twikirize JM (2014) Ethical Challenges for Social Work in Post-Conflict Situations: The Case of Africa's Great Lakes Region. *Ethics and Social Welfare*, 8(2): 135-150.

Steinberg DM (2010) Mutual Aid: A Contribution to Best Practice Social Work. *Social Work with Groups*, 33(1): 55-68.

Timpson W, Ndura E and Bangayimbaga A (2015) *Conflict, Reconciliation and Education: Moving Burundi toward a Sustainable Future*. Available at: https://books.google.bi/books?isbn =1134451733 (accessed 2 November 2017).

Twikirize J, Asingwire N, Omona J, Lubanga R and Kafuko A (2013) *The Role of Social Work in Poverty Reduction and the Realisation of Millennium Development Goals in Uganda*. Kampala: Fountain.

Wairire GG and Muiruri J (2017) Vyama in Kenya: Afrocentric Strengths-Based Approach to Community Development. In: Gray M (ed) *The Handbook of Social Work and Social Development in Africa*. New York: Routledge, 292-303.

Zastrow C (1995) *The Practice of Social Work*. Pacific Grove, CA: Brooks/Cole Publishing.

Zastrow C (2004) *Introduction to Social Work and Social Welfare: Empowering People*. Cole: Thomson and Brooks.

14

The Role of Mobile Phones in Social Work Service Delivery: A Kenyan Perspective

Elijah Macharia Ndung'u

Introduction

The mobile phone has incidentally become a revolutionary device in Africa. Once considered a gadget for the high and middle class in society, it has now been adopted by the lower class as well. The mobile phone has unquestionably transformed the livelihoods of and the mode of communication between individuals. Years ago, it was considered a symbol of prestige and luxury; however, it is now increasingly becoming a necessary device for many people. Without it, one feels cut off from society, social events, and the world in general. The mobile phone has become a transformative device gaining immense popularity among the urban and rural populace in Africa, and specifically in Kenya. Lehr (2007) alludes that the mobile phone is transforming the lives of many users in developing countries and is widely recognised as an important current and future technology platform for developing nations. Subsequently, the mobile phone's potential as a tool for economic development has been recognised by African governments, donors, mobile phone companies, and non-governmental organisations (Aker and Mbiti, 2010).

According to the Global System for Mobile Communications (2013), mobile phone users in sub-Saharan Africa spend more of their income on mobile services than in other regions of the world (15% compared to 3-5% observed in other developing markets and less than 1% in the US and Europe). This indicates that on the African continent, the use of mobile services is much higher than in other parts of the world. In some markets, mobile money is already reaching large numbers of low-income and previously unbanked customers, moving millions of households (mostly low-income) from a cash-only economy into the formal financial system. In Kenya, Madagascar, Tanzania and Uganda, where mobile network operators are allowed to offer mobile money services, the number of mobile money accounts is already higher than the number of bank accounts.[12]

In Africa, mobile phones are evolving from simple communication tools into service delivery platforms; hence, there is a paradigm shift of mobile phones from simply being gadgets for reducing communication and coordination costs to a technology with the potential to transform lives through innovative applications and services (Acker and Mbiti, 2010).

Social workers have become key users of the mobile phone in their service delivery engagements at the community level. In Kenya, social workers have a heightened awareness and uptake of the various mobile application services provided by telecommunication providers. It is, therefore, imperative that social workers fully utilise the technological platform of the mobile phone to enhance their service delivery. This is in line with the professional mandate of social work to promote social change and development, social cohesion, and the empowerment and liberation of people (IFSW, 2015).

This chapter examines the developmental impact of mobile phones as an innovative intervention strategy tool in terms of social work service delivery in Kenya. The focus is on how the mobile phone has impacted on the social work service delivery and improved the livelihoods of community members. The chapter relies on empirical findings from the PROSOWO (*Professional Social Work in East Africa*) project research conducted in Kenya. The research focus was the analysis of indigenous and innovative social work models applied by social work practitioners and social work users in Kenya. The research sample was composed of eight qualitative interviews with social workers, eight focus group discussions (FGDs) with community members and service users, three in-depth interviews and four FGDs with local community leaders, as well as interviews with five social work educators and three FGDs with social work students. The participants were drawn from Kenya's Central Region (Muranga and Kiambu County), Ukambani Region (Machakos County), and Western Region (Busia County). Thematic and content analyses were applied to the data in order to draw out major themes and categories. One of the dominant themes was the innovative use of mobile phones by both social work service providers and service users. This chapter discusses this in more detail.

An Overview of Mobile Telephony

On a global level, the mobile ecology is increasingly becoming a major driver of social and economic development. The number of users is growing at an alarming

---

[12]   http://www.gsma.com/newsroom/gsma-announces-new-global-research-that-highlights-significant-growth-opportunity-for-the-mobile-industry/#.U196iyhfb9s.

rate every year. For instance, by the end of 2015, there were 7.2 billion mobile cellular subscriptions, corresponding to a penetration rate of 98.6%, up from 7 billion recorded in 2014 (Communications Authority of Kenya, 2016). In Africa and South East Asia, the number of Global System for Mobile Communications (GSM) mobile connections doubled in the last four years, while it more than tripled in South Asia. Consequently, the total number of unique mobile subscribers stands at 3.2 billion (46% of the world's population) and is forecast to grow to 4 billion in five years.[13] Mobile phones have narrowed the digital divide and are used more than any other information and communication technology, including personal computers and fixed line telephones (Katz, 2008). In Kenya, the mobile penetration stood at 90% by the end of 2016, up from 84 % recorded at the end of 2015. Hence, Kenya's mobile penetration rate is even higher than the average continental penetration rate for Africa, which stood at 76.2% (Communications Authority of Kenya, 2016).

In Kenya, it has undoubtedly transformed the mode of communication between and the livelihoods of individuals and is increasingly becoming a natural necessity for many people. It has brought positive social and economic development for many of its users and has become a device for doing business even among the rural population. The mobile money applications commonly used in Kenya include M-Pesa, Airtel Money, and Orange Money. Equally, there are other innovative mobile application programmes that are used by both the young and the old, as well as by social workers in their service delivery at community level. These mobile applications have enhanced information acquisition and service delivery at both individual and community levels. Among the social work practitioners and social work service users, the mobile phone has become an innovative intervention strategy for service delivery, assisting them in performing their duties in the field and in their administrative roles. Thus, the mobile phone has become a crucially important innovative technological platform, transforming social work service delivery, and has lessened the burden for social work practitioners in the field.

Mobile Phone Usage in Kenya

The most visible uses of the mobile phone in Kenya, other than making calls, is sending and receiving money. Mobile money transfer services are very common and a very innovative strategy in social work service delivery. Mobile money refers to the use of mobile phones to perform financial and banking functions (IFC, 2011). It is a service that allows individuals to make financial transactions using cell phone technology. Through this platform, the individual is able to accrue savings, send and receive money, and make direct purchases of goods and services. Mobile

---

[13]   http://www.gsma.com/newsroom/gsma-announces-new-global-research-that-highlights-significant-growth-opportunity-for-the-mobile-industry/#.U196iyhfb9s

technology is a channel that, once in place, allows for the delivery of other low-cost financial services, bringing banking to previously unbanked and underserved people (IFC, 2011).

Castri (2013) notes that the full potential of mobile money has not yet been realised, with 2.5 billion people in developing countries still lacking a viable alternative to the cash economy and to informal financial services. Moreover, although 1.7 billion of them have mobile phones, the mobile industry has found it challenging to launch and scale services for the unbanked because many policy and regulatory environments are not genuinely enabling (ibid.). This notwithstanding, in developing countries, millions of poor people are using basic mobile phones to transfer money, pay for goods, and access sophisticated financial services, such as credit, insurance, and savings accounts (Donovan, 2012). With the increasing number of mobile phone users in Africa and especially in Kenya, mobile money is becoming a favourite mode of money transaction among many subscribers.

In Kenya, mobile money application services are provided by the major telecommunication providers, namely Telkom Kenya Ltd (Orange Money), Airtel Networks Kenya Ltd (Airtel Money), and Safaricom Ltd (M-Pesa). However, of the three telecommunication providers, Safaricom has the largest number of users. Its mobile service application dubbed 'M-Pesa' is one of the most used mobile money application services. The acronym 'M-Pesa' denotes M for 'mobile' and '*pesa*', a Swahili name meaning money, thus meaning 'mobile money'. Since its inception in 2007, it has grown tremendously, transforming many users' lifestyles and improving their livelihoods both socially and economically.

The mobile money platform is increasingly becoming a powerful tool for building more inclusive, stable, and secure financial sectors. It is attracting more people towards using the platform and equally enhancing people's livelihoods. According to Castri (2013), M-Pesa is now used by 18 million Kenyans (only 7 million have bank accounts) and processes 1.6 billion US\$ in payments every month. Four years after M-Pesa was launched in 2007, 86% of Kenyan households and more than 70% of Kenya's poor and unbanked households had at least one M- Pesa user (Jack and Suri, 2011).

Innovative Technologies in Promoting Social Development

Social workers, who have a mandate to liberate and empower people, especially the poverty-stricken and marginalised groups in society, need to adopt new strategies for attaining meaningful sustainable social development. As helping professionals, they need to use new intervention methods in line with emerging trends of social problems. Some of the issues that the poor and marginalised in society are facing today, include: unemployment; low wages; lack of markets for little and/or poor produce; low commodity prices; lack of supportive production and marketing institutions; lack of access to credit; inaccessibility of health services; drought; floods; human-wildlife conflict; and deforestation (Governement of Kenya, 2007 and 2001; Ndiku, 2007; Nafula et al., 2005).

The philosophy of social development is clearly accentuated by the early proponents as an intervention method geared towards socio-economic prosperity. For instance, Paiva (1977, 329) points out:

> The goal and substance of social development is the welfare of the people, as determined by the people themselves, and the consequent creation or alteration of institutions so as to create a capacity for meeting human needs at all levels (especially those at the lower levels) and for improving the quality of human relationships and relationships between people and social institutions. (Paiva, cited in Chitereka, 2009, 152)

Furthermore, Omer (1979, 15) defines social development as 'a goal and a process that aims to achieve an integrated, balanced and unified (social and economic) development of society' (Omer, cited in Chitereka, 2009, 152).

Social workers have an enormous task in promoting sustainable social development and uplifting the livelihoods of the marginalised and the poor in society. As such, social workers have started to realise the potential of mobile money platforms in helping uplift the livelihoods of these population groups. For instance, social workers are involved in facilitating income-generating activities for community members and in the mobilisation of resources. In this regard, under the guidance of the social worker, community members can contribute small amounts of money through a mobile money platform towards starting an income-generating activity. This is an efficient strategy for consolidating financial resources to help community members through self-help groups to have sustainable sources of income.

Economic stability is foundational to but not adequate for achieving sustainable social development. Subsequently, money may be at the base of many of the issues poor people are facing, but poverty's tentacles are so far-reaching and damaging that they touch multiple areas of a person's life (Hawkins and Kim, 2012). In addition, most social workers in Africa and, especially, in the East African region lack both material and financial resources to carry out their duties. This is due to the fact that social work activities are poorly supported by the incumbent governments within these countries. There are insufficient allocations of budgetary funds for social services. As Chitereka indicates, there has been a general decline in social welfare budgets throughout Africa in the last few years; yet, there are more social problems which need to be tackled. Social workers often lack basic items like offices, telephones, and computers, as well as transport to carry out home visits. This completely compromises their effectiveness to deliver services (Chitereka, 2009).

Through the use of mobile phones as a developmental intervention strategy, social workers can enhance the tradition of focusing on the poor and the oppressed to help them develop a better quality of life. Thus, the use of mobile phone platform technologies as an intervention strategy in African contexts is vital for social workers in order for social development to be achieved.

Mobile Phones in Social Work Service Delivery

In the following sections, an overview of social work interventions based on the use of mobile phones is provided. The examples are based on the empirical data from the study conducted in Kenya.

Mobile money platform

Mobile money phone-based service applications have helped many of its users to easily make transactions from their mobile phones to other users, buy airtime, and pay bills from the comfort of their seats. Social workers use mobile money to facilitate resource mobilisation, especially when initiating a community project. Community members are encouraged to accumulate funds for the community project through contributions made over the mobile money platform. This is an easy and efficient way of collecting money for development projects within the community. Owing to its user-friendliness and efficiency, it is an innovative strategy for social work clients at the community level. Social workers also utilise mobile money to send money to individuals, especially to those in dire need of financial assistance, and to settle small administrative expenses while in the field. For instance, one social worker from Kiambu County noted:

> I use M-Pesa or Airtel money to pay small bills and when sending money to a needy client while in the field and later consolidate them when I get to the office.

The use of M-Pesa services has enhanced service delivery at the local level. Findings from our study indicate that most of the community members who use M-Pesa have got immense relief from the mobile money application service, and it has lessened their social and financial burdens. For example, community members using the M-Pesa platform in relation to local resource mobilisation noted that:

> Mobile phones are used to reach many people and solicit contributions to help someone in need. For example, when having self-help groups or *chamas* [merry-go-round groups], people, instead of walking long distances to give their contributions, just send them using mobile money platforms like M-Pesa through their phones. Long journeys are cut short and that time is saved for other socio-economic activities. (Community members from Muranga and Kiambu Counties)

This was also replicated in the educational sector, whereby community members noted that the mobile money platform has assisted them in sourcing for funds from well-wishers in the community and in starting up income-generating activities. In addition, the mobile money platform has been used to assist some of the community members in dire need of financial assistance in meeting their basic needs, especially food. Many such cases have been addressed through this innovative strategy.

> We use M-Pesa and Airtel money to offer educational support to some of our relatives and friends through money for books or uniforms for their children in order for the children to continue with their education. Also, we assist those not able enough who want to start a small income-generating project etc. We have also been able to rescue some of our own in the community, especially those in financial difficulty, through sending money to them using the mobile money platform. (Community members from Muranga and Kiambu Counties)

Similar sentiments were echoed by one of the community leaders:

> This mobile money service has helped, especially in resource mobilisation. When someone in the village is affected by an issue, e.g. funeral arrangements, settling a hospital bill or school fees, community members assist by contributing their small amounts easily by sending them through M-Pesa. (Community leader from Ndeiya-Limuru, Kiambu County)

This is a clear indication that the mobile money platform has immensely transformed the lives of local community members in resource mobilisation and for offering financial support to the most vulnerable and needy in the community. It has also been utilised as an intervention strategy for supporting needy children. It is a fast and cost-efficient way of sending or receiving money for parents. They are saved the hustle and time-consuming exercise of having to walk long distances looking for sponsors to help them in paying for school fees for their children. Instead, the parents are sent money through the mobile platform by well-wishers to support their children in school. Parents who may have their child sent back from school owing to unpaid fees may appeal to well-wishers in the community to assist in raising those fees. The public can easily send money to the parents' mobile phone and help the parent child continue with his or her education through the financial support given. This reduces the high rates of school dropouts witnessed in some rural villages, especially in the area of study (Muranga County), attributed to a lack of educational materials due to chronic poverty. Such children would otherwise drop out of school and turn to the streets or engage in other maladaptive behaviours.

The mobile money platform has also improved the social work service delivery at the community level. Hence, the mobile money application is a strong innovative intervention strategy that is a key avenue for social and economic development.

Mobile applications

Mobile applications have gained acceptance among mobile users owing to the various functionalities and their user-friendliness. Several applications have been developed with services and products for specific target populations or users with the sole aim of easing and enhancing service delivery, communication and networking, and for socio-economic development initiatives. These mobile phone applications have stretched the boundaries of mobile phones from conventional uses of Short Message Texting (SMS) and making voice calls to more sophisticated uses of the device. In Africa, in general, and in Kenya, in particular, these mobile phone applications have gained tremendous acceptance and are widely used as modes of doing business and delivering services.

It is interesting to note that, unlike in the developed countries where the main focus of such mobile phone applications is on entertainment, in Africa, these applications are providing opportunities for development applications ('m-development') used in enhancing the delivery of financial, agricultural, health, and educational services, disseminating agricultural price information, monitoring health care, and transferring money (Aker and Mbiti, 2010). For example, the mobile phone as a development tool in Africa is being used for a variety of mobile health ('m-health') projects. In Kenya, Malawi, and South Africa, mobile phones are being used to send several reminders a day to HIV-positive patients about their anti-retroviral therapy schedule, as well as to allow community health workers to send information about the status of HIV patients (Aker and Mbiti, 2010). In addition, the use of SMS, the least-expensive mobile phone function, enhances communication, leading to improved delivery of health services and to better health outcomes (Zurovac, Talisuna and Snow, 2012). Thus, mobile applications are making communication much easier, more efficient, and more immediate for social workers and social work users.

The communication gap experienced by social workers has been narrowed with the advent of mobile phone applications. Social workers can monitor their clients' progress in therapeutic interventions. They can use their mobile phones to send reminders of their clients' therapy sessions and notify them if there are any changes in session timings. Hence, they can bridge the gap in terms of offering speedy interventions and enhancing efficient service delivery to their clientele. Some examples of such efficient use of mobile applications was mentioned by a social worker:

> We are using several innovations, such as WhatsApp groups for the youth or the women's enterprise fund. Through this communication, government funds can be monitored, and it ensures that defaulting is at low levels. These groups are growing and are benefitting members. (Social worker from Mavoko, Machakos County)

Social workers often work under intense pressure and are overburdened with various tasks in the field while having to make do with limited resources. At times, they conduct multiple tasks simultaneously so as to help those of their clients in need. For example, they conduct client interviews and home visits while, at the same time, still performing administrative roles. This in itself is very time-consuming and tedious for the social workers. However, the mobile phone has made it easier to take care of all these responsibilities. With various existing mobile applications, they can easily communicate and send data to their offices without having to travel long distances from the field. The use of WhatsApp and SMS has improved the transmission of information from the field to other service providers. Such applications are enhancing service delivery at the community level with improved immediacy in the referral system of emergency cases and improved follow-up of client cases.

Social workers and community health workers are also applying this innovative strategy to assist their clientele in health matters. They use such applications to offer emergency services to community members. The community health volunteers, normally involved at the village level, are using some of these health applications in the early detection of some diseases. One social worker noted this:

> Community health volunteers at the village level are being equipped with mobile phones with installed health applications that are provided by some NGOs and, therefore, are able to detect early signs of some communicable diseases such as tuberculosis and tropical diseases like malaria. They are able to get information about symptoms from the application and can then offer either emergency services or referral services to other health institutions for further treatment.

Another application that has been widely applied in Kenya and other countries is *Ushahidi*, a Swahili word meaning 'testimony'. It is a platform that allows information collection, visualisation, and interactive mapping. With the application, anyone can submit information through text messaging using a mobile phone, email, or web form.[14] *Ushahidi* is crowdsourcing[15] software that enables many individuals to enter data into a web-based system. People send a text message to report an incident of violence that is then automatically mapped on a website, using Frontline SMS (software for sending and receiving multiple text messages through a computer) and the *Ushahidi* crowdsourcing website.[16]

Ndung'u and Waema (2011) contend that mobile phones have been helpful in emergency responses and in averting security mishaps. The mobile phone has been used as a tool for alerting people about imminent dangers or insecurities within their areas of residence. *Ushahidi* employs the same ideology in consolidating information to address security concerns in society through the use of the mobile phone interface. Social workers are also utilising such platforms to identify potential conflict or crisis areas and to mobilise emergency rescue teams or agencies.

---

[14]   www.ushahidi.com

[15]   Crowdsourcing is a specific sourcing model in which individuals or organisations use contributions from internet users to obtain needed services or ideas.

[16]   www.ushahidi.com

The *Ushahidi* platform has been used in identifying and reporting hotspots prone to violence in order to assist government authorities, including the police force, to take immediate and appropriate measures to address the issues. For instance, in Kenya, social workers and other psycho-social service providers were able to report incidents of violence and emergency situations during the recent election period of 2017. Several incidents of post-election violence were reported via social media platforms, such as WhatsApp, Facebook, and Twitter. Such information was widely shared through social media, and government authorities were able to easily intervene and avert violence from escalating. Much of this was done through individuals' smartphones that are compatible with such mobile applications. Hence, social workers and other psycho-social service providers are utilising mobile applications on their phones to offer immediate, reliable, and effective services to their clientele.

Social workers are equally applying these technological innovations to help with child protection. This is done through sending text messages or photos about incidents of violence, child abuse, child marriage, sexual harassment, and other child-related abuses on WhatsApp, Facebook, and Twitter on their phones. This information is transmitted to various social work agency service providers, government authorities, and child helpline services. For instance, child helpline services in Kenya have gained popularity among social work practitioners and have assisted in the rescue of children from abuse in most parts of the country. This helpline service began in 2009 as a landline phone service. However, since the inclusion of an SMS, the demand for helpline services has increased twentyfold (Mattila, 2011). This indicates the power mobile phone applications can have in enhancing social work service delivery to society.

Social cohesion and integration

Mobile phones play a pivotal role in connecting people and in enhancing social cohesion among individuals in a society. The application increases social networks and may be used to reduce crime and household exposure to risk. Mobile phones have a direct, and prominent, impact at the micro and macro levels through interconnecting people for personal, business, or community purposes. Equally, mobile phones save individuals' time and money. For example, this is evidenced through the use of mobile money platforms that enable efficiency in transactions, lower travel costs, and save time. Mobile phones are also important in that they have strengthened social ties at the micro level and in allowing families to easily link up and interact with their family members more easily and more efficiently. Where issues arise, the mobile phone has been used as an innovative tool for intervention by community and family members in conflict resolution and in offering social support to afflicted individuals. For example, one of the community members that were interviewed noted:

> Phones play a major role. Through the use of the phone, one can reach a large population and pass on relevant information. (Interview with community members from Machakos County)

This was equally noted by the social workers we interviewed when they said that social interactions had grown through the use of mobile phones in communicating with various groups through group SMS. For instance, one social worker from Kathiani noted that 'a message can be easily relayed to young people, women, or the elderly for any urgent meetings.'

Sentiments relayed by the social work students we interviewed indicate that mobile phones are indeed playing an integral part in social work service delivery. For instance, one student from Busia pointed out:

> The use of technology, for example through mobile phones, is one of the key factors that has contributed to the emergence of innovative ways of dealing with community issues.

Another social work student argued:

> Since we are part of a modern world where people live in different and diverse societies, traditional ways have become very difficult or impossible to be applied.

This indicates that mobile phone technology is well positioned at the centre of social work service delivery.

Social workers are utilising the mobile phone in the transmission of crucial field information and data, especially regarding vulnerable and abandoned children. This is achieved through linking children to resources, services, and emergency assistance. According to Mattila (2011), information about vulnerable children is collected through mobile phones (rapid SMS for signalling and reporting cases) and smartphones, or through web-based applications that allow for uploading more complex child and family assessment forms. Social workers use such platforms in inter-agency referrals and for the provision of child protection services. Thus, they assist in case management and in offering immediate intervention strategies to the children. It also assists in the referral to rehabilitation centres or in their reintegration process with their primary caregivers. Such platforms also assist social workers in the identification and assessment of organisations and service providers within a much faster and more efficient timeframe. An example of such innovative use of mobile phones in the rescue of vulnerable children was given by one of the social workers we interviewed:

> Through the innovative ways, rescue cases have been very successful. For example someone recently rescued a young man who had been hidden for 28 years in the Mitaboni area. The young man has his rights, which had been violated for a long

time; he has now been put into a cash transfer programme. This was achieved through constant communication with the elders by the use of a phone which, via various training sessions, had helped educate them. For example, they are now aware of all the human rights. (Social worker from Kathiani)

Facilitating social work service delivery

As innovative tools of social work service delivery, mobile phones are being applied by social workers to support and enhance the communication, coordination, and sharing of information between organisational staff and other stakeholders in development, including community groups, NGO partners or agencies, policy makers, and social welfare service providers. This helps social workers with ensuring the delivery of services in a timely and appropriate manner. For example, mobile phones are used to gather, consolidate, and share information relating to the design, monitoring, and implementation of projects and programmes; to communicate programme goals and impacts and to build sponsorship and funding relationships; and to support and facilitate timely responses to emergencies (Beardon, 2009). For example, one social worker we interviewed noted:

> Using digital tools like laptops and mobile phones to upload and document information acquired in the field has assisted us in the implementation of programme work. (Social work practitioner from Thika, Kiambu County)

In addition, a social work educator in Nairobi noted:

> The use of mobile phones and laptops/tablets is also a very important and innovative way which social workers can utilise in social work service delivery, for example in using it for the documentation of cases, for case profiling, and for making communication easier.

Therefore, mobile phones improve working with social work programmes, especially in the dissemination of information, the monitoring and evaluation of programmes, and in emergency response work. Additionally, via the use of SMS, organisations are able to publicise and to advocate for their programmes more effectively.

Consequently, information about various aspects of social and civic education, human rights awareness, and health-related issues can be made easily accessible via mobile phone applications. This, in turn, assists social workers in reaching more people in order to raise awareness about various issues. According to Beardon (2009), development based on mobile phone applications encompasses a broad range of work, including supporting citizens and communities in accessing information about their rights, influencing policy makers, enhancing communication and cooperation between actors, or developing new methodologies, tools, and resources.

Social workers are also able to upload information from their mobile phones to their organisation's websites via the internet from their phones. This has eased the transmission of urgent information. For example, internet-based blogging and photo sharing are commonly used to share views, news, and updates (Beardon, 2009). Such platforms can be useful as innovative strategies for the dissemination of information and the progress of social work programmes to stakeholders, agency partners, and community members.

Challenges

The use of mobile phones as innovative tools and strategies in social work service delivery faces a number of challenges. Some of these are due to the existing technological divide between users and even between devices that are being used. Most of these mobile phone applications require the use of a smartphone, which may be out of reach for many users, especially at the community level. Many users of social work services may not be able to afford such devices, given that they are often faced with a myriad of other socio-economic issues, including poverty. Network and internet availability is another challenge in the use of mobile phone applications. Some of these applications require connectivity to the internet, which may be unavailable in some areas. In addition, some mobile applications may require money to purchase internet bundles, which would create an extra cost for users and which would cut off those who cannot afford this from accessing information from such platforms.

Additionally, there is a challenge in terms of sustainability for mobile phone applications, in that there needs to be continuing political will to cultivate and enhance awareness among users. Some of them may not fully understand the purpose of such innovative strategies. Therefore, there is a need for an increased partnership with relevant public and private sectors in order to strengthen the linkages between their programmes towards sustainability (Beardon, 2009).

Another challenge refers to the issue of data security, which is an immanent risk when using mobile phones and social media platforms. Here, social workers have to deal with a delicate balance between utilising the benefits of such devices, on the one hand, and safeguarding their clients' privacy as an ethical imperative of their daily work, on the other hand.

Potential for Upscaling Mobile Phone Usage in Social Work Service Delivery

Development efforts that involve the use of mobile phones have demonstrated both creativity and a possibility for the improvement of the quality of life for their users. There is great potential for increased partnerships that focus on the nexus between bottom-up and top-down development in order to cultivate a productive feedback loop between the various actors involved, to conjoin needs identification with appropriate technology and sustainable models for delivering services (Hosman and Fife, 2012). Mobile phones have great potential in social work service delivery if used holistically to address the issues affecting most of the individuals at the community level. They ought to encompass all the spheres, including socio-economic, political and psychological, in order to effectively address societal issues. Subsequently, mobile phones are a vital tool, especially for emergency responses as well as crisis and disaster rescue missions. They are also crucial in humanitarian assistance and the coordination of the activities of social work programmes at the organisational and community levels.

Therefore, social workers ought to enhance the integration of mobile phones as an innovative strategy into their programme work to effectively and efficiently deliver their mandate of addressing social issues, including poverty alleviation and improving the livelihoods of their clientele.

Conclusion

The chapter provided a descriptive overview of how mobile phones are an essential tool that enhances effective and efficient social work service delivery. Among the most commonly used mobile phone applications in Kenya is the M-Pesa mobile money platform. This platform has transformed many users' livelihoods for the better and has equally aided social workers in their service delivery and benefitted community members at large.

Mobile phone applications have transformed the way in which services are delivered by social workers at the community level. Mobile phones have also enhanced the resolution of issues, and benefitted social integration and cohesion at micro, meso, and macro levels. This indicates that the mobile phone has improved and uplifted many individual users' livelihoods and enhanced the delivery of the activities of social work programmes. Thus, through the integration of mobile phone technologies, social workers are using innovative developmental strategies in enhancing their service delivery, enhancing their clients' capability to attain socio-economic and psychological wellbeing, and thus fostering sustainable social development.

References

Aker JC and Mbiti IM (2010) Mobile Phones and Economic Development in Africa. CGD Working Paper 211. *Journal of Economic Perspectives,* 24(3): 207-232.

Beardon H (2009) *Mobiles for Development: How Mobile Technologies Can Enhance Plan and Partners' Work in Africa.* Helsinki: Plan Finland.

Castri S (2013) *Mobile Money: Enabling Regulatory Solutions.* London: GSMA.

Chitereka C (2009) Social Work Practice in a Developing Continent: The Case of Africa. *Advances in Social Work,* 10(2): 144-156.

Communications Authority of Kenya (2016) *Annual Report 2015-2016*. Available at: http://www.ca.go.ke/images//downloads/PUBLICATIONS/ANNUALREPORTS/Annual%20Report%20for%20the%20Financial%20Year%202015-2016.pdf (accessed 15 August 2017).

Donovan KP (2012) Mobile Money, More Freedom? The Impact of M-PESA's Network Power on Development as Freedom. *International Journal of Communication*, 6: 2647-2669.

Government of Kenya (2001) *Poverty Reduction Strategy Paper 2001*. Nairobi: GoK.

Government of Kenya (2007) *Basic Report of Fourth Participatory Poverty Assessment Report (PPA-IV)*. Nairobi: GoK.

Hawkins RL and Kim EJ (2012) The Socio-economic Empowerment Assessment: Addressing Poverty and Economic Distress in Clients. *Clinical Social Work Journal*, 40: 194-202.

Hosman L and Fife E (2012) The Use of Mobile Phones for Development in Africa: Top-Down-Meets-Bottom-Up Partnering. *Journal of Community Informatics*, 8(3).

International Federation of Social Workers (IFSW) *IFSW's Policies 2015*. Berne: IFSW.

International Finance Corporation (IFC) (2011) *IFC Mobile Money Study 2011 Summary Report*. Washington, DC.

Jack W and Suri T (2011) *Risk Sharing and Transaction Costs: Evidence from Kenya's Mobile Money Revolution*. Available at: http://www.uh.edu/~bsorense/risk_sharing_and_transactions_costs.pdf (accessed 24 August 2018).

Katz J (Ed.) (2008) *Handbook of Mobile Communication Studies*, Cambridge, Mass. MIT Press.

Lehr D (2007) *Going Wireless: Dialing for Development*. (Working paper). Available at: http://mobileactive.org/dialing-development new-report-mobile-phone-use-base-pyramid.

Mattila M (2011) *Mobile Technologies for Child Protection: A Briefing Note*. Dakar. UNICEF WCARO.

Nafula NN, Onsomu EN, Mwabu G and Muiruri S (2005) *Review of Policy Options for Poverty Reduction in Kenya*. Nairobi: Kenya Institute for Public Policy Research and Analysis.

Ndiku JM (2007) The Issue of Poverty in the Provision of Quality Education in Kenyan Secondary Schools. *Educational Research and Review*, 2(7): 157-164.

Ndung'u MN and Waema TM (2011) Development Outcomes of Internet and Mobile Phones Use in Kenya: The Households' Perspectives. *Info*, 13(3): 110-124.

Zurovac D, Talisuna AO and Snow, RW (2012) Mobile Phone Text Messaging: Tool for Malaria Control in Africa. *PLoS Med*, 9(2). Available at: http://journals.plos.org/plosmedicine/article?id=10.1371/journal.pmed.1001176 (accessed 26 July 2018).

15

Towards Integrating Indigenous Knowledge and Problem Solving into Contemporary Social Work in Africa

Helmut Spitzer and Janestic M. Twikirize

In this concluding chapter, we reiterate the enduring relevance of indigenous knowledge systems and problem-solving approaches and the need for modern social work to build on this knowledge base. Africa has a long history of traditional problem-solving systems and approaches that go back to the precolonial era. Outstanding examples are the family and kinship system, mutual aid groups, and other forms of reciprocity, solidarity, and alliance. With colonialisation and the introduction of formal services, these systems and approaches were widely ignored or even suppressed. In the post-independence period, when social work began to emerge as formal professional services, it almost exclusively relied on Western sciences and methods instead of building on local knowledges and practices. Actually, indigenous, culture-specific forms of helping, coping, resilience building and problem solving are still underrepresented in contemporary social work education, theory, practice, and policy in many African countries.

The discussions in this publication are testament to a resurgence of interest in these local knowledge systems and approaches, which points to the need to reposition social work to intently draw on the wealth of indigenous knowledge and to reclaim important African philosophical principles such as *ubuntu* to strengthen and make social work more appropriate. The argument to strongly draw on indigenous models and approaches ties in well with a collectivist-communalist ontological perspective that is commonly associated with social work in the Global South (Ornellas, Spolander and Engelbrecht, 2018). Innovative models by development agencies are already building on indigenous knowledge systems to deliver more socially accepted, effective, and sustainable products and services, thus contributing to sustainable social change (see for example the *akabondo* model in Uganda as discussed in Chapter 8 of this volume).

The indigenous models presented in this book demonstrate that the poor and people in vulnerable circumstances are not devoid of knowledge, and neither are they passively waiting on external interventions. They actively harness their resources, potentials, and social networks, and draw from the wealth of their long-held value systems to address challenges in their communities and environments. For social work professionals, it is helpful to understand that social values in a given geographical location include language, oral traditions, taboos, rituals, music, dance, knowledge forms, art, folklore, riddles, idioms, and cultural spaces (Mawere, 2015), all of which can be incorporated into social work education and practice upon thorough reflection on their respective relevance and applicability.

As argued by Mangaliso (2005, cited in Osei-Hwedie and Rankopo, 2008, 206), in a globalising world, societies must develop their own unique knowledge, values, and resources that they can use as their source of comparative advantage and the basis of their own development. As a way forward, we propose that social work researchers and academics in East Africa (and Africa in general) need to intensify efforts in a number of interrelated realms:

- Research on indigenous knowledge to inform theory and model-building;
- Curriculum development that effectively integrates indigenous knowledge and culture-specific practices; and
- Integration of local knowledge systems into policy and practice.

Research on the Link between Indigenous Knowledge and Social Work

The low research capacity and output, particularly in the field of social sciences, has been a major challenge for scholars in sub-Saharan Africa (Tettey and Puplampu, 2000). This not only affects the contribution towards knowledge generation but also the lack of a thorough investigation of context-specific phenomena that is important for designing locally relevant interventions. Scholars in Africa have an obligation to ensure that this research is directed towards addressing the needs of the poor and marginalised populations. This will require an intensification of practice- and action-oriented research that is conducted in partnership with community members and social development practitioners not as objects of the research but as partners actively participating in the design, execution, and analysis and sharing of the research and generated data. This is especially important when researching and theorising local indigenous practices.

Butterfield and Abye (2013, 214), in their plea that international social work scholars can learn a lot from their colleagues based in Africa, uphold certain strengths that they identified when working with African researchers:

- Outline the specific setting of their research, its locale and environmental conditions, its cultural context and community setting;
- Bridge the distance between local projects and national policy;
- Interpret their research to challenge and inform global policies and practice; and
- Obtain first-hand accounts from vulnerable populations, and propose innovative and radically different analyses and responses that are relatively unattended to in the international literature.

Some of these strengths can also be seen in this volume, and they might serve as a motivation for scholars, students and practitioners alike to intensify their research agenda, despite the limited resources and lack of institutional support which can be observed in many African universities and organisations.

With regard to research on the link between indigenous knowledge systems and social work, we wish to recommend a selection of potential areas for future studies which pertain to the East African context, but which may also apply to other African contexts (in alphabetical order):

- Care systems for the elderly
- Death and dying and the role of hospice social work
- Ethical and gender perspectives in indigenous models and approaches
- Gender and empowerment of girls and women
- Indigenous and innovative ways of dealing with trauma, healing, and reconciliation in contexts of collective violence
- Indigenous knowledge for sustainable development and the protection of ecosystems
- Indigenous knowledge regarding child protection and family welfare
- Indigenous people and social work
- Issues pertaining to handicapped people and people with albinism
- Issues pertaining to minority groups (e.g. homosexual and transgender people)
- Links between traditional healing, religion, and social work
- Mental health issues

- Social work supervision
- Social work's role in the transformation of social and cultural norms
- Traditional practices of coping and mourning in the face of   the AIDS pandemic

Research is critical for theory building. While presenting our findings on indigenous and innovative social work approaches in East Africa at the *Global Social Work and Social Development Conference* in Dublin in 2018, a participant raised this question: 'Have you developed any theories to support indigenous social work practice so far?' In fact, one of the key challenges for social work in African contexts is to develop theories of its own; hence, there is dire need for a thorough scientific base rooted in African knowledge systems. Such theories will subsequently inform practice interventions, which, in turn, must be culturally relevant and provide meaningful responses to the socio-economic realities and corresponding challenges in African societies (Spitzer, 2014).

To fully understand, theorise and apply the nuggets on indigenisation, indigenous knowledge and practices, the need for ongoing quality research cannot be overstated. This is important in increasing the body of knowledge, but also to support policy development and social work practice that is relevant for the communities we work with.

Integration of Indigenous and Innovative Approaches in Education and Training of Social Workers

Relevant education is a critical foundation for appropriate social work practice. Hence, in order to engender effective integration of indigenous knowledge, perspectives, and approaches, there has to be a deliberate effort to integrate these into social work curricula. The design and delivery of the social work curriculum has to go beyond reliance on international frameworks to incorporate local knowledge. The challenge to this process has been, according to Kreitzer (2012, 11), the 'remnants of western teaching, the wish to be at par with European universities, and the desire to be black on the outside and European on the inside'. Chigbu, Izugbara and de Vries (2018) characterise such loss of culture as the total or partial disappearance of aspects of culture that give unique identities to a community. This has been largely blamed on forces of modernisation, urbanisation, and globalisation, and has been cited in almost all the case examples presented in this book as threatening the effective adoption of indigenous models of problem solving. This loss or weakening of traditional cultural identity negatively affects interactions, participation, commitment, and place-attachment. McGrath and Brennan (2011, cited in Chigbu, Izugbara and de Vries, 2018, 109) advocate cultural preservation, social inclusiveness, and community-based solutions to local problems as relevant for avoiding a loss of community in many locales. This is as applicable to practice as it is to education and training.

The inclination towards an internationally informed curriculum is exemplified by various incidents of resistance against efforts to indigenise the curriculum at the University of Botswana in the early 1990s (Osei-Hwedie and Rankopo, 2008). In the Botswana case, university authorities, learners and some members of the social work faculty showed little interest in decolonising or indigenising the curriculum owing to a desire to remain internationally competitive and marketable. Another cause was that university lecturers wished to attain international recognition. There was also a lack of consensus on whether Western theories and models were really irrelevant to the local context. Thus, whilst the localised curriculum had the intent of inclining counselling and issues of death and dying from a largely African perspective, in practice, there remained a strong inclination towards Western-oriented concepts, such as psychodynamic theories.

The case study from Botswana tells us a story about a prevalent tendency in many academic institutions, both in Africa and elsewhere: While Western knowledge is considered to be rational and scientific, and thus superior, African indigenous knowledge is best seen as an unscientific accumulation of native wisdom, and thus as inferior (Ogungbure, 2013).

Whilst the above tensions are understandable, the development and delivery of social work curricula informed by a local knowledge base does not have to imply a total disregard of everything Western but rather paying more attention to local realities and indigenous knowledges. A promising example can be cited from Makerere University, Uganda. Although its social work curriculum was historically linked to the institution's colonial past and the 1960s, it has been revised over the years through a series of curriculum reviews to make it more contextually relevant. The programme is designed within the social development framework and prioritises pressing issues within the country and region, particularly poverty and community-oriented interventions. A newly developed Master of Social Work (MSW) (2018) has been largely informed by empirical research conducted under the auspices of the PROSOWO project on the role of social work in poverty reduction and social development as well as the current practice needs. This project on the promotion of professional social work in East Africa was conducted in partnership with universities in Kenya, Rwanda, and Tanzania, as well as a European partner from Austria. While the Western partner acted as overall coordinator of the project, it is worth noting that during the entire project span, no single moment was spent on discussing social work methods and theories deriving from the partner's context;

on the contrary, all project-related activities, including curriculum development, exclusively focused on the respective East African perspectives. Today, the MSW curriculum at Makerere University addresses the need for specialised training in the areas of child protection, health and wellbeing, livelihoods and social enterprise development, as well as social work in conflict and emergency situations.

The integration of indigenous knowledge and approaches will also require a systematic documentation and use of case studies, which relate to the everyday experiences of the local people. Whilst this might sound obvious, it is sometimes not always applied in the classroom due to a lack of systematic documentation and dissemination of such case studies. Yet, most of these case studies can be easily collected from students' fieldwork reports and grey literature produced by social development agencies and government departments. Another curriculum-related component that should potentially provide an opportunity for the mainstreaming of indigenous and innovative approaches and models in social work is that of fieldwork or field practice education. Besides agency-based placements of students, an innovative model of fieldwork can involve block placement of groups of students in a particular community to work for a specified period of time with local community-based organisations. This would help students learn and appreciate the knowledge, values, and practices of the local community and how they relate to and could be integrated into social work. The learning objectives as well as the supervision and assessment framework for field practice education could also be designed to deliberately reflect components of indigenous knowledge systems and values as well as issues such as cultural competence.

Indigenous Approaches in Social Work Practice: Community Organising and Developmental Social Work

Social workers are increasingly acknowledging the important contribution that culturally informed interventions make in advancing social development (Twikirize et al., 2013). The social development paradigm, upon which developmental social work has been founded, itself is predicated in part on a validation and adoption of practical interventions that are meaningful to the local communities and which acknowledge and make use of clients' strengths and resources (Midgley and Conley, 2010). According to Midgley and Conley (2010), developmental social work stresses the role of community-based practice interventions and upholds the belief that the vast majority of social work's clients can be served in community settings and, despite the challenges many face, they can live independently in the community. In essence, this argument is a validation of the importance of identifying and working with the already available indigenous, local material and non-material resources often wrapped in the daily practices, principles, and value systems within communities.

The wealth of knowledge, resources, and strengths within local populations at the community level is a common thesis that emerges from many chapters of this book. The people are experts in assessing and understanding their own social situations, their contexts, and the daily challenges they experience. They also possess invaluable ideas regarding what might constitute relevant and effective interventions.

In advancing the importance of indigenous approaches, we are, however, not naively suggesting that they are adequate by and within themselves, since that would beg the question as to the persistence of innumerable social problems, including pervasive poverty and deprivation in most communities in Africa. We are well aware that many people in Africa continue to suffer from poverty and inequality due to a lack of tangible resources and multiple vulnerabilities that keep them in a cycle of deprivation and marginalisation. Rather, we suggest that social and community development interventions, and community-oriented social work functions in general, would be more effective if they built on existing knowledge and concepts and worked in an integrative partnership approach with community members, validating and utilising their strengths and resources rather than claiming expert knowledge. This is in line with developmental social work's emphasis on giving a voice to people to engage in and influence their own development (Lombard, 2014, 49). Social work practitioners need to carefully study the salient organising elements of such community structures such as *bataka* groups in Uganda (see Chapter 9 in this book) or the *msaragambo* model in Tanzania (see Chapter 7) to understand how they rally whole communities and continue to play a diversity of roles fairly successfully compared to the short-term project-based organising efforts spearheaded by formal social work and social development agencies. How can these positive elements be harnessed to achieve sustainable social change within communities?

A common characteristic of the indigenous approaches as presented in this publication is their role and efficacy in community organising. Although most of these approaches lack formal structures of operation, they continue to demonstrate effectiveness in rallying community members around a common goal. According to Staples (2016), grassroots community organising entails the collective action by community members, drawing on the strength of their numbers, participatory processes, and indigenous leadership to decrease power disparities and achieve shared goals for social change. Staples (2016, 2) elaborates the key elements underlying this activity as follows:

- Community members make their own decisions about social change – what needs to be added, altered, or eliminated to make their lives better. There is a basic assumption that they have the right, necessity, and capacity to define their own goals and objectives as well as to speak and act on their own behalf.

> Thus, organising is a bottom-up philosophical approach to social change, and not simply a method to achieve it.
>
> - Community members take collective action that employs 'people power' to achieve shared goals, resolve common problems, and gain a greater measure of control over the circumstances of their lives.
>
> - The community provides its own leadership for the change effort. The operative assumption is that effective leadership should and will emerge from within the community, rather than from the outside.

Staples (2016) further emphasises the role of collective action (seen in all the indigenous approaches presented in this book) and the strength of numbers in achieving social solidarity. This solidarity is important in promoting community sustainability, stability, and where necessary, social change. In this process, the inclination towards a collective good underlies the motivation for social solidarity. These attributes seem to be present in sub-Saharan African societies, where, as stated by Chigbu, Izugbara and de Vries (2018, 103), the consciousness of the community 'goes beyond the individual self-consciousness to communal consciousness of culture – as an essential part of the community development'. Hence, the organising role of the community associated with indigenous problem-solving models can be effectively harnessed to promote community development.

Link to the Global Agenda for Social Work and Social Development

A systematic analysis of indigenous knowledge and models makes significant sense within the framework of the Global Agenda for Social Work and Social Development. Launched by the three global social work organisations (International Association of Schools of Social Work, International Federation of Social Workers, and International Council on Social Welfare), the Global Agenda focuses on four major pillars:

> - Promoting social and economic equality;
> - Promoting the dignity and worth of peoples;
> - Promoting community and environmental sustainability; and
> - Strengthening the recognition of the importance of human relations.
>
> (Jones and Truell, 2012)

Whilst indigenous knowledge and approaches are directly relevant to all the four pillars of the Global Agenda, we provide an illustration of pillars three and four.

Both of these pillars directly demand that we pay attention to indigenous knowledge systems and approaches.

Globally, there is recognition of the role that indigenous communities play in preserving the environment, based on the fact that most of these communities maintain a special relationship with nature, including its elements, such as land, water, forests, and mountains (United Nations, 2007; Maathai, 2009). At the same time, these communities at the grassroots level suffer most from the effects of climate change and the destruction of the natural habitat, which often occurs through industrialisation and other modern practices undertaken in the name of economic development. As social work takes increasing interest in environmental justice and green social work (cf. Dominelli, 2012; Ramsay and Boddy, 2017), there is even more reason to research and integrate indigenous approaches. Jones, Powers and Truell (2018) aver that social workers working to promote sustainable communities and environments can gain useful insights by drawing from the wealth of knowledge and practice of indigenous peoples. For social work in African contexts, it is paramount to integrate an ecological perspective into its thinking and to link social and environmental dimensions in its practice in order to make a tangible difference when working with communities adversely affected by environmental degradation (Spitzer and Twikirize, 2014). The knowledge and expertise of the people living at the grassroots level cannot be left out in this process.

Similarly, community sustainability has to be based on what the communities know and value, and the communities themselves have to be actively involved in sustaining their entities and structures. The *ubuntu* ethic that characterises indigenous approaches and practices will need to be further researched so that rather than being left to dissipate, innovative ways of reinvigorating and entrenching it in modern social work practice are found and applied. In this regard, Kalinganire, Gilkey and Haas (2017) state that the social work profession will need to lead the way in developing culturally responsive interventions, methods, and practice approaches to promote societal wellbeing, strengthen family and community systems, and secure cultural values and government commitment to ensure sustainability.

The culturally informed indigenous approaches and practices, as presented in this book, strongly demonstrate the importance of human relationships as exemplified best among communities at the grassroots level and their local value systems and practices. Hence, it is hoped that with this stirring up of interest in indigenous approaches, they can form a crucial element of the framework for analysing, documenting, and reporting on the Global Agenda for Social Work and Social Development in Africa. In other words, as scholars and practitioners reflect on their work, they should pay attention to the extent to which the integration of indigenous and innovative models of problem solving are positively contributing to the different pillars of the Global Agenda, including the promotion of the importance of human relationships, which will be the subject of the Global Agenda report in 2020. This discourse could also form some of the reflections on the key pillars of the post-2020 Global Agenda for Social Work and Social Development.

Concluding Remarks

In our efforts to professionalise social work in the countries of the East African Community, we – a consortium of schools of social work[17] – deliberately decided to establish a *centre of excellence* in order to push further the social work agenda in the region. This centre – the East Africa Centre for Research and Innovation in Social Work (CRISOWO)[18] – is the first of its kind in this part of the world. It provides a forum for mutual learning, innovation, and knowledge transfer at the local, regional, and international levels, and serves as a coordination mechanism for social work research, capacity-building, networking, and advocacy within the East African Community.

The following country-specific publications on our study on indigenous and innovative social work approaches were about to be available at the time of finalising this book:

- For Burundi: Muchiri SW, Nzisabira SC and Murekasenge J (forthcoming) *Indigenous and Innovative Models of Social Work Practice in Burundi*. Bujumbura: Hope Africa University.

- For Kenya: Wairire GG, Ndung'u EM and Nungari S (forthcoming) *Indigenous and Innovative Social Work Approaches in Kenya*. Nairobi: University of Nairobi Press.

- For Rwanda: Uwihangana C, Hakizamungu A, Bangwanubusa T and Rutikanga C (forthcoming) *Indigenous and Innovative Models for Social Work Practice in Rwanda*. Kigali: University of Rwanda.

- For Tanzania: Mabeyo ZM and Mvungi A (forthcoming) *Indigenous and Innovative Models of Social Work Practice in Tanzania*. Dar es Salaam: Mkuki na Nyota.

- For Uganda: Twikirize JM, Luwangula R and Twesigye J (forthcoming) *Social Work Practice in Uganda: Learning from the Indigenous and Innovative Models of Problem Solving*. Kampala: Fountain.

---

[17]   Representatives come from Hope Africa University (Burundi), University of Nairobi (Kenya), University of Rwanda, Institute of Social Work (Tanzania), Makerere University (Uganda), and Carinthia University of Applied Sciences (Austria).

[18]   www.crisowo.org

However, this is not an end in itself. There is a need to incorporate relevant themes related to indigenous and innovative approaches into the research agendas of schools of social work in the region, and indeed in Africa as a whole, as well as to regularly ensure that conferences and related events continue to reflect on these issues.

It is our hope that *Social Work Practice in Africa. Indigenous and Innovative Approaches* will serve as a valuable resource and inspiring catalyst for future initiatives to further the case of meaningful social work practice on the African continent.

References

Butterfield AK and Abye T (2013) Learning from Africa: Publication and Research: In: Butterfield AK and Abye T (eds) *Social Development and Social Work: Learning from Africa.* New York: Routledge, 211-2017.

Chigbu U, Izugbara CO and de Vries WT (2018) Land, Culture Loss and Community. Rural Insights from Sub-Saharan Africa. In: Keny S, McGrath B and Phillips R (eds) *The Routledge Handbook of Community Development. Perspectives from Around the Globe.* New York: Routledge, 98-114.

Dominelli L (2012) *Green Social Work: From Environmental Crises to Environmental Justice.* Cambridge: Polity.

Jones DN and Truell R (2012) The Global Agenda for Social Work and Social Development: A Place to Link together and be Effective in a Globalized World. *International Social Work*, 55(4), 454-472.

Jones DN, Powers M and Truell R (2018) Global Overview. In: Jones DN (ed) *Global Agenda for Social Work and Social Development: Third Report. Promoting Community and Environmental Sustainability.* Rheinfelden: IFSW, 1-51.

Kalinganire C, Gilkey SL and Haas LJ (2017) Social Work Practice in Rwanda: The Challenge of Adapting Western Models to Fit Local Contexts. In: Gray M (ed) *The Handbook of Social Work and Social Development in Africa.* London: Routledge, 315-328.

Kreitzer L (2012) *Social Work in Africa: Exploring Culturally Relevant Education and Practice in Ghana.* Calgary: University of Calgary Press.

Lombard A (2014) A Developmental Perspective in Social Work Theory and Practice. In: Spitzer H, Twikirize JM and Wairire GG (eds) *Professional Social Work in East Africa. Towards Social Development, Poverty Reduction and Gender Equality.* Kampala: Fountain, 43-55.

Maathai W (2009) *The Challenge for Africa.* London: Arrow Books.

Mawere M (2015) Indigenous Knowledge and Public Education in Sub-Saharan Africa. *Africa Spectrum*, 50(2): 57-71.

Midgley J and Conley A (2010) Introduction. In: Midgley J and Conley A (eds) *Social Work and Social Development: Theories and Skills for Developmental Social Work*. New York. Oxford University Press, xiii-xx.

Ogungbure AA (2013) African Indigenous Knowledge: Scientific or Unscientific? *Inkanyiso. The Journal of Humanities and Social Sciences*, 5(1): 12-20.

Ornellas A, Spolander G and Engelbrecht LK (2018). The Global Social Work Definition: Ontology, Implications and Challenges. *Journal of Social Work*, 18(2): 222-240.

Osei-Hwedie K and Rankopo MJ (2008) Developing Culturally Relevant Social Work Education in Africa: The Case of Botswana. In. Gray M, Coates J and Yellow Bird M (eds) *Indigenous Social Work around the World: Towards Culturally Relevant Social Work Education and Practice*. Aldershot: Ashgate, 203-218.

Ramsay S and Boddy J (2017) Environmental Social Work: A Concept Analysis. *The British Journal of Social Work*, 47(1): 68-86.

Staples L (2016). *Roots to Power: A Manual for Grassroots Organizing*. Santa Barbara. Praeger.

Spitzer H (2014) Social Work in African Contexts: A Cross-Cultural Reflection on Theory and Practice. In: Spitzer H, Twikirize JM and Wairire GG (eds) *Professional Social Work in East Africa. Towards Social Development, Poverty Reduction and Gender Equality*. Kampala: Fountain, 15-28.

Spitzer H and Twikirize JM (2014) A Vision for Social Work in East Africa. In: Spitzer H, Twikirize JM and Wairire GG (eds) *Professional Social Work in East Africa. Towards Social Development, Poverty Reduction and Gender Equality*. Kampala: Fountain, 373-84.

Tettey, WJ and Puplampu, KP (2000) Social Science Research and the Africanist: The Need for Intellectual and Attitudinal Reconfiguration. *African Studies Review*, 43(3): 81-102

Twikirize JM, Asingwire N, Omona J, Lubanga R and Kafuko A (2013) *The Role of Social Work in Poverty Reduction and the Realization of Millennium Development Goals in Uganda*. Kampala: Fountain.

United Nations (2007) *United Nations Declaration on the Rights of Indigenous Peoples*. United Nations.

Glossary of Key Indigenous Terms and Concepts

abashingantahe/bashingantahe/mushingantahe: Wise men of integrity, whose primary role is the solving of conflicts at different levels of Burundian society, particularly at the grassroots level. *Bashingantahe* refers to the institution itself, while *mushingantahe* is a singular form of *abashingantahe*.

agatuku k'abagabo: A concept used in relation to the institution of *bashingantahe* in Burundi, which means voluntary participation.

akabondo: A Luganda word from Uganda literally meaning a shell or sack that contains eggs of a jigger. It is used symbolically in some communities to refer to the household cluster approach.

bataka: A concept from Western Uganda meaning community members or neighbours. *Bataka* groups are common mutual assistance groups that serve multiple purposes, such as burial societies.

chamas: A Kiswahili word meaning 'merry-go-round' or self-help groups (also referred to as *vyama* in correct Swahili grammar).

engozi: A word from Western Uganda meaning a stretcher, mainly used as a local ambulance in rural, hilly communities owing to the absence of modern ambulances.

gacaca: An informal conflict settlement arrangement at the grassroots level in Rwanda. The literal meaning of the Kinyarwanda term is 'grass'.

girinka munyarwanda: One cow per family programme in Rwanda.

harambee: A Kiswahili concept from Kenya used to describe activities that unite people around a common goal. The literal meaning is 'to pull on one string'.

ikibiri: A concept of mutual assistance used in Burundi, literally meaning 'working together' in Kirundi.

jando: Initiation rite in Tanzania, referring to boys.

masale: A particular type of leaf that is perceived as a sacred object with magical powers among the Chagga community in Tanzania. It is used to deter people from giving false information during conflict resolution with a fear that if they do so, they will be cursed and die instantly.

mato oput: A conflict resolution and reconciliation ritual among the ethnic group of the Acholi in Northern Uganda. It literally means 'drinking the bitter herb' (from the *oput* tree).

mbege: A local beer in Kilimanjaro region, Tanzania, that is taken while people are working together.

msaragambo: A model of community organising among the Chagga people in Tanzania.

mwami: A Kirundi word meaning 'king'.

nkwatiraako: A self-help group approach mainly used in Rakai District in Uganda. The Luganda term literally means 'give me a helping hand'.

Nta ntahe y'umugore: A Kirundi expression, meaning that a woman should not be a judge while resolving conflicts in the community.

saiga: A local name for self-help groups in Mara Region of Tanzania.

samuragwa: A Kirundi label for a child who inherits the father's authority within the family and could inherit his father's seat in the *bashingantahe* institution.

susu: Mutual aid groups serving economic functions in Ghana.

twesitule: A Luganda word literally meaning 'let us uplift ourselves'. In this book, the term is referred to the *Twesitule* Women's Group in Kyotera, Rakai District.

ubudehe: A culture-based social protection system of intra-community cooperation based on collective actions in Rwanda.

ubuntu: A term denoting humanness and reflecting the collective nature of African societies. It can be found in variations in many African languages.

ujamaa: A Kiswahili concept from Tanzania which refers to the ideal of familyhood. It formed the basis of President Julius Nyerere's social and economic development policies after Tanzania gained independence from Britain in 1961.

umudugudu: A Kinyarwanda term for the lowest administrative unit in Rwanda, also referred to as a village (plural *imidugudu*).

umuganda: A term for communal work in Rwanda. As a government policy, it is practised every last Saturday of the month.

umugoroba w'ababyeyi: A Kinyarwanda concept literally meaning 'parents' evening forum'. It is geared towards the socio-economic wellbeing of the population.

umupfasoni: A Kirundi term for the wife of a *mushingantahe*, who is seen as a wise woman in Burundi.

umutahira: A Kinyarwanda word used to refer to people who are in charge of the civic education academy.

unyago: An initiation rite in Tanzania, referring to girls.

urugwiro: A Rwandan word referring to the president's office.

ushahidi: A Kiswahili word meaning testimony, also referring to an internet-based crowdsourcing platform.

vyamas: A Kiswahili word meaning 'merry-go-round' or self-help groups (singular: chama).

wachili: Local community leaders in Kilimanjaro Region, Tanzania.

washenga: Dowry negotiators during marriage ceremonies in Kilimanjaro Region, Tanzania.